The *Beginner's* Book of SENIOR ACTIVITIES

36 Fun Events for TODAY'S Senior Adults

Lisa C. Deutsch

ISBN-13: 978-0-9964347-3-7

ISBN-10: 0-9964347-3-9

The Beginner's Book of Senior Activities - 36 Fun Events for TODAY's Senior Adults

Copyright © Lisa C. Deutsch 2016

All rights reserved. No part of this publication may be reproduced (with the exception of the handouts on the PDF), stored in a retrieval system, or transmitted in any way by any means—electronic, mechanical, photocopy, recording, or otherwise—without the prior permission of the copyright holder, except as provided by USA copyright law.

Cover and Layout design by Holly Hyde
Posy Creative
www.posycreative.com

Scripture quotations are taken from:
THE HOLY BIBLE, NEW INTERNATIONAL VERSION®, NIV®
Copyright © 1973, 1978, 1984, 2011 by Biblica, Inc.™
Used by permission. All rights reserved worldwide.

This book is a compilation of ideas, stories, jokes, and activities collected from numerous sources over many years. Any use of original material that is unauthorized is unintentional. Unless otherwise attributed, the origin and authorship of jokes, stories, and poems is unknown and assumed to be in the public domain. Credit is given to as many original sources as are known.

Acknowledgments

Special thanks to Carol and Nancy for believing in this project and for contributing typing, activities, art, and ideas taken from lifetimes of ministry.

Thanks to Laura and Terri for their typing and ideas, to Beverly for her proofing, to the Christian Communicator Manuscript Service for their editing and guidance and lastly to Dolores and Nina for sharing their ideas, proofing, and information taken from their care giving ministries.

Also, thanks to Chaplain Bart, Herb, Anna, Marvin, and Steve for their collections of jokes, all taken from years of joyful ministry and to Holly for all of her help and encouragement!

And especially to my family (Paul, Anna, and Jared) for allowing me the time to work on this project. I love you!

table of CONTENTS

1 Introduction
Why 50+ Programs: Who Are the Baby Boomers?

2 Chapter 1
A Step-by-Step Guide to Starting a 50+ Program

10 Chapter 2
Monthly or Weekly Club Ideas

16 Chapter 3
Volunteer Ideas for Seniors

22 Chapter 4
Monthly Ideas for Meetings/Activities Index:

A. January.................28
B. February................38
C. March..................52
D. April 64
E. May 78
F. June 100
G. July 114
H. August 128
I. September 138
J. October 152
K. November 160
L. December 172

189 Appendix
Activity Sheets Index

Introduction
Why 50+ Programs: Who Are the Baby Boomers?

Ministering to today's seniors is far different than ministering to past generations. We live in the age of the baby boomers, and the seniors today are a force to be reckoned with! Today's 50+ers want more information, more professional programs, and more creativity in their activities. With advances in medicine and education, today's seniors are living longer, and they want interesting activities for their retirement years. Today's seniors want to enjoy their golden years!

In 2006 the first of the baby boomers (born between 1946 and 1964) began to turn 60 years old. According to the U.S. Census, the number of people 65 years and older on July 1, 2009, was 39.6 million (13 percent of the total population). By 2050 it is estimated to be 88.5 million (20 percent of the total population). 1It is easy to see that vibrant senior ministry programs are more needed today than at any other time in history.

The Bible commands us to respect and honor our parents "… so that it may go well with you and that you may enjoy long life on the earth" (Eph. 6:3). Even Jesus when on the cross made provision for his mother to be looked after. Can we do any less for the older members of our society?

God bless you as you minister to this precious segment of our society, churches, and communities. These are their golden years, and you have the opportunity to help them discover, develop, and deploy their talents to truly make these years "golden."
(www.census.gov/newroom and www.census.gov/population)

Stay tuned to Senior Program Resources . . . there are many more activities on the way!

CHAPTER 1

A STEP-BY-STEP GUIDE TO STARTING A 50+ PROGRAM

Chapter 1
A Step-by-Step Guide to Starting a 50+ Program

Whether you are a pastor, retirement community coordinator, senior day care director, or a nursing home administrator, starting a senior ministry from the ground up can be a daunting task. This is a simple, easy outline to follow regardless of your situation and resources.

1. **Have the seniors fill out a survey:** While surveys have limited usefulness, conducting one does give the group a say in their activities and helps you get to know your group. A healthy and long-lasting program will have to contain a combination of educational and spiritual activities, as well as those just for fun. Outings should also be included. For a survey, **(see appendix page 192).**

2. **Create a mailing list:** All group members who are 50 and over need to be included.

3. Create a logo and where applicable, a theme: Examples are: "50+ Ministries: Serving Christ and the Community," "Primetimers Ministry: Using Our Time for the Lord," "Fifty-Plus: Continuing in Growth and Service," "Young at Heart Ministry: Serving the King," "50 Plus Ministry: Serving and Empowering our Seniors," "BYF: Best Years Fellowship," "TNT: Tried and True," "Classic Club," "Pacesetters," "Keen Agers," etc.

4. Banners: If possible have at least two banners made up. These can be done relatively inexpensively at a local copy store or online at a poster/banner site … (Outreach.com is a good source.) Put one banner in the information area of the vestibule and the other where the seniors will actually be meeting. It is surprising how groups will feel a sense of ownership when they have an "official" logo and see it displayed.

5. Budget: Have a good budget established, one that will subsidize event costs at least in part. Seniors are usually on fixed incomes that limit what they can spend on non-essential activities.

6. Newsletter: While we are in the paperless generation, seniors (50+) still like to get items in the mail, especially something from the church/community. If a monthly newsletter of local events/topics of interest to 50+ers (including the featured 50+ event) with logo can be created; it will hasten the feeling of belonging to the group and ministry. However, don't assume that 50+ers aren't on Facebook or don't have email; many do. You can also ask for supplies for upcoming events in the newsletter. This will cut down on costs if you are able to borrow some of the decorations and props! For newsletter topics (see appendix page 193).

7. Monthly meetings/events: Depending on the size of your ministry and the resources available, it is best to have at least one big event per month advertised in the newsletter. This gives the group a fellowship event to look forward to and plan for. The idea is to alternate between a dinner/event at the church or community center and an outing the following month so that events don't get monotonous (except for December–March, when in colder climates indoor events are better because of weather concerns). Sometimes the older members will only come to the familiar surroundings of the church or other meeting place especially during cold weather or after dark.

8. Signing up for events: Having sign-ups can be challenging, but it is a necessary part in planning for the monthly event. Sign-ups are advertised first in the 50+ newsletter, followed by either:

a. **A notice in the bulletin with a tear-off section for signing up for the event.** The benefit of this is that the sign-up and payment can be placed in the offering plate/bag. This is the easiest process but makes it more difficult to get detailed information out to people about the event.

b. **A notice in the church bulletin along with a sign-up table in the vestibule or designated area.** Decorate the table with items related to the theme or topic of the month's meeting or event. If you have a sign-up sheet and people pre-pay when they sign up, there is less chance they will cancel at the last moment. Ideally, someone will need to be at the table before and after each service with an envelope to make change for payments. The other option is to pay at the door. For the sample sign-up sheet, **(see appendix page 194).**

9. Meeting time: Keep meetings short (two hours maximum) and try to adjourn before it gets dark, as many seniors are hesitant to drive after dark! Optimal time is from 5–7 p.m. People who work can come directly from work to eat dinner, enjoy the evening, and still get home at a reasonable hour.

10. Meetings/Food: Food is an important draw, especially when a ministry is new and trying to get established with its members. For inside meetings, use the best local caterers and include the menu for each meeting in the newsletter. It is surprising how important that is! The cost of the meal may need to be subsidized to an affordable cost for the seniors ($8-$10/meal). You will need to increase the cost according to the meeting speaker/theme, but hopefully no more than $10/meeting. Depending on the budget, the group may still have to do potlucks or cheaper meals such as chili night, soup and salad night, stuffed potato night, pancakes and sausage, chicken and dumplings, or "super sandwich night."

11. Decorations: Try to make each event festive with decorations that match the theme. For example, a gospel bluegrass band evening could be decorated with a country farm theme, complete with lots of hay bales, washboards, old timey bedpans, etc.

Prepare the tables in advance - pre-set with tablecloths, centerpieces, napkins, cutlery, and cups (a small bottle of water nested in each cup is an option.) Having the table preset will make less items for people to carry along with their plates. It also shows them that they are special since someone has decorated and fixed their places so nicely for them. Candlelight for each meal adds quaintness and gentleness to the meal. Oftentimes people don't know exactly what to talk about or say to one another, but they need to relax so they can visit.

You can always ask for decorative items needed the month before the event. For example, ask for old bows (specific colors) and use them as the centerpieces and/or cut up some for confetti for the tables.

12. Volunteers: Having a few people to volunteer during the dinner is a must. You will need someone at the sign-in table to take money and give name tags. If possible it is better to pre-print the name tags in large, easy-to-read lettering (first name only is easier for them to remember). Several volunteers are needed to assist in getting drinks and clearing plates after dinner, assist with games, and then cleaning up at the conclusion of the event. Different groups in the church can do this occasionally: youth, young adult, homeschooled children/their parents, and home groups. (It doesn't hurt to advertise for volunteers in the bulletin as well.)

13. Prizes: We all like to get a deal — something for free! So when possible have "give-away" prizes to give a fun aspect to the gathering. These can be as simple as dollar store items for the home, shop, or items donated by church members who were cleaning out their homes of excess items. These can be given away through such means as:

> a. The oldest member there/the youngest member there.
> b. Who went to a one-room schoolhouse?
> c. Anniversaries that month (even if widow or widower).
> d. Who traveled the longest distance?
> e. Who was born at home?
> f. Who has a picture of their spouse in their wallet/purse?
> g. Who has had the most surgeries?
> h. Who has the sticker under their napkin?
> i. Who grew up using an outhouse?
> j. Who has written a love poem to their spouse (in the last year)?
> k. Birthdays during that month.
> l. The table that won the game.
> m. Or purchase a double ticket roll (available at party stores) and give a ticket to each person entering and then place the matching ticket in a container for drawing later (this is a good method because it isn't based on winning a game — the same for everyone)!

Some suggested gifts are:

• duct tape	• sugar-free candy	• notepads	• crossword books
• pens	• word find books	• stamps	• kitchen utensils
• plants	• stationary/cards	• pencils	• chip clips
• lip balm	• hand lotion	• flowers	• sticky notes
• jelly/jam	• regular tape	• teas	• coffees

14. Games: Most people like to laugh and learn; so at each meeting try to combine both aspects with a game of some sort. Always have a "conversation starter" at each place (relating to the topic of the evening). Having the conversation starter while waiting for all members to arrive will help to both generate conversation and fill time until the event begins. (See individual monthly meeting ideas for examples.)

15. Monthly meetings: Remember the same venue will become boring and old hat. With the exception of the winter months where in many climates most events will be inside, trips and outside events also need to be included. The monthly events section will give ten suggestions for each month of meetings and trips that can be taken by seniors. (They will surprise you with what they can do!)

16. Specialty Stores (for decorating and party supplies): Since most people are on a budget, here are a few good suppliers to help with the inexpensive purchasing of unique decorating and party supplies:

1. Oriental Trading: By far, this is the best and cheapest source for specialty party supplies. They will mail out free catalogues upon request. Their contact info is Oriental Trading, P.O. Box 2308, Omaha, NE 68103-2308, www.orientaltrading.com, 1-800-228-2269.
2. Stumps: An event planner supply catalog that is very reasonably priced. They have themed party supplies, www.stumpsparty.com, 1-800-348-5084.
3. Dollar General Store: It is amazing what decorations can be found at the local dollar store.
4. Hobby Lobby or Michael's: Both have good party sections.
5. Critic's Choice: This is a great source for ordering DVDs of both new and old movies/TV shows: Critic's Choice Video & DVD, P.O. Box 642, Itasca, IL 60143-0642, www.ccvideo.com, 1-630-919-2246, 1-800-367-7765.

17. Need to Buy: Before your first meeting you will need:

1. Supply Storage: Purchase a few clear plastic tubs to store your dinner or event supplies in. Try to give away as much as possible of the table decorations as gifts, or use disposable paper items to keep storage to a minimum. Seasonal items such as Christmas, holidays, fall, and spring decorations can be kept. You will need a designated area for your clearly marked 50+ tubs to be stored.
2. Candle Holders: These will be used over and over. A small size such as the tea-sized candle holders are the best and cheapest to use. Places like Walmart carry these for under a dollar each.
3. Pencils: Buy as many pencils as you have participants. These will be used repeatedly for games at meetings.

18. Meeting Format - Each leader will have his or her own individual format; the following is just an example:

9am: Decorate the tables as early in the day as you can in case something unexpected happens or you need to make changes. Put napkins, silverware, cups, and the pre-dinner conversation starter (with pencils if needed) at each place setting. Make sure drink tables have extra cold and hot cups, sugar, diet sweetener, creamer, stirrers, and ice. Have a sound check prior to the event to ensure the sound/video is ready and working.

4pm: Put on instrumental Christian or classical music (not too loud, but enough volume to avoid having an awkward silence in the room).

4:30pm: Have a sign-in table set up by the door with name tags for all. This will help people learn one another's names (especially when they should know each other's names but may have forgotten). Depending on the payment plan that is chosen (in advance or at the door) there will need to be someone to take the payments.

4:35pm: Light candles on tables.

5pm: Welcome and express thanks to attending guests, caterer, and speaker.

5:05pm: Read a short joke or story while more people are arriving, or show a funny video or YouTube clip. This should be something light to begin the evening with cheer. The pre-dinner conversation starter could also be discussed at this time.

5:10pm: Prayer over dinner. Encourage people to fix their plates, enjoy the

5:11pm:	meal, and fellowship with one another. Begin music again and continue during dinner.
5:12–5:45pm:	Have volunteers check with each of the tables, offering to get drinks, taking finished plates, and generally waiting on them.
5:30–5:45pm:	Once everyone has finished going through the line to get their dinner, stop the music before beginning the program.
5:45pm:	While people finish their dinners, it is the perfect time for another joke, story, or reading that relates to the evening, and perhaps also a game.
6pm:	Introduce main speaker/entertainment (usually 45 minutes to one hour is a good period for the main event).
7pm:	Thank speaker and all attending. Announcements such as: 1. Designate what items can be taken home on the table, 2. Announce the activity and date for the next meeting, 3. Indicate any items needed for the next meeting, and 4. Say a prayer for a safe journey home.
7:10pm:	Clean up room/tables, using volunteers.

CHAPTER 2

WEEKLY OR MONTHLY CLUB IDEAS

Chapter 2
Weekly or Monthly Club Ideas

Specialty clubs or groups can be a valuable outreach and social outlet in addition to regularly scheduled monthly meetings.

1. A Weekly Bible Study: For men, women, or both together, a Bible study is a great reason to get together. There is a specific Bible study designed for seniors (in large print editions as well) by Lifeway Christian resources. Lifeway.com/senioradults or call 800-458-2772. There are also several organized national Bible studies that are first rate: Community Bible Study (www.communitybiblestudy.org) is an excellent one. For a more "tech savvy" Bible Study try the Explorer's Bible Study online at http://iStudyEBS.org.

2. A Quilting Group: This might be a specialized group, but even ladies who do not quilt can come along for a social time. Sometimes companies like Hobby Lobby or Jo-Ann's Fabrics will donate materials.

3. A Book Club: This is where the participants all read the same book (a chapter a week or a book a month) and discuss it together.

4. A Music Group: This can be a simple get-together at a set time once a month or once a week for those who play an instrument or sing. This could be held in a community area where others can come and listen, for example at a nursing home or senior center.

5. A Cooking Club: This group can take several forms where once a month they get together for a cooking related topic or to exchange recipes. Occasional trips could be made to various restaurants to see their kitchens and possibly learn a new recipe (for example, to a Chinese restaurant to learn or see how noodles are made or to a bakery to see how bread is made). Martha Stewart also has a cooking school on PBS with step-by-step instructions based on her book Martha Stewart's Cooking School: Lessons and Recipes for the Home Cook. Reading or watching Martha's cooking tips and recipes always provides good instruction and rewards!

6. Bowling Club: For those avid and not so avid bowlers, this can be a fun time together once a month.

7. Pilates or Tai Chi: Having age-appropriate exercise classes can be such a motivating activity for seniors who find it difficult to get enough exercise.

8. A Senior Adult Choir: Often seniors don't want to be in a formal performing choir, but a fun, casual one still meets their love of singing. A good resource for this is:

Well-Seasoned Praise by Marty Parks. Published by Word Music, 2011. This choral song book (UPC 080689460173) also comes with CD trax split, practice trax.

9. Crocheting/Knitting Group: Even if people are working on their own individual projects, it is still fun to get together with others and visit, especially for those who live alone. If the group wanted to do a project together, there are organizations such as Afghans for Angels to which completed projects can be donated.

10. Reader's Drama Group: For a fun and different type of group, a reader's drama group is one that performs drama through reading from script dramas prepared for such groups. Some resources are:

    A. *Seniors Center Stage* by Gail Blanton, Lillenas Publishing Co., 1997
    B. Jules Abram, Senior Theatre Resource Center, www.seniortheatre.com
    C. Pioneer Drama Service, www.pioneerdrama.com

11. Word Game Group: This group is perfect for those wanting to stimulate their mind and keep their brains sharp. Have a group that does word games such as: "find a word," "finish a word," or "make a word" games. For games to utilize, go to:

Lumosity.com	brainbashers.com	brainden.com
Incredibar.com/Sudoku	fillthevoid.org/games	twopaths.com/crossword
braingle.com	brainteasers.org	billsgames.com/brain-teasers

12. Coupon Clippers Club: Seniors love a bargain and often have the time to look for sales and coupons. Have a coupon cut, keep, and/or swap club.

13. The College Club: This group can do a short course together, meeting regularly to discuss it. The Great Courses (on DVD and CD) has courses on many topics. A few examples are: "Optimizing Brain Fitness," "How to Listen to and Understand Great Music," and "The History of European Art." 1-800-832-2412 www.greatcourses.com 4840 Westfield Blvd. Suite 500, Chantilly, VA 20151. A catalog of courses is available upon request. (Many libraries have these as well.)

14. Chess/Checkers/Scrabble Club: Classic board games have somewhat gone out of vogue with today's youth, but playing them will bring back wonderful memories for seniors.

15. Dominoes Club: Dominoes is another classic game that many seniors grew up playing. It is an easy game - fun, and mentally stimulating for all.

16. Terrific TV Tune-in Club: Classic TV shows can bring back great memories and be a fun time together with the addition of something special like desserts or coffee. Some suggestions are:

Green Acres	*Mr. Ed*	*McHale's Navy*
Ozzie and Harriet	*The Rifleman*	*I Dream of Jeannie*
Petticoat Junction	*Bill Cosby Show*	*I Love Lucy*
The Partridge Family	*Gomer Pyle, USMC*	*Bonanza*
Hogan's Heroes	*Happy Days*	*Daniel Boone*
The Andy Griffith Show	*The Big Valley*	*Get Smart*
Family Affair	*The Beverly Hillbillies*	*The Flying Nun*
My Three Sons	*The Dick Van Dyke Show*	

Critic's Choice: This is a great source for ordering DVDs of both new and old movies/TV shows: Critic's Choice Video & DVD, P.O. Box 642, Itasca, IL 60143-0642, www.ccvideo.com, 1-630-919-2246, 1-800-367-7765.

17. Gardeners Club: Gardeners will love to get together and learn new plant-related topics. Speakers can come and talk about plant care, or projects can be done together such as making bottle gardens or growing fruit trees from seeds (which can later be donated to a local park/garden).

18. Card Ministry Club: Card making is such a popular pastime these days. Have those who are gifted in card making get together to make cards (or donate cards). Others can address and write the cards to shut-ins in the community or church group.

19. Once a Month Nursing Home Visit Team: There are many, many activities that a church group can do for local nursing homes. The staff of most nursing homes are glad to have help with activities that make the residents' lives better. Here are some ideas for a team of people willing to give a couple of hours once a month:

A. Church/Prayer Service: If there are resources to do a service, a short message, and music, then this activity would be the most beneficial. If there are ministry students who need an opportunity to preach, this would be an ideal opportunity or perhaps retired ministers or chaplains could volunteer.

B. Music Groups: One of the most cherished activities by residents is a musical time. They don't have to do anything but just sit back and listen. Perhaps there are musicians in the church or group who could participate in a once a month or an every other month session.

C. Craft Time: Simple crafts such as paper stained glass coloring done with colored markers or foil etching can be so fun. Hobby Lobby, Michaels, and most craft stores have these types of crafts.

D. Current Events Time: Just because many nursing home patients' bodies have worn out doesn't necessarily mean their minds have as well. Having a weekly or monthly current events time where top news headlines can be discussed would keep them involved and informed of world events. Having a bigger perspective outside one's own world is always healthy.

E. Video Series: Having a weekly or monthly video series would give opportunity for growth and education. Learning something new and being challenged keeps life interesting. Christian comedy and inspirational videos would be good as well!

F. Special Food Time: Once a month "treat time" could be planned. Serve items such as watermelon, root beer floats, cheese and crackers, or tea and cookies. The staff will have to supervise this, as some of the residents' diets may be restricted.

CHAPTER 3

VOLUNTEER IDEAS FOR SENIORS

Chapter 3
Volunteer ideas for seniors

Sometimes seniors lose sight of their value after they have retired. They can become isolated and depressed because they feel they are too old to be of use anymore. Providing seniors with volunteer ideas that they can become involved in, even for a couple of hours a week, is very important. This will help both seniors and society too!

> "A man without A PURPOSE is like a ship without a rudder.
> — Thomas Carlyle

Some examples are:

- Hospice volunteer
- Reading to the elderly who cannot read anymore (homebound, nursing home, vision-impaired)
- Providing rides (doctor visits, grocery shopping, and rides in the country for the homebound)
- Hospital volunteer (hospitals have a variety of volunteer positions)
- Nursing home visitation (crafts, fingernail painting, music, church service)
- Local food pantry volunteer
- Animal shelter/rescue volunteer
- Handyman ministry
- Card ministry (sympathy, homebound, encouragement, birthday, college students)

- Women's abuse shelter volunteer
- Fall leaf raking for homebound/elderly
- Low-income childcare center volunteer
- Senior adult day care volunteer
- Local homeless shelter volunteer
- Prayer group member
- Reading with kids (through library or school programs)
- Funeral/memorial dinner cooking/coordination
- Church office volunteer
- Church maintenance volunteer
- Girls and boys ministry volunteer (participant or providing snacks)
- Nursery worker
- Landscaping/cleaning church volunteer
- Volunteer with local services for the vision and hearing impaired
- Foster care organizations volunteer (fundraising, clothing pantry, etc.)
- Hospital visitation (for church/group members)
- Knitting/crocheting prayer blankets (to give to cancer patients)
- Greeter, usher, counter volunteers at church services
- Music (choir, helping photocopy music, set up, and/or take down)
- Financial counseling
- Marriage counseling
- Sunday school teacher
- Vacation Bible School volunteer (snacks, crafts, or teaching)

- Foster grandparent (look for a single mom who needs help)
- Compile church directory or cookbook
- Missions volunteer (letters to missionaries, fundraising for missions, such as yard sales)
- Communion volunteer (prepare and clean up, also can take to shut-ins)
- Local boys and girls club volunteers
- Thrift shop volunteers (Salvation Army, Goodwill, etc.)
- Habitat for Humanity volunteer
- State fair volunteer (or pay for a needy family to go)
- Library volunteer (church or local)
- Volunteer to clear driveways (For the elderly, snow is a huge concern for those in bad health, especially when they need to get to doctor appointments or to the pharmacy.)
- Veteran ministry (provide rides, visits, cooking)
- Apprentice/teaching volunteers for boys and girls: changing a tire, building skills (such as framing, wiring, plumbing, sheet rocking, taping, mudding, staining, lacquering), sewing, knitting, embroidery, gardening, and computer hardware and software.
- Drama (participate in local plays or skits at church)
- Teach music lessons (to someone who can't afford them)
- Organize a children's voice or hand bell choir
- Tax preparation assistance/volunteer
- Voting station volunteer
- Teach gardening or fishing to a child (who doesn't have a local grandparent)
- Kids/youth camp volunteer (or pay for a needy child to go)

- Museum volunteers (art, history, local historical site)
- Thank you cookies for the church staff, local firemen, police or sheriff's offices.
- Coaching recreational and sports league
- Serving as wedding consultant and/or coordinator
- Local pregnancy resource center volunteer
- Meals on Wheels volunteer
- Senior center volunteer
- Stephen Ministry: minister to those going through grief or hurting via cards and visits. To learn more visit www.stephenministries.org
- Sewing ministry (making costumes for church or local dramas)
- Flower ministry (raise and take flowers to shut-ins, nursing homes, hospice or palliative care patients. See www.thebloomproject.org for an example of the ministry of bringing beauty and joy to those in end-of-life care.)
- Nature center volunteer
- Foreign student friend (host or befriend an international student)
- Volunteer for meals (volunteer to provide a meal for a new mom or someone dealing with illness or bereavement)
- Volunteer as a court appointed special advocate (CASA) for children.
- Red Cross or American Cancer volunteer
- Fire Department volunteer or emergency responder
- Organize a group to take a course (photography, sewing, exercise, music, pottery, painting, computer, etc.). Many community colleges and universities will waive tuition if an individual is over 65 years of age.

CHAPTER 4

MONTHLY IDEAS FOR MEETINGS & ACTIVITIES

Chapter 4
Monthly Ideas for Meetings/Activities: Laugh, Learn, Serve, and Have Fun

Seniors both love to and need to get together and enjoy fellowship. Most churches provide ample Bible teaching in their regular services so the activities listed below are not intended for Bible study but rather for relaxed fellowship and service opportunities. There are seven different activity suggestions for each month! Use the ideas listed below to serve as a springboard for planning monthly meetings that will be fun, varied, and educational.

Monthly Ideas Index

JANUARY

1. Sight and Sound Night: Large Screen Biblical Plays — 28
Date used: _____

2. Super Bowl Party with a Chili Cook off/Dessert Night — 29
Date used: _____

3. Numismatics Night — 34
Date used: _____

FEBRUARY

1. "Love Those Grandkids" Night (Intergenerational: Kids) — 38
Date used: _____

2. A Carbonaro Night — 41
Date used: _____

3. Photography Night — 44
Date used: _____

MARCH

1. March Madness/St. Patrick Theme   52
Date used: _____

2. Square Dancing Performance/History Night   55
Date used: _____

3. Genealogy Night   59
Date used: _____

APRIL

1. Science and the Bible (Intergenerational: Youth)   64
Date used: _____

2. Testimonies and Taters   69
Date used: _____

3. A Night on the Trail: Old West Evening Theme   73
Date used: _____

MAY

1. Oooh LaLa Day/Pillowcase Making for Kids with Cancer   78
Date used: _____

2. Fun with Fondue Night   85
Date used: _____

3. Mother's Day: Thrift/Resale Store Shopping Trip/Lunch   90
Date used: _____

JUNE

1. "Art is Ageless" Evening: Local Artist as Speaker   100
Date used: _____
2. Lunch and Learn (with Beans and Greens)   104
Date used: _____
3. Trip to Botanical Garden
(with lunch prearranged inside the Garden)   109
Date used: _____

JULY

1. Red, White and Blue BBQ: Veterans' Stories   114
Date used: _____
2. A Night in Jolly Ol' England   117
Date used: _____
3. A USO Tribute to Bob Hope with Patriotic Pictionary   121
Date used: _____

AUGUST

1. "Keep your mind sharp with AARP"   128
Date used: _____
2. Senior Fraud Protection: State Attorney
General's Office Speaker   131
Date used: _____
3. Rodeo/On the Trail Night/Back Yard Chef
Cook-off (Intergenerational: Kids/Youth)   135
Date used: _____

SEPTEMBER

1. Political Candidates Speaker/Debate Dinner   138
Date used: _____

2. Farm (Fruit, Animal, or Dairy) Tour/Lunch Out   141
Date used: _____

3. Family Feud Game Night (Intergenerational: Kids)   146
Date used: _____

OCTOBER

1. "What not to Wear" Fashion Show (by local shops)   152
Date used: _____

2. National Quartet Competition/Creation Museum Trip (Bus Trip)   155
Date used: _____

3. Apple or Pumpkin Picking/Sorghum Making/Hayride and Bonfire (Intergenerational: Kids)   156
Date used: _____

NOVEMBER

1. A Charlie Brown Thanksgiving   160
Date used: _____

2. Outlet Mall Shopping Trip: Beat the Christmas Rush   164
Date used: _____

3. Duck Dynasty Night   165
Date used: _____

DECEMBER

1. Animals for Alzheimer's – (super soft stuffed animals to give to Alzheimer's patients).   **172**

Date used: _____

2. Christmas Dinner with Local Orchestra/Group   **176**

Date used: _____

3. Dinner Theatre for the Holidays   **182**

Date used: _____

Appendix: Activity Sheets   **188**

JANUARY
Monthly Ideas

January
Monthly Ideas

1. Sight and Sound Night: Large Screen Biblical Plays

The Sight and Sound theatres in Pennsylvania and Missouri have created amazing live shows using the latest technology. Fortunately they have videotaped the shows which can be ordered and shown on a large screen (use sheet on a wall if needed). There are stories such as: Jonah, Noah, Joseph, Ruth, Moses or "In the Beginning," which can be ordered from www.sight-sound.com – or by phone at 800-377-1277.

Remember, you will need a movie license to show a movie to a group. These can be obtained from: Christian Video Licensing Corporation (CVLI), www.cvli.com or call 1-888-771- CVLI.

Pre-dinner Conversation Starter:
Have popcorn, candy and bottled drinks ready for people as they come in.

Quote for the Month/Event:
"As we grow older in life, years somehow seem to shorten and New Year's Day approaches with an ever increasing tempo. The more mature we get, the more we realize that time is only relative; how we live means more than how long we live. Happily, also we do not live by years, but by days. In His wisdom God does not show us all that lies ahead. So we enter a new year to live it day by day. What is past is past. Today we start anew, and what we do today will make our life for tomorrow. Chin up, shoulders straight, eyes agleam, let us salute the New Year, and each day let us follow more faithfully, more courageously, more daringly the lead of our great Captain who bids us follow Him." – William Thomson Hanzsche

"One resolution I have made, and try always to keep, is this: to rise above the little things."
- John Burroughs

Reading:
1. For the Conclusion of the Evening:

My God has been faithful
In my moments of fear,
Through every pain, every tear,
There's a God who's been faithful to me.

When my strength was all gone,
When my heart had no song,
Still in love, He's proved faithful to me.

Every word that he's promised is true;
What I thought was impossible, I see God do.
He's been faithful to me.

Looking back through my life, I now understand,
That all the time I was in God's hand.
My God has been Faithful to Me!
(www.laughandlift.com. Used by permission.)

Scripture for the Month: (Can put in newsletter to encourage memorization)
"Whatever you do, work at it with all your heart, as working for the Lord, not for human masters, since you know that you will receive an inheritance from the Lord as a reward. It is the Lord Christ you are serving" (Colossians 3:23-24).

2. Super Bowl Party & Chili Cook off/Dessert Night

Gathering together for an event such as the super bowl can be fun. Add a chili cook off followed by the group's best desserts and it will be an enjoyable time!

Pre-dinner Conversation Starter:
While waiting for the game to begin, having snacks and just visiting, a game of trivia could be played by just asking group or by playing individually with prizes given out for the most correct. For Super Bowl Trivia (see appendix page 195).

Decorations:
Football related decorations. Most party stores will have football napkins, plates and often nuts and party mixes in a football shaped container.

Quote for the Month/Event:
"Youth is when you're allowed to stay up late on New Year's Eve. Old age is when you're forced to."
– Bill Vaughn

Joke/Story:
1. For those who like Cajun food!
You might be from New Orleans if:

- The crawdad mounds in your front yard have overtaken the grass.
- You greet people with "Howzyamomma'an'dem?" and hear back "Dey fine!"
- Every so often, you have waterfront property.
- When giving directions, you use words like "uptown," "downtown," "backatown," "riverside," "lakeside," "other side of the bayou," or "other side of the levee."
- When you refer to a geographical location "way up North," you are referring to places like Shreveport, Little Rock, or Memphis, "where it gets real cold."
- You don't worry when you see ships riding higher in the river than the top of your house.
- You judge a po-boy by the number of napkins used.
- The waitress at your local sandwich shop tells you a fried oyster po-boy "dressed" is healthier than a Caesar salad.
- You know the definition of "dressed."
- You "wrench" your hands in the sink with an onion bar to get the crawfish smell off.
- You're not afraid when someone wants to "ax you something."
- You don't learn until high school that Mardi Gras is not a national holiday.
- Your last name isn't pronounced the way it's spelled.
- You have spent a summer afternoon on the Lake Pontchartrain seawall catching blue crabs.
- You like your rice and politics dirty.
- You know those big roaches can fly, but you're able to sleep at night anyway.
- You assume everyone has mosquito swarms in their backyard.
- You realize the rainforest is less humid than Louisiana.

(GCFL.net, info@gcfl.net. Used by permission.)

2. Bubba's Prayer
Bless this house, oh Lord, we cry,
please keep it cool in mid-July.
Bless the walls where termites dine,
while ants and roaches march in time.
Bless our yard where spiders pass,
fire ant castles in the grass.
Bless the garage, a home to please-
carpenter beetles, ticks and fleas.
Bless the love bugs, two by two,
the gnats and mosquitoes that feed on you.
Millions of creatures that fly or crawl,
in Arkansas, Lord, you've put them all!
But this is home, and here we'll stay,
so thank you Lord, for INSECT SPRAY!!

3. Bubba looks for a job:
- Bubba was trying out as a teller at the local bank; his first customer hands him a withdrawal slip for $400.00 and says "May I have large bills, please?" Bubba looked at him with a strange look and said "Sir, all the bills are the same size." He didn't get the job.
- Bubba was trying out for a job at an automobile dealership. A couple came to pick up their car, and was told the keys had been locked in it. They went to the service department and found Bubba working feverishly to unlock the driver side door. As they watched from the passenger side, they tried the door handle and discovered that it was unlocked.
"Hey," they said to Bubba, "its open!"
Bubba said: "I know. I already got that side."
He didn't get that job either.
- Bubba lives in a rural area. He recently decided to run for town mayor – his platform – the removal of all DEER CROSSING signs on their city roads. At the town picnic, he gave the reason for his platform: "Too many deer are being hit by cars out here! I don't think these are good places for them to be crossing anymore." The crowd (being animal lovers and hunters) burst into applause. Bubba got the job and is now mayor!

4. Bubba goes to the vet:
Bubba goes to the vet with his new the pet goldfish. I think it's got epilepsy," Bubba tells the vet. The vet takes a look and says, "It seems calm enough to me." The airhead replies, "Wait, I haven't taken it out of the bowl yet."

Game/Activity:
Watching the game is the main activity. Dessert can be served during the half time show. Have people decide what commercial they thought was the best and discuss that at the end of the game.

Reading:
1. Wisdom from the Easy Chair.
- Wouldn't it be great if we could put ourselves in the dryer for ten minutes, come out wrinkle-free and three sizes smaller?
- Last year I joined a support group for procrastinators. We haven't met yet!
- I don't trip over things, I do random gravity checks!
- Old age is coming at a really bad time!
- When I was a child I thought naptime was a punishment ... now, as a grown-up, it just feels like a small vacation!
- The biggest lie I tell myself is. . ."I don't need to write that down, I'll remember it."
- Lord, grant me the strength to accept the things I cannot change, the courage to change the things I can, and the friends to post my bail when I finally snap!
- I don't have gray hair. I have "wisdom highlights." I'm just very wise.
- My people skills are just fine. It's my tolerance to idiots that needs work.
- I'm going to retire and live off of my savings. Not sure what I'll do that second week.
- I've lost my mind and I'm pretty sure my kids took it!
- Even duct tape can't fix stupid. . . but it can muffle the sound?
- Of course I talk to myself – sometimes I need expert advice!

2. How Cold Is It?
60 degrees - Californians put on sweaters.
50 degrees - Miami residents turn on the heat.
45 degrees - Vermont residents go to outdoor concert.
40 degrees - You can see your breath.
             Californians shiver uncontrollably.
             Minnesotans go swimming.
35 degrees - Italian cars don't start.
32 degrees - Water freezes.
30 degrees - You plan your vacation in Australia.
25 degrees - Ohio water freezes.
             Californians weep pitiably.
             Minnesotans eat ice cream.
             Canadians go swimming.
20 degrees - Politicians begin to talk about the homeless.

                 New York City water freezes.
                 Miami residents plan vacation further south.

15 degrees - French cars don't start.
                 Cat insists on sleeping with you.

10 degrees - You need jumper cables to get the car going.

5 degrees - American cars don't start.

0 degrees - Alaskans put on T-shirts.

-10 degrees - German cars don't start.
                 Eyes freeze shut when you blink.

-15 degrees - You can cut your breath and use it to build an igloo.
                 Arkansans stick tongues on metal objects.
                 Miami residents cease to exist.

-20 degrees - Cat insists on sleeping in pajamas with you.
                 Politicians actually do something about the homeless.
                 Minnesotans shovel snow off roof.
                 Japanese cars don't start.

-25 degrees - Too cold to think.
                 You need jumper cables to get the driver going.

-30 degrees - You plan a two week hot bath.
                 Swedish cars don't start.

-40 degrees - Californians disappear.
                 Minnesotans button top button.
                 Canadians put on sweater.
                 Your cat helps you plan your trip south.

-50 degrees - Congressional hot air freezes.
                 Alaskans close the bathroom window.

-80 degrees - Polar bears move south.
                 Green Bay Packer fans order hot cocoa at the game.

-90 degrees - Canadian buildings turn off air conditioning.

Scripture for the Month: (Can put in newsletter to encourage memorization)

"For physical training is of some value, but godliness has value for all things, holding promise for both the present life and the life to come" (I Timothy 4:8).

3. Numismatics Night

What is numismatics? Simply, it is the study of coins. Have a coin collector/buyer come and give a short lecture on old coins/money facts. Allow people to bring two or three coins to have them appraised. They will need to be tagged, numbered, and entered on a list when they come in (small plastic jewelry bags or sandwich bags can be used to place each coin in). The speaker can write the value on each tag/bag, and then choose several of the more interesting ones to speak on. A question and answer time at the end of the presentation would be a good idea.

Pre-dinner Conversation Starter:
Have copies of "Coin Collecting: How Much Do You Know?" at each place setting (see appendix pages 196-197).

Decorations:
Use a green theme with play money (which can be purchased at a dollar store or Walmart), scattered around the center of the table. Also have some candy coins for each place setting.

Quote for the Month/Event:
"In Rome many people maintain the custom of throwing something out the window on New Year's Eve. What a relief to get rid of every old resentment, every old fear, old prejudices, old notions, old ways of doing things." – Dr. Norman Vincent Peale

"Many people buy cemetery plots in advance but do nothing about preparing a home in heaven." – Anonymous

Joke/Story:
1. Kiss the Frog
Billy Bob is 77 years old and loves to fish. As he was sitting in his boat one day he heard a voice say, "Pick me up." He looked around and couldn't see anyone. He thought he was dreaming but then again he heard the voice say "Pick me up." He looked in the water and there, floating on the top, was a frog.

The man said, "Are you talking to me?" The frog said, "Yes, I'm talking to you." "Pick me up, then kiss me, and I'll turn into the most beautiful woman you have ever seen. I'll make sure that all your friends are envious and jealous because I will be your woman." The man looked at the frog for a short time, reached over, picked it up carefully, and placed it in his front breast pocket. Then the frog said, "What, are you, nuts? Didn't you hear what I said? I said kiss me and I will be your beautiful bride." He opened his pocket, looked at the frog and said, "Nah, at my age I'd rather have a talking frog."

2. Airplane Ride

Fred and his wife Edna went to the state fair every year. Every year Fred said, "Edna, I'd like to ride in that there airplane." And every year Edna would say, "I know, Fred, but that airplane ride costs ten dollars, and ten dollars is ten dollars."

One year Fred and Edna went to the fair and Fred said, "Edna, I'm 71 years old. If I don't ride that airplane this year, I may never get another chance." Edna replied, "Fred, that there airplane ride costs ten dollars, and ten dollars is ten dollars."

The pilot overheard them and said, "Folks, I'll make you a deal. I'll take you both up for a ride. If you can stay quiet for the entire ride and not say one word, I won't charge you, but if you say one word, it's ten dollars." Fred and Edna agreed, and up they went. The pilot did all kinds of twists and turns, rolls and dives, but not a word was heard. He did all his tricks over again, but still not a word.

They landed and the pilot turned to Fred. "Well, I did everything I could think of to get you to yell out, but you didn't." Fred replied, "Well, I was gonna say something when Edna fell out, but ten dollars is ten dollars."

3. All Dressed Up

The rural Baptist church has a small congregation of mostly very faithful people. "Mostly," because one brother, Shep Thomas, had quit coming to church. The pastor became concerned about him, so he decided to take a trip out to his farm and see why he had stopped coming.
"Well, preacher, I outgrew my funeral suit and I only have these overalls and old shirt. I can't go to the Lord's house dressed like this." "I can remedy that," the preacher said with great compassion. "I've got a spare shirt, sports coat and slacks that I'll give to you if you'll come back to church." The man agreed, and the pastor came back that afternoon with the clothes. Next Sunday Shep Thomas didn't show up again, so the pastor went out to the farm and asked, "Shep, I gave you all those clothes, why didn't you come to church?" "Well preacher," Shep responded, "I got up and showered and shaved, and put on those nice duds. I looked in the mirror and looked so good that I went to the Episcopal Church in town!"

Game/Activity:

1. Advertise in Advance: Members can be encouraged to bring their personal coin collections to share with their respective tables. Table participants then try to guess what country the coins are from.

2. Read the "Dementia Test" (see appendix pages 198-199) to the group and wait briefly after each question to give them time to think and then give the answer.

Video/YouTube Clip:

There are some very good YouTube tutorials on how to start a coin collection if something prior to the beginning of the event is desired.

Reading:

1. Read some excerpts from Jeff Foxworthy's "You Might Be a Redneck If…" available over the Internet.

2. Give out copies of "Tips for a Positive New Year" to take home (see appendix pages 200-201).

Scripture for the Month: (Can put in newsletter to encourage memorization)

"Rejoice always, pray continually, give thanks in all circumstances; for this is God's will for you in Christ Jesus" (1 Thessalonians 5:16–18).

FEBRUARY
Monthly Ideas

February
Monthly Ideas

1. "Love Those Grandkids" Night
(Intergenerational: Kids)

One variant on the love theme for February is having an intergenerational meeting with the grandkids! It will be something young and old can do together during the winter months. Grandparents love their grandkids and grandkids love their grandparents, so play games, laugh, and have lots of candy on hand.

Entertainment/speaker:
This has to be a fun evening, so make it a game night, or have a children's ministry team come, a clown that does tricks or balloons, a Christian comedian or a combination of the above.

Pre-dinner Conversation Starter:
1. Have sheets with tic-tac-toe, dots, and seek and find word games to play before dinner (see appendix page 202). Don't forget to put pencils on the tables as well. Grandparents may get to know their grandkids more and vice versa with "My Favorite Things to Do," and "Valentine Word Search" activity (see appendix pages 203-204). You could also have paper airplane sheets for children to make; see www.funpaperairplanes.com.

2. Photo Booth: Have an area set up for photos to be taken of people when coming in. You could have a professional come in or just a good photographer from the group who doesn't mind taking pictures would be fine. Then send each person a 5x7 copy of the picture later, after they have all been developed, as a gift for coming.

Decorations:
Valentine theme: use red and pink with paper cups (Valentine muffin liners would be perfect) for candy at each place. (Candy will be given out after each game and through the evening for placement in their cups.) For a centerpiece, you could use children's valentines

or chocolate kisses sprinkled around. Also, packs of children's games can be purchased inexpensively at Oriental Trading or most dollar stores.

Quote for the Month/Event:

"Too often we underestimate the power of a touch, a smile, a kind word, a listening ear, an honest compliment, or the smallest act of caring, all of which have the potential to turn a life around." –Leo Buscaglia

Joke/Story:

1. There is the story of a woman who was in the bathroom, putting on her makeup, under the watchful eyes of her young granddaughter, as she'd done many times before. After she applied her lipstick and started to leave, the little one said, "But Grandma, you forgot to kiss the toilet paper good-bye!" Children say the cutest things! We will probably never put lipstick on again without thinking about kissing the toilet paper good-bye.

2. A grandmother was telling her little granddaughter what her own childhood was like: "We used to skate outside on a pond. I had a swing made from a tire that hung from a tree in our front yard. We rode our pony. We picked wild raspberries in the woods." The little girl was wide-eyed, taking this all in. At last she said, "I sure wish I'd gotten to know you sooner!"

3. One grandmother was telling that she didn't know if her granddaughter had learned her colors yet, so she decided to test her. She would point out something and ask what color it was. The granddaughter would tell her and was always correct. It was fun for the grandmother, so she continued. At last, the little girl headed for the door, saying, "Grandma, I think you should try to figure out some of these yourself!"

4. A second grader came home from school and said to her grandmother, "Grandma, guess what? We learned how to make babies today." The grandmother, more than a little surprised, tried to keep her cool. "That's interesting," she said, "How do you make babies?" "It's simple," replied the girl. "You just change 'y' to 'i' and add 'es.'"

5. A grandfather was delivering his grandchildren to their home one day when a fire truck zoomed past. Sitting in the front seat of the fire truck was a Dalmatian dog. The children started discussing the dog's duties. "They use him to keep crowds back," said one child. "No," said another. "He's just for good luck." A third child brought the argument to a close. "They use the dogs," she said firmly, "to find the fire hydrants."

6. Little Johnny's new baby brother was screaming up a storm. He asked his mom,

"Where'd we get him?" His mother replied, "He came from heaven, Johnny." Johnny says, "WOW, I can see why they threw him out!"

7. One lady tells of a certain time when she was sitting in the reception area of her doctor's office. A woman rolled an elderly man in a wheelchair into the room. As she went to the receptionist's desk, the man sat there, alone and silent. Just as she was thinking she should make small talk with him, a little boy slipped off his mother's lap and walked over to the wheelchair. Placing his hand on the man's hand he said, "I know how you feel. My mom makes me ride in the stroller too."

Game/Activity:

1. Play "Famous Animals" (see appendix pages 205-206).

2. Make a valentine together for a parent, friend or to give away to a shut-in.

Video/YouTube Clip:

Playing a couple funny children's video clips would be a good break throughout the evening.

Reading:

1. "A Child's View of Grandma and Grandpa"

- A grandmother is a lady who has no children of her own, so she likes other people's kids.
- A grandfather is a man grandmother. He likes to go on walks with kids and talk about fishing and things like that.
- Grandmas don't have to do anything but be there. They're old, and so they shouldn't play hard or run. They let you ride the "pretend horse" at Kmart and they always have plenty of quarters.
- When they take you for walks, they always stop for things like caterpillars and pretty leaves. Grandmas never say, "Hurry up."
- Usually they are fat, but not too fat to tie your shoes. They wear glasses and funny underwear. They can do neat things like take out their teeth.
- They can always answer questions like, "Why do dogs hate cats?" and "How come God isn't married?"
- They don't talk baby talk like visitors do, because they know it's hard to understand.
- When they read to you, they don't skip. And they never mind reading the same story over again.
- Everybody should try to have a grandma or grandpa, because they're the only grown-ups who seem to always have time for you.

Handout to take home:
Hand out copies of "Biblical Attributes to Pray for Your Grandchildren" (see appendix pages 207-208).

Scripture for the Month: (Can put in newsletter to encourage memorization)
"Yet to all who did receive him, to those who believed in his name, he gave the right to become children of God" (John 1:12).

2. A Carbonaro Night
(from the Carbonaro Effect - You Tube Series)

Play several episodes from the Carbonaro Effect, You Tube Series for the group – interspersed with games. Carbonaro is a great magician and he always leaves you wondering how he did each trick! Lots of fun.

Pre-dinner Conversation Starter:
Play "Riddle Your Brain" (see appendix page 209).

Decorations:
Shiny, glitzy and magician like decorations. Could have shiny magic wands as decorations or cone hats in the middle with stars on them. The heart theme could be used as well since it is February.

Quote for the Month/Event:
"A marriage may be made in heaven, but regular maintenance must be done on earth."
- Anonymous

Joke/Story:
1. The Silent Treatment
A man and his wife were having some problems at home and were giving each other the silent treatment. The next week, the man realized that he would need his wife to wake him at 5:00 AM for an early morning business flight to Chicago. Not wanting to be the first to break the silence (AND LOSE), he wrote on a piece of paper, "Please wake me at 5:00 AM."

The next morning the man woke up, only to discover it was 9:00 AM and that he had missed his flight. Furious, he was about to go and see why his wife hadn't awoken him when he noticed a piece of paper by the bed. The paper said, "It is 5:00 AM. Wake up."

2. "Husbands Listen Up"
There is the story of a husband and wife who had not been out together in quite some time. One Saturday, as the wife was finishing the dinner dishes, the husband stepped up behind her. "Would you like to go out, girl?" he asked enthusiastically. Not even turning around, the wife quickly replied, "Oh, yes, I'd love to!" The next evening they went out to a fancy restaurant, like they had in their dating days, had a wonderful evening, and it wasn't until the end of it that the man confessed. His question had actually been directed to the family dog, lying near the woman's feet on the kitchen floor! That confirmed that the honeymoon was definitely over!

3. Marital Trust
One day a man drove his secretary home after she fell quite ill at work. Although this was an innocent gesture, he decided not to mention it to his wife, who tended to get jealous easily.

Later that night the man and his wife were driving to a restaurant. Suddenly he looked down and spotted a high-heel shoe half hidden under the passenger seat. Not wanting to be conspicuous, he waited until his wife was looking out her window before he scooped up the shoe and tossed it out of the car. With a sigh of relief, he pulled into the restaurant parking lot.

That's when he noticed his wife squirming around in her seat. "Honey," she asked, "have you seen my other shoe?"

Game/Activity:
1. Play "Bible Pairs" (see appendix page 212).

2. Call people up randomly (and give them a prize) after they answer a question. Use the "Get to know you Questions," (see appendix pages 210-211).

Reading:
1. The Most Beautiful Flower
The park bench was deserted as I sat down to read,
Beneath the long, straggly branches of an old willow tree.
Disillusioned by life with good reason to frown,
For the world was intent on dragging me down.

And if that weren't enough to ruin my day,
A young boy out of breath approached me, all tired from play.

He stood right before me with his head tilted down,
And said with great excitement, "Look what I found!"
In his hand was a flower, and what a pitiful sight,
With its petals all worn - not enough rain, or too little light.
Wanting him to take his dead flower and go off to play,
I faked a small smile and then shifted away.

But instead of retreating he sat next to my side,
And placed the flower to his nose,
And declared with overacted surprise,
"It sure smells pretty and it's beautiful, too.
That's why I picked it; here, it's for you."

The weed before me was dying or dead.
Not vibrant of colors: orange, yellow or red.
But I knew I must take it, or he might never leave.
So I reached for the flower, and replied, "Just what I need."

But instead of him placing the flower in my hand,
He held it mid-air without reason or plan.
It was then that I noticed for the very first time,
That weed-toting boy could not see: he was blind.

I heard my voice quiver; tears shone in the sun
As I thanked him for picking the very best one.
"You're welcome," he smiled, and then ran off to play,
Unaware of the impact he'd had on my day.

I sat there and wondered how he managed to see
A self-pitying man beneath an old willow tree.
How did he know of my self-indulged plight?
Perhaps from his heart, he'd been blessed with true sight.

Through the eyes of a blind child, at last I could see
The problem was not with the world; the problem was me.
And for all of those times I myself had been blind,
I vowed to appreciate every second that's mine.
And then I held that wilted flower up to my nose

And breathed in the fragrance of a beautiful rose
And smiled as I watched that young boy,
Another weed in his hand,
About to change the life of an unsuspecting old man.
(www.laughandlift.com Used by permission.)

Video/YouTube Clip:
Play selections from An Evening of Comedy with Tim Lovelace, Can You Glither? 2009, Crosswoods Music. (The section of friends by Aaron Wilburn.) He is a Christian comedian who does a comedy set about aging – perfect for seniors! Available from TimLovelace.com, 1-800-614-5163.

Scripture for the Month: (Can put in newsletter to encourage memorization)
"Call to me and I will answer you and tell you great and unsearchable things you do not know" (Jeremiah 33:3).

3. "Photography Night"

At this activity, have a local photography studio and several photographers come and speak for 15 minutes each on topics such as "How to Take Clear Pictures," "Comparison between Black and White Photography and Color: Which Is the Best?" or "The History of Photography." Each of the businesses represented will set up tables and displays showing examples of their photography (good for business) AND will have staff on hand to clean/examine people's cameras for free.

Attendees are encouraged to bring their cameras for the staff at the tables to review and clean. (These will need to be tagged with their names upon entering.)

Pre-dinner Conversation Starter:
A fun idea is to have disposable cameras at each table for the people to take pictures of each other together. Developed pictures will be sent to table members afterward. Have a note on the cameras saying to take pictures of those at your table (see appendix page 214).

Also have wedding pictures of couples in the group (photocopied previously and the originals returned) placed around the center of the table. Try to guess the couples. For "Name That Couple" (see appendix page 213).

Search YouTube for "Classic Commercials of the '70s, and about 10 minutes before the event play the video.

Decorations:

Do Las Vegas style with glitzy decorations and shiny confetti sprinkled around the tables, shiny metallic helium balloons, the camera, and pictures. If wedding pictures are not used, then put pictures of camera-related scenes (see appendix page 214).

Quote for the Month/Event:

(On trying something new)

"If one advances confidently in the direction of his dreams and endeavors to live the life which he has imagined, he will meet with a success unexpected in common hours. If you have built castles in the air, your work need not be lost. That is where they should be. Now put the foundations under them." – Henry David Thoreau

"The only place people ain't happy is in hell; and I've made arrangements not to go there! So. HA HA HA!" – Jerry Clower

Joke/Story:

1. NEWSFLASH: "In order to help save the economy, the government announced this week that the Immigration department will start deporting seniors, (instead of illegal immigrants) in order to lower Social Security and Medicare costs. They justified their decision by saying older people are easier to catch and will not remember how to get back home. I was very upset when I heard this - thinking of you all. Then it dawned on me. . . oh rats, I'll see you on the bus!

2. Ah, those dating days. . . On a lonely, moonlit country road the engine coughed and the car came to a halt. "That's funny," said the young man. "I wonder what that knocking was?" "Well, I can tell you one thing for sure," the girl answered icily. "It wasn't opportunity."

Boy: "You know, sweetheart, since I met you, I can't eat…. I can't sleep … I can't drink." Girl: "Why not?" Boy: "I'm broke!"

Boy: "Aww, look at the cow and the calf rubbing noses in the pasture. That sight makes me want to do the same." Girl: "Well, go ahead … it's your cow."

Boy: "Gladys, do you love me?" Girl: "Yes." Boy: "Would you be willing to live on my income?"

Girl: "Yes, if you'll get another one for yourself!"

John: "Don't you think I'm rather good looking?" Judy: "In a way." John: "What kind of way?"
Judy: "Away off."

3. A priest, a Pentecostal preacher, and a rabbi all served as chaplains at a major university. Every week they would get together for coffee and to talk about their ministry cases. One day, someone made the comment that preaching to people isn't really all that hard. It would be much harder to preach to a bear. So they all decided to participate in an experiment. They would go out into the woods, find a bear, and see which of them could convert it.

A week later they found themselves in the hospital discussing their experiences. Father Flannery, on crutches and with a big bandage around his head, said, "Well, I went into the woods to find a bear. When I found him, I blessed him, called on the saints, and began reading from the Catechism, and he wanted nothing to do with that. He batted me around until I could grab my holy water, sprinkle him, and say 'Holy Mary Mother of God.' When I did, he became gentle as a lamb. Next week the bishop is coming to give him first communion."

Rev. Billy Bob, the Pentecostal preacher, was next. He was in a wheelchair with one arm in a sling and one leg in a cast and hooked up to an IV drip. In his best pulpit voice, he said, "Well, brothers, you know I don't have nothing to do with holy water and sprinkling. I found me a bear and read to him from God's Holy Word. Satan was behind him and he pushed the bear into me. He commenced scratchin' and bitin' until we rolled down the hill into a crick. As soon as we did, I quick dunked him down and baptized him. He became gentle as a lamb and we was praisin' God together."

They both looked at the rabbi, who was in intensive care with a full body cast and tubes all over. The rabbi glances up and strains to say, "I've decided that the next time, I won't try to start things out with circumcision!"

4. Super Bowl Time
It was Super Bowl Sunday, and in church the time for the Sunday tithes and offerings was approaching. The minister, an avid sports fan, was obviously excited about the day. After he blessed the offering, he reached into his pocket, grabbed a quarter, flipped it into the air, glanced at it as it landed, then in referee fashion announced, "The ushers have elected to receive!"

Game/Activity:

1. Photo Contest: Advertise in advance to have members bring their photos that they have taken, put them on display around the room, number them, and then have the members vote on first, second, and third place.

2. Play "Heart Words" or "Valentine's Day Crossword" (see appendix pages 215-217).

3. Old Hat Surprise: Ask each guest to bring an old hat to the party, or collect them yourself before the party with the help of members and friends. Any kind of old hat can be used, the greater the variety the better — men's felt, straw or silk hats, visor caps, farmer's hats and all varieties of women's hats (will need enough for everyone attending). Have each table put one hat in front of each person. Then someone starts the music and as long as the music continues the hats are passed around the table from left to right. When the music ceases each person decides if he wants to keep the hat or not. If he is satisfied with his hat he puts it on and drops out of the game. If not, he puts it back on the table in front of him and the process is repeated twice more. At the end of the third round everyone must keep whatever hat he has and wear it for the rest of the evening. (And do take pictures of each other!) The hats that are left over at the end of the evening must either be reclaimed by the owners or donated ones given to charity.

4. Laugh Out Loud Silhouettes: Have two sheets set up in an area with lights behind them. Have teams (by table) come up with a shadow pose. Have judges to vote on the best one!

Video/YouTube Clip:
Search YouTube for "Classic Commercials of the '70s;" it will bring back memories!

Reading:
1. "What Love Means to 4 to 8 Year-Olds"
Touching words from the mouths of babes.
A Group of professional people posed this question to a group of children between the ages of four and eight: "What does love mean?" See what you think:

- "When my grandmother got arthritis, she couldn't bend over and paint her toenails anymore… so my grandfather did it for her all the time, even when his hands got arthritis too. That's love." Rebecca – Age 8

- "Love is when a girl puts on perfume and a boy puts on shaving cologne and they go out and smell each other." Karl – Age 5

- "Love is when you go out to eat and give somebody most of your french fries without making them give you any of theirs." Chrissy – Age 6

- "Love is when Mommy makes coffee for Daddy and she takes a sip before giving it to him to make sure the taste is OK." Danny – Age 7

- "Love is what's in the room with you at Christmas if you stop opening presents and listen." Bobby – Age 7 (Wow!)

- "If you want to learn to love better, you should start with a friend who you hate." Nikka – Age 6 (we need a few million more like Nikka on this planet)

- "Love is when you tell a guy you like his shirt, then he wears it every day." Noelle – Age 7

- "Love is like a little old woman and a little old man who are still friends even after they know each other so well." Tommy – Age 6

- "During my piano recital, I was on a stage and I was scared. I looked at all the people watching me and saw my daddy waving and smiling. He was the only one doing that. I wasn't scared anymore." Cindy – Age 8

- "Love is when Mommy gives Daddy the best piece of chicken." Elaine – Age 5

- "Love is when your puppy licks your face even after you left him alone all day." Mary Ann – Age 4

- "I know my older sister loves me because she gives me all her old clothes and has to go out and buy new ones. Lauren – Age 4

- "When you love somebody, your eyelashes go up and down and little stars come out of you." Karen – Age 7

- And the final one: The winner was a four-year-old child whose next-door neighbor was an elderly gentleman who had recently lost his wife. Upon seeing the man cry, the little boy went into the old gentleman's yard, climbed onto his lap, and just sat there. When his mother asked what he had said to the neighbor, the little boy said, "Nothing. I just helped him cry."

2. There once was a king who offered a prize to the artist who would paint the best picture of peace. Many artists tried. The king looked at all the pictures, but there were only two that he really liked, and he had to choose between them.

One picture was of a calm lake. The lake was a perfect mirror for peaceful, towering mountains that were all around it. Overhead was a blue sky with fluffy, white clouds. All who saw this picture thought that it was a perfect picture of peace.

The other picture had mountains too, but these were rugged and bare. Above was an angry sky from which rain fell and lightning played. Down the side of the mountain tumbled a foaming waterfall. This did not look peaceful at all, but when the king looked, he saw behind the waterfall a tiny bush growing in a crack in the rock. In the bush a mother bird had built her nest. There, in the midst of the rush of angry water, sat the mother bird on her nest. . .perfect peace. The king chose the second picture.

When he was asked why, he explained, "Peace does not mean to be in a place where there is no noise, trouble, or hard work. Peace means to be in the midst of all those things and still be calm in your heart. That is the real meaning of peace."

3. When we are thinking of photography and also looking at the wonder of nature, it gives us just a small picture of God's glory, as seen in his creation. Give a copy of "Awesome" to take home (see appendix pages 218-219).

Scripture for the Month: (Can put in newsletter to encourage memorization)
"A new command I give you: Love one another. As I have loved you, so you must love one another. By this everyone will know that you are my disciples, if you love one another" (John 13:34–35).

MARCH
Monthly Ideas

March
Monthly Ideas

1. March Madness/Saint Patrick Theme

This night honors all the hard-working immigrants who have made this country strong. To add a fun atmosphere, make sure you have good Scottish/Irish music playing when people come in. This music is peppy and will create anticipation and excitement. If there is a local bagpiper who could come and perform, that would be a treat. (Try calling the local fire station for a reference.) If there are cloggers or square dancers locally, have them come and do a demonstration. Have a local speaker come - a local historian on the city/area to discuss the origins of the city or town. The local fire chief or a city official would be good speakers as well.

Pre-dinner Conversation Starter:
Do statistics on the percentages of country of origin in your particular state, county or city. Visit the following to find local statistics:

> www.city-data.org   www.infoplease.com
> Local Chamber of Commerce or historical society

Decorations:
Use a green and white color theme with clovers and shamrocks, etc. for St. Patrick's Day. Dollar stores commonly have green and white clover or shamrock decorations in March. Small flags from different countries can be ordered inexpensively on the Internet. Another idea is to look on the Internet under Google or Bing images for different flags of Ireland, England, Scotland, France, etc., to copy and scatter around the center of the tables. Be sure to watch for trademark, registration or copyright information that may restrict the image usage.

Quote for the Month/Event:

"Never let yesterday use up today." – Anonymous

"You may have to fight a battle more than once to win it." – Margaret Thatcher

Joke/Story:

1. Two 90-year-old men, Joe and Tom, have been friends all their lives. Joe is dying, so Tom comes to the hospital to visit him. "Joe," says Tom, "you know how we both loved baseball all our lives. Joe, you have to do me a favor, ol' friend. When you go, somehow you've got to tell me if there's baseball in heaven." Joe looks up at Tom from his deathbed and says, "Tom, you've been my friend for many years. I'll do that for you." And with that, he passes on. It is midnight a couple of nights later. Tom is sound asleep when a loud voice calls out to him, "Tom ... Tom…." "Who is it?" Tom says, sitting up suddenly in bed. "Who is it?" "Tom. It's Joe." "Come on, you're not Joe. Joe died." "I'm telling you," insists the voice, "It's me, Joe." "Oh, Joe? My friend, is that you? Where are you?" "I'm in heaven," says Joe, "and now I've got to tell you, I've got some good news and some bad news." "Tell me the good news first," says Tom. "The good news," says Joe, "is that there really is baseball in heaven." "Really?" says Tom. "What's the bad news?" "You're pitching Tuesday!"

2. There were two very wealthy brothers who were known for their dishonesty and worldly ways. They were hated by most all the people in the town. Suddenly one of the brothers dropped dead of a heart attack. Not being church-going folks, the surviving brother went to a local minister and asked if he'd do the funeral. He told the pastor that he was prepared to make a very large donation to the church, on one condition, that during the funeral the minister must tell everyone that his brother was a saint. The minister thought it over for a little bit and agreed to preach the funeral.

The day of the funeral the pastor stood behind the pulpit and said, "The man you see lying here before your eyes was a womanizer, a drunkard, liar, cheat, and a totally heartless man, but compared to his brother he was a saint."

3. Supposedly this is a true story from Tennessee. See if any of you heard about this. There was a man who wanted to build a bar in the town. A church congregation that was next door strongly opposed it, but construction of the bar went on. Just before it was finished, however, lightning struck the bar and it burned to the ground.

The church congregation gloated and credited the Lord. The bar owner sued the church, claiming that the congregation's prayers had cost him his building, but the church leaders denied having anything to do with it. The case went to court and the local judge was said not to know how to rule on the matter. He said he had a bar owner who believed in the power of prayer and a church congregation that didn't!

Game/Activity:
1. "Saint Patrick: How Much Do You Know?" (see appendix pages 220).
2. "March Madness:" Word Game (see appendix page 221).

Video/YouTube Clip:
For traditional Irish dancing, watch a YouTube video of the group Riverdance.
For a beautiful Irish ladies' group, watch Celtic Women singing "Amazing Grace" with bagpipe accompaniment on YouTube.

Reading:
1. "Irish Blessing for Weddings"
May the road rise to meet you.
May the wind be always at your back.
May the sun shine warm upon your face,
The rains fall soft upon your fields.

May the light of friendship guide your paths together.
May the laughter of children grace the halls of your home.
May the joy of living for one another trip a smile from your lips,
A twinkle from your eye.

And when eternity beckons, at the end of a life heaped high with love,
May the good Lord embrace you with the arms that have nurtured you
the whole length of your joy-filled days.

May the gracious God hold you both in the palms of His hands,
And, today, may the Spirit of Love find a dwelling place in your hearts. (Traditional)

2. "I am a Christian"
When I say that 'I am a Christian', I am not shouting that 'I am clean living.' I'm whispering 'I was lost, but now I'm found and forgiven.'
When I say 'I am a Christian,' I don't speak of this with pride. I'm confessing that I stumble and need Christ to be my guide.
When I say 'I am a Christian,' I'm not trying to be strong. I'm professing that I'm weak and

need His strength to carry on.

When I say 'I'm a Christian,' I'm not bragging of success. I'm admitting I have failed and need God to clean my mess.

When I say 'I am a Christian,' I'm not claiming to be perfect. My flaws are far too visible, but God believes I am worth it.

When I say 'I am a Christian,' I still feel the sting of pain. I have my share of heartaches, so I call upon His name.

When I say 'I am a Christian,' I'm not holier than thou. I'm just a simple sinner who received God.

Scripture for the Month: (Can put in newsletter to encourage memorization)

"This is the confidence we have in approaching God: that if we ask anything according to his will, he hears us. And if we know that he hears us — whatever we ask — we know that we have what we asked of him" (1 John 5:14–15).

2. Square Dancing Performance/History Night

Square dancing is a part of U.S. history and is a fun dance to just watch. When this event is advertised, be sure to state that it will be a demonstration, and attendees are not required to participate! Research to see if a square dancing group is close by or for more info see below:

> United Square Dancers of America: www.usda.org/folkdn.htm
> Western Square Dancing: www.dosado.com

Pre-dinner Conversation Starter:

"Square Dancing Trivia" (see appendix page 222).

Reading: Background

A square dance is a dance for four couples (eight dancers) arranged in a square. Square dances were first documented in seventeenth-century England but were also done in France and throughout Europe. They came to North America with the European settlers and through preservation and repetition; square dances have attained the status of a traditional U.S. folk dance. In most American forms of square dance, the dancers are prompted or cued through a sequence of steps by a caller to the beat or the wording of music. Twenty-one U.S. states have designated it as their official state dance.

A few other examples of state dances are:

Hawaii: The Hula
Pennsylvania and Wisconsin: The Polka
Virginia: The Reel
North Carolina: The Shag
New York: Lindy Hop
Ohio: The Charleston
Texas: The Texas Two Step
Massachusetts: The Hokie Pokie

Decorations:
Use a western country theme — bandanas and tin cans (beans, corn, black-eyed peas, hominy) in the center with small candles placed in glass holders on can tops. Cans may be taken home by the people at the table or donated to a local food pantry.

Quote for the Month/Event:
"Life is not about waiting for the storms to pass… it's about learning how to dance in the rain." – Anonymous

Joke/Story:
1. A young man who left his home in Texas at an early age finally purchased his own ranch in Oklahoma. He invited his father out for a visit and took him on a tour of the property. While they were driving along in the son's pickup truck, a jack rabbit hopped onto the road in front of them. The son stopped the truck to let the rabbit pass, and the father queried, "What in tarnation is that?" The son incredulously replied, "That's a jackrabbit Dad; what did you think it was?" The father shrugged and said, "We grow 'em a lot bigger back home in Texas." So they went on and a little farther down the road they came to a few buffalo roaming the range. The son stopped the truck and the father again said in a puzzled tone, "What are those?" The son hesitantly said, "Those are buffalo, Dad. You gotta be kidding me. You really don't recognize them?" The father replied, "Well, I guess they're kinda familiar — it's just that we grow 'em so much bigger back in Texas."

The son, a bit disgruntled, drove on in silence. At length they approached a low part in the road with marshy wetlands on either side. A large snapping turtle lumbered onto the road. The father peered intently at the creature and said, "Now what on earth is that thing?" Without missing a beat, the son replied, "a wood tick"…

2. An old man is sitting on a park bench crying his eyes out. A young jogger comes by and asks him what the matter is. The old man says, "I'm a multimillionaire. I have a great big

house and the fastest car in the world, and I just married a beautiful blonde bombshell." The young jogger says, "Man, you have everything I have ever dreamed for in my life. What could be so wrong in your life that you are sitting here in the park crying?" The old man says, "I can't remember where I live."

3. Billy and Bubba, two farmers from a small town outside of Little Rock, Arkansas, were walking home together after each had purchased a pig. Billy said to Bubba, "How are we going to tell them apart?" Bubba answered, "We'll cut the left ear off of your pig." And so they did. After a while, the pigs got into a fight and they had bitten off each other's ears. Billy asked, "Now what are we going to do?" "Well, how about if we cut the tail off of my pig?" Bubba replied. "That sounds like a good plan to me," Billy agreed. A little while later, the pigs got into another fight, and when it was over, they were both missing their tails. "What will we do now?" Bubba asked Billy. After giving it some thought, Billy replied, "Well, we could cut the leg off of yours." "That's not humane!" Bubba cried. So after some more thought, Billy said, "Well, let's do this. We'll just call the white one yours and the black one mine."

4. Three buddies died in a car crash. In heaven, St. Peter asked each one what he'd like to hear his friends and family say when they passed his casket at the wake. "I'd like to hear them say I was a great family man," said the first. "I'd like to hear them say what a wonderful father and teacher I was," said the second. The last fellow replied, "I'd like them to say, 'Hey look, He's moving!'"

Game/Activity:
Play "Take Your Foot out of Your Mouth!" (see appendix page 223). Be sure and have prizes!

Video/YouTube Clip:
If desired, a YouTube video of traditional square dancing can be played before the event begins.

Reading:
1. Read "I Double Dog Dare You" (see appendix page 224).

2. "Ramblings of a Retired Mind"
~ I was thinking about how a status symbol of today is a cell phone that everyone has clipped on their belt. I can't afford one, so I'm wearing my garage door opener. Now everyone thinks that I'm cool too!
~ I was thinking that women should put pictures of deadbeat missing husbands and fathers on beer cans.
~ I was thinking about old age and decided that it is when you still have something on the

ball but you are just too tired to bounce it.
- ~ You know when people see a cat's litter box, they always say, "Oh, have you got a cat?" Just once I want to say, "No, it's for company."
- ~ Employment application blanks always ask who is to be notified in case of an emergency. I think you should write, "A Good Doctor."
- ~ Why do they put pictures of criminals up in the Post Office? What are we supposed to do - write to these people? Why don't they just put their pictures on the postage stamps so the mail carriers could look for them while they delivered the mail?
- ~ Why do people constantly return to the refrigerator with the hopes that something new to eat will have materialized?
- ~ Why do people keep running over a string a dozen times with their vacuum cleaner, then reach down, pick it up, examine it, then put it down to give their vacuum one more chance?
- ~ Why is it that NO plastic garbage bag will open from the end on your first try?
- ~ I saw a sign in a travel window that said, "Please go away."
- ~ Life is like a doughnut . . . you're either in the dough or in the hole.

Scripture for the Month: (Can put in newsletter to encourage memorization)
"*…a time to weep and a time to laugh, a time to mourn and a time to dance*" (Ecclesiastes 3:4).

3. Genealogy Night

Often people would like to know their family history, but most don't know how to begin the research. Find a speaker on genealogical research and have them come and present a "how to" for beginners. A good place to begin, in the search for a speaker, would be with the local historical society, library or the state genealogical association.

Pre-dinner Conversation Starter:
Have a packet prepared by the speaker at each place setting or use the handouts: "Genealogy 101: How to get Started"; and "Favorite Websites"; (see appendix pages 225-226) and "Family Group Sheets" available from familysearch.org.

Decorations:
Go with an antique theme, using brown napkins and glass Coke bottles with flowers in them for the centerpieces. If there is an antique shop nearby, ask them to be the sponsor, bringing in antiques for decorations (and sales). If needed, use old black and white pictures downloaded from Google or Bing images on the Internet to copy, cut, and scatter around tables — but be sure to watch for trademark, registration or copyright information that may restrict the image usage.

Quote for the Month/Event:
"It's not where you start – it's where you finish that counts." – Zig Ziglar

Joke/Story:
1. Walking up to a department store's fabric counter, a pretty young girl tells the clerk, "I want to buy this material for a new dress. How much does it cost?" "Only one kiss per yard," replied the smirking male clerk. "That's fine," replies the girl. "I'll take ten yards." With expectation and anticipation written all over his face, the clerk hurriedly measures out and wraps the cloth, then held it out teasingly. The girl snapped up the package, pointed to a little old woman standing beside her, and smiling, says: "Grandma is paying the bill."

2. Three boys are in the school yard bragging about their fathers. The first boy says, "My Dad scribbles a few words on a piece of paper, he calls it a poem, they give him $50." The second boy says, "That's nothing. My Dad scribbles a few words on a piece of paper, he calls it a song, and they give him $100." The third boy says, "I got you both beat. My Dad scribbles a few words on a piece of paper, he calls it a sermon, and it takes eight people to collect all the money!"

3. An elderly woman died last month. Having never married, she requested no male pallbearers. In her handwritten instructions for her memorial service, she wrote, "They wouldn't take me out while I was alive; I don't want them to take me out when I'm dead."

Game/Activity:
1. In advance, get childhood pictures of people who will be attending and copy or scan them and return. If it is possible, scan the pictures then show on an overhead and let the group guess who they are. Otherwise photocopy the pictures, return the originals, and then place copies on the tables for people to look at and guess who they are (same ones on each table).

2. Get to Know Each Other
This game is a list "Get to Know Each other" that is handed out to each table where the scores are tallied and the person with the highest number wins! (see appendix page 227).

Video/YouTube Clip:
From Mark Lowry's DVD Mark Goes to Hollywood, 2005, Spring House Productions (well worth buying), play "Lord of the Dance" by Lordsong. (The song has amazing harmony and gives a wonderful presentation of how we should celebrate life.)

Reading:

1. "Senior Citizens Lament"

Thought I'd let my doctor check me
Cause I didn't feel quite right,
All those aches and pains annoyed me
And I couldn't sleep at night.
He could find no real disorder,
But he wouldn't let it rest,
What with Medicare and Blue Cross
It wouldn't hurt to take some tests.
To the hospital he sent me
Though I didn't feel that bad,
He arranged for them to give me
Every test that could be had.
I was fluoroscoped and cystoscoped
My aging frame displayed,
Stripped upon an ice-cold table
While my gizzards were x-rayed.
I was checked for worms and parasites
For fungus and the crud,
While they pierced me with long needles
Taking samples of my blood.
Doctors came to check me over
Probed and pushed and poked around,
And to make sure I was living,
They wired me for sound.
They finally concluded
(Their results have filled a page),
What I have will someday kill me
My affliction is OLD AGE…

2. My family coat of arms ties at the back. Is that normal?
- My family tree is a few branches short! All help appreciated.
- My ancestors must be in a witness protection program!
- Shake your family tree and

watch the nuts fall!
- My hobby is genealogy; I raise dust bunnies as pets.
- I looked into my family tree and found out I was a sap.
- I'm searching for myself; have you seen me?
- A family tree can wither if nobody tends its roots.
- A new cousin a day keeps the boredom away.
- After 30 days, unclaimed ancestors will be adopted.
- Any family tree produces some lemons, some nuts, and a few bad apples.
- FLOOR: The place for storing your priceless genealogy records.
- Gene-Allergy: It's a contagious disease, but I love it.
- Genealogy is like playing hide and seek: They hide ... I seek!
- "Crazy" is a relative term in my family.
- A pack rat is hard to live with but makes a fine ancestor.
- I want to find ALL of them! So far I only have a few thousand.
- I should have asked them BEFORE they died!
- I think my ancestors had several "bad heir" days.
- Only a genealogist regards a step backwards as progress.
- Heredity: Everyone believes in it until their children act like fools!
- It's an unusual family that hath neither a lady of the evening nor a thief.
- Many a family tree needs pruning.
- Snobs talk as if they had begotten their own ancestors!

Bright ideas

- That's strange: half my ancestors are WOMEN!
- Genealogists live in the past lane.
- All right! Everybody out of the gene pool!
- Always willing to share my ignorance!
- Documentation . . . the hardest part of genealogy.
- Genealogy: chasing your own tale!
- Genealogy . . . will I ever find time to mow the lawn again?
- That's the problem with the gene pool: NO lifeguards.
- I researched my family tree . . . and apparently I don't exist!

(GCFL.net, info@gcfl.net. Used by permission.)

Scripture for the Month: (Can put in newsletter to encourage memorization)
"Trust in the Lord with all your heart and lean not on your own understanding; in all your ways submit to him, and he will make your paths straight" (Proverbs 3:5–6).

APRIL
Monthly Ideas

April
Monthly Ideas

1. "Science and the Bible" (Intergenerational: Youth)

This is an evening where we focus on science and the Bible. There are many great resources for this topic from a Christian perspective. One such resource is an organization called "Answers in Genesis," which has great teaching material and also speakers who will do presentations for groups.

This is a youth night, where the seniors have the teens in the church to join in the lesson. If a live speaker is not an option then a good alternative is Ken Ham in the DVD Science Confirms the Bible made by Answers in Genesis. This video is a very fast-paced and funny approach geared for teens. It is available from Answers in Genesis for $12.99.

Take a few minutes to honor the retired ministers or chaplains from the group. Mention that they have dedicated their lives to teaching the word of God and we honor and appreciate them.

(For introduction) George Burns said:
"I don't worry about getting old. I'm old already. Only young people worry about getting old."

Pre-dinner Conversation Starter:
Have handouts "Evolution vs. Creation" on the table for people to read when arriving (see appendix pages 228-229).

Decorations:
Church/crosses theme: If possible make little milk box churches, spray painted white with a small gold or bronze cross (available at craft stores) to decorate the steeple. Gospel tracts

can be scattered around the center of the table and then taken at the end of the dinner.

Billy Graham's Peace with God is a simple and classic tract that touches the simple human need of how to have peace with God (which comes only through salvation in Jesus). It is available from www.crossway.org or www.billygrahambookstore.com.

Another idea, since it is April, would be to have a vase of spring flowers on the table with a nature springtime color theme.

Quote for the Month/Event:
"Art demands an artist. Random change has never explained a waltz or a symphony, a physical equation or an epic poem. It cannot." – Thomas Dubay

"If man evolved from monkeys and apes, why do we still have monkeys and apes?"
– Anonymous

Joke/Story:
1. One day a group of scientists got together and decided that man had come a long way and no longer needed God. So they picked one scientist to go and tell Him that they were done with Him. The scientist walked up to God and said, "God, we've decided that we no longer need you. We're to the point that we can clone people and do many miraculous things, so why don't you just go on and get lost."

God listened very patiently and kindly to the man. After the scientist was done talking, God said, "Very well, how about this? Let's say we have a man-making contest." To which the scientist replied, "Okay, great!" But God added, "Now, we're going to do this just like I did back in the old days with Adam." The scientist said, "Sure, no problem" and bent down and grabbed himself a handful of dirt. God looked at him and said, "No, no. You make your own dirt!"

2. I've often wondered what an atheist would do if stuck behind a car that wasn't moving at a green light that had a bumper sticker on it that said, "Honk if you love Jesus!"

3. I have the King Dude's Version of the Bible…it starts off by saying: "In the beginning, there was like…NADA! Then the Big Guy Upstairs separated the beach from the ocean, and on the seventh day, there were some gnarly waves, Dude!" It goes on to say, "And Moses went down into Egypt and said, 'This captivity is BOGUS…let my people GO, Sandman!'"

4. A teacher is using the "scientific method" to teach the class about evolution...
TEACHER: Tommy, do you see the tree outside?
TOMMY: Yes.
TEACHER: Tommy, do you see the grass outside?
TOMMY: Yes.
TEACHER: Go outside and look up and see if you can see the sky.
TOMMY: Okay. (He returned a few minutes later.) Yes, I saw the sky.
TEACHER: Did you see God?
TOMMY: No.
TEACHER: That's my point. We can't see God because he isn't there. He doesn't exist.
A little girl spoke up and wanted to ask the boy some questions. The teacher agreed and the little girl questioned the boy.
LITTLE GIRL: Tommy, do you see the tree outside?
TOMMY: Yes.
LITTLE GIRL: Tommy, do you see the grass outside?
TOMMY: Yessssss (getting tired of the questions this time).
LITTLE GIRL: Did you see the sky?
TOMMY: Yesssssss.
LITTLE GIRL: Tommy, do you see the teacher?
TOMMY: Yes
LITTLE GIRL: Do you see the teacher's mind?
TOMMY: No.
LITTLE GIRL: Then according to what we were taught today in school, she must not have one!

5. An atheist was taking a walk through the woods, admiring all that naturalism and evolution had created. "What majestic trees! What powerful rivers! What beautiful animals!" he said to himself. As he was walking alongside the river, he heard a rustling in the bushes behind him.

As he turned to look, he saw a seven-foot grizzly charge toward him. He ran as fast as he could up the path. He looked over his shoulder and saw that the bear was closing in on him. He tried to run even faster, so scared that tears were coming to his eyes. He looked over his shoulder again and the bear was even closer. His heart was pumping frantically as he tried to run even faster, but he tripped and fell on the ground.

He rolled over to pick himself up and saw the bear right on top of him raising his paw to kill him. At that instant he cried out "Oh my God!" Just then, time stopped. The bear froze, the forest was silent, and the river even stopped moving. A bright light shone upon the man, and a voice came out of the sky saying, "You deny my existence all these years, teach others I don't exist, and even credit my creation to a cosmic accident and now do you expect me to help you out of this predicament? Am I to count you as a believer?"

The atheist, ever so proud, looked into the light and said, "It would be rather hypocritical to ask to be a Christian after all these years, but could you make the bear a Christian?" "Very well," said the voice. The light went out, the river ran, the sounds of the forest continued, and the bear put his paw down. The bear then brought both paws together, bowed his head, and said, "Lord I thank you for this food that I am about to receive."

Game/Activity:
1. See how much science you know by playing "Science and the Bible" – Parts I and II (see appendix pages 230-231).

Video/YouTube Clip:
Take a few minutes before the dinner begins to watch a YouTube video of pictures from the Hubble Telescope. There are many different videos and these types of pictures masterfully show the glory of God's creation.

Reading:
1. "He was just a little boy"
He was just a little boy,
on a week's first day;
wandering home from Bible school,
and dawdling on the way.
He scuffed his shoes into the grass;
he even found a caterpillar;
he found a fluffy milkweed pod,
and blew out all the 'filler.'
A bird's nest in a tree overhead,
so wisely placed up so high;
was just another wonder,
that caught his eager eye.
A neighbor watched his zigzag course,
and hailed him from the lawn;
asked him where he'd been that day
and what was going on.
'I've been to Sunday School,'

he said, and turned a piece of sod...
he picked up a wiggly worm, replying,
'I've learned a lot about God.'
'M'mm, very fine way,' the neighbor said,
'for a boy to spend his time;'
'if you'll tell me where God is,
'I'll give you a brand new dime.'
Quick as a flash the answer came,
nor were his words faint;
'I'll give you a dollar, Mister,
if you can tell me where God ain't!'

2. Origins of April Fool's Day
The group can be asked if they know the origins of April Fool's Day. As they will probably not know, read the article by David Emery on April Fool's Day at www.about.com.

3. Blessing on Group
Have all the pastors come to the front of the group at the end of the meeting and assign one blessing to each of the pastors to speak over the group. For a list of blessings (see appendix pages 232-233).

Scripture for the Month: (Can put in newsletter to encourage memorization)
"The heavens declare the glory of God; the skies proclaim the work of his hands" (Psalm 19:1).

2. Testimonies and Taters

Having personal testimonies (one or two) is always a very interesting topic. Combine this night with a potato bar with all the toppings. Several potato casseroles, potato soup, potato salads, tator tots, French fries, etc. can be done as well.

Prizes: Can be potato peelers, containers of Pringles or small bags of chips.
Advertise in advance: People are to bring copies of their favorite potato recipe to share.

Pre-dinner Conversation Starter:
Have copies of "Senior Student Exam" (see appendix page 236) to play before event begins.

Decorations:
Have a large baking potato in the center with, fabric scraps, cotton balls, buttons, shiny glitter glue, yarn, pins and scissors (will be used later for a game).

Quote for the Month/Event:
"The one proof of a life beyond the grave is the resurrection of Jesus Christ. Therefore, let us be glad with the gladness of men plucked from a dark abyss of doubt and uncertainty, and planted on a rock of solid certainty; and let us rejoice with joy unspeakable, and laden with a prophetic weight of glory, as we ring out the ancient Easter morning's greeting, 'The Lord is risen indeed!'"
- Alexander Maclaren

Joke/Story:
1. An old geezer, who had been a retired farmer for a long time, became very bored and decided to open a medical clinic. He put a sign up outside that said: Dr. Geezer's clinic. "Get your treatment for $500, if not cured get back $1,000."

Doctor "Young," who was positive that this old geezer didn't know beans about medicine, thought this would be a great opportunity to get $1,000. So he went to Dr. Geezer's clinic. This is what transpired. Dr. Young: -"Dr. Geezer, I have lost all taste in my mouth. Can you please help me?"

Dr. Geezer: "Nurse, please bring medicine from box 22 and put 3 drops in Dr. Young's mouth."
Dr. Young: "Aaagh! This is Gasoline!"
Dr. Geezer: "Congratulations! You've got your taste back. That will be $500."
Dr. Young gets annoyed and goes back after a couple of days figuring to recover his money.
Dr. Young: "I have lost my memory. I cannot remember anything."
Dr. Geezer: "Nurse, please bring medicine from box 22 and put 3 drops in the patient's mouth."
Doctor Young: "Oh no you don't! That is Gasoline!"
Dr. Geezer: "Congratulations! You've got your memory back that will be $500."
Dr. Young (after having lost $1000) leaves angrily and comes back after several more days.
Dr. Young: "My eyesight has become weak! I can hardly see!
Dr. Geezer: "Well, I don't have any medicine for that so, "Here's your $1000 back."
Dr. Young: "But this is only $500..."
Dr. Geezer: "Congratulations! You got your vision back! That will be $500."
Moral of the story – just because you're "Young" doesn't mean that you can outsmart an old "Geezer!"

2. What kind of tater are you?
Emma Tater: tries to be like everyone else.
Ira Tater: annoys everyone else.
Facili Tater: leads and moves things along.
Agie Tater: always stirring up trouble.
Hezzie Tater: never gets around to doing anything.
Dick Tater: likes to give orders but doesn't want to soil their own hands.
Comment Tater: is not willing to help themselves, but quick to criticize those who are.
Speck Tater: content to sit on the sidelines and not participate in any ministry.
Ampu Tater: cuts themselves off from church and everything around them.
Sweet Tater: always willing to help, brings sunshine to lives of others and displays fruit of the Spirit.

3. It's Tax Season
A father walks into the market followed by his ten-year-old son. The kid is spinning a 25-cent piece in the air and catching it between his teeth. As they walk through the market, someone bumps into the boy at just the wrong moment and the coin goes straight into his mouth and lodges in his throat. He immediately starts choking and going blue in the face and Dad starts panicking, shouting and screaming for help. A middle-aged, fairly unremarkable man in a gray suit is sitting at a coffee bar in the market reading his newspaper and sipping a cup of coffee. At the sound of the commotion he looks up, puts his coffee cup down on the saucer, neatly folds his newspaper and places it on the counter. He gets up from his seat and makes his unhurried way across the market. Reaching the boy (who is still standing, but only just) the man takes hold of the kid and squeezes gently but firmly. After a few seconds the boy coughs up the quarter, which the man catches in his free hand. The man then walks back to his seat in the coffee bar without saying a word. As soon as he is sure that his son is fine, the father rushes over to the man and starts effusively thanking him. The man looks embarrassed and brushes off the thanks. As he's about to leave, the father asks one last question. "I've never seen anybody do anything like that before - it was fantastic - what are you, a surgeon or something like that?"
"No" the man replies, "I work for the income tax department, getting people to cough it up is my business."

4. One night the father comes home from work and knowing it was report card day says to his son, "I would like to see your report card." The son sheepishly grins and says "Sorry dad, it's not here - my friend just borrowed it. He wants to scare his parents."

5. Cheerful Giver

On one particular Sunday, the pastor was emphasizing the importance of everyone giving their tithes and offerings. He went on to challenge the people to give enthusiastically because II Corinthians 9:7 says that "God loves a cheerful giver." As the plate was passed, a little boy in the second pew quickly slipped off his neck tie and placed it into the offering plate. His mother, absolutely mortified, asked him what in the world he thought he was doing. The boy replied, "The pastor said put your ties in the offering plate and do it joyfully. I love that man!"

Game/Activity:

1. Potato show: Each table takes the decorations that are scattered and decorates the potato for a fashion show. Have prizes for the most creative, most "hot" potato, etc.

2. Hot Potato: Every person says their name, describes something interesting about themselves when "caught" by the potato.

3. Purse Scavenger Hunt: Play a scavenger hunt in cooperation by tables for items in ladies purses! For a List of "Scavenger Hunt" items (see appendix page 234).

Reading:

1. Since April is tax month:
"Taxes"
Tax his land, tax his wage,
Tax his bed in which he lays.
Tax his tractor, tax his mule,
Teach him taxes is the rule.
Tax his cow, tax his goat,
Tax his pants, tax his coat.
Tax his ties, tax his shirts,
Tax his work, tax his dirt.
Tax his car, tax his gas
Tax the roads he must pass.
Tax his hunting, tax his deer,
if he cries, tax his tears.
Tax his bills, tax his trash,
Tax his notes, tax his cash.
Tax him good and let him know
that after taxes, he has no dough.
If he hollers, tax him more,
Tax him until he's good and sore.
Tax his coffin; tax his grave,
Tax the sod in which he lays.
Put these words upon his tomb,
"Taxes drove me to my doom!"
And when he's gone, one won't relax,
they'll still be after the inheritance TAX!
(www.laughandlift.com - Used by permission.)

2. Devotion: Short devotion can be about being part of the body of Christ. Use Mr. Potato Head to illustrate what happens when we are not fulfilling our God-designed role in the church body. (You end up with 4 ears or 3 feet or all jumbled in the wrong places;) simple but funny and effective.

Video/YouTube Clip:

The 2012 YouTube video of Larnell Harris and Sandi Patti singing "I've Just Seen Jesus" is amazing. As they have gotten older their voices have matured to a just beautiful pitch. Since this is Easter month – this is a very appropriate song to play.

Scripture for the Month: (Can put in newsletter to encourage memorization)

"Whatever happens, conduct yourselves in a manner worthy of the Gospel of Christ." (Philippians 1:27-29).

3. A Night on the Trail: Old West Evening Theme

An "Old West" evening is always fun and usually there is a bluegrass group within a couple of hours that will come and play for the evening. Food should be "Old West" type," beans, biscuits, smoked meat or barbeque is appropriate with apple pie or fruit cobblers. One wonderful bluegrass gospel band that is reasonably priced and well worth inviting is:
The Harper Family
(harperfamilymusic.com)
Gallon or Katrina Harper

Pre-dinner Conversation Starter:
Have copies of the "Old West Trivia" game at each place setting (see appendix page 235).

Decorations:
Use lots of cowboy hats, red lanterns, ropes, old barrels, split-rail fencing, and hay bales with saddles on them if possible. Make homemade barn scenes or Oriental Trading has a great inexpensive Old West theme set. For a centerpiece put red bandanas underneath vases made out of tin cans (beans, tomatoes, vegetables) with simple flowers like daisies, black-eyed Susans or goldenrod. Another fun centerpiece idea would be to use cowboy boots filled with black-eyed Susans (if you know people you can borrow boots from)!

Dress:
Advertise in advance that there will be prizes for the best dressed cowboy, cowgirl or farm hand!

Quote for the Month/Event:
"Well done is better than well said." – Benjamin Franklin

"People are like tea bags — you have to put them in hot water before you know how strong they are." – Anonymous

Joke/Story:
1. City Slicker on the Farm: A young man from the city went to visit his farmer uncle. For the first few days, the uncle showed him the usual things — chickens, cows, crops, etc. After three days, however, it was obvious that the nephew was getting bored, and the uncle was running out of things to amuse him with. Finally the uncle had an idea. "Why don't you grab a gun, take the dogs, and go shooting." This seemed to cheer the nephew up and with enthusiasm, off he went, dogs in trail. "How did you enjoy that?" asked the uncle upon his return. "It was great!" exclaimed the nephew. "Got any more dogs?"

2. A farmer goes to his vet and says, "Doc, I need some more potency pills for my bull." The doc asks, "Do you recall what kind I gave you last time?" The old farmer says, "No, but they taste like chocolate."

3. A farmer was asked what he would do if he inherited $1,000,000.
"Oh," he said, "I'd jest keep farmin' 'til it was all gone."

4. A little prospector wearing clean new shoes walked into a saloon. A big Texan said to his friend standing at the bar, "Watch me make this dude dance." He walked over to the prospector and said, "You're a foreigner, aren't you? From the East?" "You might say that," the little prospector answered. "I'm from Boston and I'm here prospecting for gold." The big Texan said, "Now tell me something. Can you dance?" "No sir. I never did learn to dance." "Well, I'm gonna teach you. You'll be surprised how quickly you can learn." With that, the Texan took out his gun and started shooting at the prospector's feet. Hopping, skipping, and jumping, the little prospector was shaking like a leaf by the time he made it to the door. About an hour later the big Texan left the saloon. As soon as he stepped outside the door, he heard a click. He looked around and there, four feet from

his head, was the biggest shotgun he had ever seen. And the little prospector said, "Mr. Texan, have you ever kissed a mule?" "No," said the quick-thinking Texan, "but I've always wanted to."

5. Three burly fellows on huge motorcycles pulled up to a highway café, where a truck driver, just a little guy, was perched on a stool quietly eating his lunch. As the three fellows came in, they spotted him, grabbed his food away from him, and laughed in his face. The truck driver said nothing. He got up, paid for his food, and walked out.

One of the three cyclists, unhappy that they hadn't succeeded in provoking the little man into a fight, commented to the waitress: "Boy, he sure wasn't much of a man, was he?" The waitress replied, "Well, I guess not." Then, looking out the window, she added, "I guess he's not much of a truck driver, either. He just ran over three motorcycles."

Game/Activity:

1. Cow Milking Contest: Have a cow milking contest! This can be done with live or homemade wooden cows (with calf feeder bottles attached from behind). There will be lots of laughter at seeing the antics of this activity. Use a timer and have little measuring cups to keep track of who is the "best milker."

2. Cow Patty Toss: Paper or Styrofoam plates painted all brown can be thrown frisbee style into a barrel in the center of the tables. The table with the most plates in the barrel wins!

3. Potato Guess: Have a good-sized basket of potatoes on display. Upon arrival, have each person write down their name and guess as to how many potatoes are in a good-sized basket on display. Give a prize to the nearest guess.

4. Shoot 'em straight: This will need to be set up in advance, in an area out of the way (on a stage behind a curtain, for example). Several long tables will need to be set up with candles on top and plastic underneath (several tarps would be perfect). The object of the game is to use the water guns to try to put the flame out. Each table selects one person to represent them; the first one to get their candle out wins prizes for their tables.

5. Name That Tune: Have short clips from these classic Old West songs and see how many people can guess:

"Old Susanna" "Camptown Races" "Juanita
"The Old Chisholm Trail" "My Old Kentucky Home" "Old Man River"

"Old Folks at Home"   "Love's Old Sweet Song"   "Virginia Reel"
"You Are My Sunshine"   "Old McDonald Had a Farm"   "Clementine"
"Sweet Alice Ben Bolt" "Silver Threads among the Gold"
"She'll Be Coming 'Round the Mountain"

6. Old West Words: Give each table a piece of paper and pencil and ask them to come up with as many Old West words as they can in three minutes. Prizes: men's or ladies' straw hats or Bag Balm® (udder salve) from a local farm store!

Video/YouTube Clip:
Before the event begins, just for fun, show a YouTube video on how to milk a cow.

Reading:
1. For farmers, the weather is so much more important than to most of us. Take the town in Nebraska where there had been no rain for such a long time that the fields were brown, the crops were dying, and the ponds and watering sources were drying up. This was a desperate time for the farmers there. They did what people used to do when they needed help; they called for a special prayer service at the church. The minister requested that the people bring something that expressed their faith in God.

The minister was touched to see all the fervent prayers and expressions of faith from those in attendance. People had brought crosses, bibles, rosaries, and pictures of Jesus. They sang and prayed, and as if on cue at the end of the service, a soft rain began to fall. Cheers echoed through the church, and people began pouring out of the doors dancing in the rain. But the most special faith seemed to shine out when a small 7-year-old boy walked out the front doors of the church with an umbrella he had brought.

Scripture for the Month: (Can put in newsletter to encourage memorization)
"Whatever you do, work at it with all your heart, as working for the Lord, not for human masters, since you know that you will receive an inheritance from the Lord as a reward. It is the Lord Christ you are serving" (Colossians 3:23–24).

MAY
Monthly Ideas

May
Monthly Ideas

1. "Oooh LaLa" Day - Pillowcase Making for Kids with Cancer

This is "salon day" where local hairdressers come and do hair for the group. Usually hairdressers are looking for new clientele, so this could be billed as a way to get new customers. Hopefully they will donate several hours free of charge or at a small cost, supplies only, perhaps. This activity can consist of hot oil treatments or haircuts. Centers will have to be pre-set up around the area to be used. The hair stylists will bring their own equipment, but they will need places to set supplies and chairs for the people to sit.

Give people numbers when they arrive so the hairdressers can call the numbers in order. To fill in time while waiting for hairdressers, the people will need activities to do, so have other centers set up (complete with supplies; see below.) Some sample ideas are: 1. Manicures and pedicures, 2. Homemade Lipstick, 3. Grey Hair No More, 4. Coconut Feet, 5. Neck and back massages, 6. Homemade sugar scrubs, 7. Homemade lotion, and 8. Pillowcases for Kids with Cancer.

Encourage people in advance, to bring needed supplies for the event: fingernail polish to share, crayons for lipstick, (crayons can be old broken ones but nice colors for lipstick); their own plastic shower caps; an extra pair of socks and the pillow material of their choice – ¾ yard for the pillowcase and 1/3 yard for the border with matching thread). If possible, have all other supplies provided. See below for further instructions.

Decorations:

Tables will need to be set up around the room for people to sit and work on their activities. Decorate tables with vases of flowers or small baskets filled with nail files, nail polish, and lipstick or chapstick as gifts.

Refreshments:

There will need to be refreshments and snacks. This event would be perfect combined with a tea and coffee time: have different kinds of coffees and teas to be tried out on a nicely decorated table, with cookies.

Quote for the Month/Event:

"People are like stained glass windows. They sparkle and shine when the sun is out, but when the darkness sets in their true beauty is revealed only if there is a light from within."
– Elisabeth Kubler-Ross

"I don't think of all the misery but of the beauty that still remains." – Anne Frank

Joke/Story:

1. Women will never be equal to men until they can walk down the street with a bald head and a beer gut and still think they are sexy.

2. Mrs. Franklin had been called for jury duty. She declined to serve because, she said, she did not believe in capital punishment. The judge tried to persuade her to stay. "Madam," he said, "This is not a murder case. It is merely a case in which a wife is suing her husband because she gave him $4,000 she had saved to buy her a new fur coat and he lost it all at the racetrack instead." "I'll serve," agreed Mrs. Franklin. "I could be wrong about capital punishment."

3. A man timidly walked into the ladies' department of JC Penney and shyly said to the woman at the counter, "I'd like to buy a bra for my wife." "What type of bra?" asked the clerk in a businesslike tone. "Type?" inquired the man. "There's more than one type?" "Look around," said the saleslady, as she pointed out a sea of bras in every shape, size, color, and material imaginable. "Actually," she said, "even with all of this variety, there are really only four types of bras to choose from." Relieved, the man asked about the types. The saleslady replied, "There are the Catholic, the Salvation Army, the Presbyterian, and the Baptist types. Which one would you prefer?" Now befuddled again, the man asked about the differences between them.

The saleslady responded, "It's really quite simple. The Catholic type supports the masses. The Salvation Army type lifts the fallen, the Presbyterian type keeps them staunch and upright, and the Baptist type makes mountains out of molehills."

4. A mom tells the story of one Mother's Day at church when there were rows of little potted flowers beside the altar. The pastor asked all the children to come forward

and pick out a plant for their mother. This family had been through a difficult year and survived some very hard times, and the mom was thinking that this special bit of appreciation was just what she needed. She was surprised, however, when her children presented her with a small, bedraggled flower plant. But she saw the joy and pride in their eyes, and asked them, out of all those beautiful flowers, what had made them pick this plant for her? Her son said, "We all agreed this one looked like it needed you, Mom." Moms make a difference!!

5. The room was full of pregnant women with their husbands. The instructor said, "Ladies, remember that exercise is good for you. Walking is especially beneficial. It strengthens the pelvic muscles and will make delivery that much easier. Just pace yourself, make plenty of stops and try to stay on a soft surface like grass or a path." "Gentlemen, remember – you're in this together. It wouldn't hurt you to go walking with her. In fact, that shared experience would be good for you both."

The room suddenly became very quiet as the men absorbed this information. After a few moments a man, name unknown, at the back of the room, slowly raised his hand. "Yes?" said the Instructor. "I was just wondering if it would be all right, if she carries a golf bag? Brings a tear to your eye, doesn't it? This level of sensitivity can't be taught.

Activity Tables: (Have a take-home sheet with the instructions below as well as ones to use during the activity.)

1. "Homemade Lipstick with Crayons"

There are many recipes out there, but the most inexpensive and convenient one is to mix half a crayon with a half tsp. of oil (vegetable oil is suggested). The only other ingredient needed is a ¾-inch-size piece of some type of greasy solid such as Crisco, or shea butter which actually has more benefits for your lips (as a moisturizer). One optional thing that can be added is a drop of some type of essential oil (like peppermint, available at craft stores); but for something sweeter, vanilla works as well. Just heat it up in the microwave until it is all melted, pour it immediately into the container, and wait for it to harden. This is more like a lip gloss than lipstick and would be fine for children to use as well.

There will need to be microwaves, microwavable containers, and small containers set up on a table for people to use to put lipstick in.

2. "Grey Hair No More"

For darker hair: make strong tea, 1 cup per person, and put on hair (then put shower/plastic cap on). Blackberry, Raspberry or Pomegranate tea will give a slight auburn highlight look. Let sit two hours if possible. Shampoo. For lighter hair: use honey and 3 tbsp. fresh lemon juice and put on selected parts of hair. Leave on one hour, then shampoo.

3. "Coconut Feet": A great foot softener is coconut oil available at Walmart stores. Rub on feet and let sit; put an extra pair of socks on.

4. Homemade sugar scrubs and lotion (see appendix pages 237-238)

5. "Pillowcases for Kids with Cancer:" to be donated afterward Ask people, in advance, to bring sewing machines to use, and have instructions pre-printed from the website: conkerrcancer.org/pillowdirections.html

Video/YouTube Clip:
1. Play the YouTube clip of Anita Renfroe's "All the Wrinkled Ladies," a parody of Beyonce's "All the Single Ladies."

2. Show "For Heaven's Sake" a ladies barbershop group with great singing and comedy, on YouTube.

Reading:
1. "To Mothers"
This is for the mothers who have sat up all night with sick toddlers in their arms, wiping up barf laced with Oscar Mayer wieners and cherry Kool-Aid, saying, "It's okay, honey, Mommy's here."
Who have sat in rocking chairs for hours on end soothing crying babies who can't be comforted.
This is for all the mothers who show up at work with spit-up in their hair and milk stains on their blouses and diapers in their purses.
For all the mothers who run carpools and make cookies and sew Halloween costumes.
And all the mothers who DON'T.

This is for the mothers who gave birth to babies they'll never see. And the mothers who took those babies and gave them homes.

This is for the mothers whose priceless art collections are hanging on their refrigerator doors.

And for all the mothers who froze their buns on metal bleachers at football or soccer games instead of watching from the warmth of their cars.

And when their kids asked, "Did you see me, Mom?" they could say, "Of course, I wouldn't have missed it for the world," and meant it.

This is for all the mothers who yell at their kids in the grocery store, and swat them in despair when they stomp their feet and scream for ice cream before dinner. And for all the mothers who count to ten instead, but realize how child abuse happens.

This is for all the mothers who sat down with their children and explained all about making babies. And for all the (grand)mothers who wanted to, but just couldn't find the words.

This is for all the mothers who go hungry so their children can eat.

For all the mothers who read "Goodnight, Moon" twice a night for a year. And then read it again. "Just one more time."

This is for all the mothers who taught their children to tie their shoelaces before they started school. And for all the mothers who opted for Velcro instead.

This is for all the mothers who teach their sons to cook and their daughters to sink a jump shot.

This is for every mother whose head turns automatically when a little voice calls "Mom?" in a crowd, even though they know their own offspring are at home — or even away at college or have their own families.

This is for all the mothers who sent their kids to school with stomachaches, assuring them they'd be just FINE once they got there, only to get calls from the school nurse an hour later asking them to please pick them up right away.

This is for mothers whose children have gone astray, who can't find the words to reach them. For all the mothers who bite their lips until they bleed when their 14-year-olds dye their hair green.

For all the mothers of the victims of recent school shootings, and the mothers of those who did the shootings. For the mothers of the survivors, and the mothers who sat in front of their TVs in horror, hugging their children who just came home from school safely. This is for all the mothers who taught their children to be peaceful, and now pray they come home safely from a war.

What makes a good mother anyway? Is it patience? Compassion? Broad hips? The ability to nurse a baby, cook dinner, and sew a button on a shirt, all at the same time?

Or is it in her heart?

Is it the ache you feel when you watch your son or daughter disappear down the street, walking to school alone for the very first time?

The jolt that takes you from sleep to dread, from bed to crib at 2 a.m. to put your hand on the back of a sleeping baby?

The panic, years later, that comes again at 2 a.m. when you just want to hear their key in the door and know they are safe again in your home?

Or the need to flee from wherever you are and hug your child when you hear news of a fire, a car accident, a child dying?

The emotions of motherhood are universal and so our thoughts are for young mothers stumbling through diaper changes and sleep deprivation, and mature mothers learning to let go.

For working mothers and stay-at-home mothers.

Single mothers and married mothers.

Mothers with money, mothers without.

This is for you all. For all of us…

Hang in there. In the end we can only do the best we can.

Tell them every day that we love them. And pray and never stop being a mom.

(GCFL.net, info@gcfl.net. Used by permission.)

2. A man came home from work and found his three children outside, still in their pajamas, playing in the mud, with empty food boxes and wrappers strewn all around the

front yard. The door of his wife's car was open, as was the front door to the house and there was no sign of the dog. Proceeding into the entry, he found an even bigger mess. A lamp had been knocked over, and the throw rug was wadded against one wall. In the front room the TV was loudly blaring a cartoon channel, and the family room was strewn with toys and various items of clothing. In the kitchen, dishes filled the sink, breakfast food was spilled on the counter, the fridge door was open wide, dog food was spilled on the floor, a broken glass lay under the table, and a small pile of sand was spread by the back door.

He quickly headed up the stairs, stepping over toys and more piles of clothes, looking for his wife. He was worried she might be ill, or that something serious had happened. He was met with a small trickle of water as it made its way out the bathroom door. As he peered inside he found wet towels, scummy soap, and more toys strewn over the floor. Miles of toilet paper lay in a heap and toothpaste had been smeared over the mirror and walls. As he rushed to the bedroom, he found his wife still curled up in the bed in her pajamas, reading a novel. She looked up at him, smiled, and asked how his day went. He looked at her bewildered and asked, "What happened here today?" She again smiled and answered, "You know every day when you come home from work and you ask me 'what in the world did you do all day?'" "Yes," was his incredulous reply. She answered, "Well, today I didn't do it."

Scripture for the Month: (Can put in newsletter to encourage memorization)
"Finally, brothers and sisters, whatever is true, whatever is noble, whatever is right, whatever is pure, whatever is lovely, whatever is admirable—if anything is excellent or praiseworthy—think about such things" (Philippians 4:8).

2. Fun with Fondue Night

Most seniors will remember fondue from the 1960s and '70s when it was a popular fad, and is now beginning to make a comeback. A fondue meal is a LOT of kitchen prep but is so special and fun! If possible, have it catered but if not, all the food will need to be cut up in advance. Have some nice music playing in the background to add atmosphere. Playing a few games and a special musical performance halfway through the evening would make this a very special time.

The Meal:
The meal is served in three courses: cheese and bread, meat and vegetables, and lastly dessert. Survey the group to see how many pots, (minus skewers) can be borrowed. Check

with local caterers as well to see if they have fondue pots that could be rented or borrowed. Ceramic pots need to be used for cheese and dessert fondues with metal pots for the meat fondue. Either vegetable broth or oil can be used for cooking the meat in the metal pots. Lots of wood skewers will need to be purchased for each table. The skewers used for the cheese and desserts may be cut in half as they don't need to be used to cook but just dip. Participants will need to use a new stick for each bite, to cut down on the spreading of germs, so no double dipping!

Course One: Different types of bread cut into chunks are dipped into the cheese fondue.

Course Two: Meat and Vegetables: the meats should be pre-prepared on skewers as they will take the longest to cook. The vegetables are in a bowl for the people to choose and place on their skewers. Can do several at a time (onions, zucchini, squash, green beans, carrots, etc.).

Course Three: Dessert: Small pieces of pound cake, strawberries, pineapple chunks, banana chunks are all dipped into the chocolate fondue.

Pre-Dinner Conversation Starter:
"Bible Testing" Time (see appendix page 239).

Decorations:
It is May and this evening deals with moms as well as Bible facts. Decorate with the Spring/flower motif. Hawaiian leis can be taken apart and the flowers scattered around the center of the table. Or tissue paper flowers can be made with the large ones as wall decorations and smaller ones used as a centerpiece.

Quote for the Month/Event:
"If you have a Bible that's falling apart, you'll have a life that's not." – Anonymous

"You know you're getting older when you stoop to tie your shoes and wonder what else you can do while you're down there." – George Burns

"I wake up every morning at nine and grab for the morning paper. Then I look at the obituary page. If my name is not on it, I get up." – Benjamin Franklin

Joke/Story:

1. A minister spoke to a deacon and said, "I'm told you went to the ball game instead of church this morning." The deacon thought for a minute and replied with indignation "That's a lie," he said, "and here's the fish to prove it."

2. Bible Trivia –
Who was the most successful physician in the Bible?
Job. He had the most patience.
Who was the best financier in the Bible?
Noah. He floated his stock while the whole world was in liquidation.
Who is the straightest man in the Bible?
Joseph. Pharaoh made a ruler out of him.

3. A conscientious minister decided to get acquainted with a new family in his congregation, so he called on them unannounced. Not knowing that the husband was on his way home from work and was expected any moment, his knock was answered by a teasing voice from within calling, "Is that you, Angel?" "No," replied the minister, "But I'm from the same department."

4. "Roof Repairs" - The minister was preoccupied with thoughts of how he was going to ask the congregation to come up with more money than they were expecting for repairs to the church building. Therefore, he was annoyed to find that the regular organist was out that Sunday and a substitute been brought in at the last minute. The substitute wanted to know what to play.

"Here's a copy of the service," he said impatiently. "But, you'll have to think of something to play after I make the announcement about the finances." During the service, the minister paused and said, "Brothers and sisters, we are in great difficulty: the roof repairs cost twice as much as we expected and we need to raise $4,000 more. Any of you who can pledge $100 or more, please stand up." At that moment, the substitute organist played "The Star Spangled Banner." And that is how the substitute became the regular organist.

5. For the moms in the group:

A teacher gave her class of second graders a lesson on the magnet and what it does. The next day in a written test, she included this question: "My full name has six letters. The first one is M. I am strong and attractive. I pick up things. What am I?" When the test papers were turned in, the teacher was astonished to find that almost 50 percent of the students answered the question with the word "Mother."

Game/Activity:

1. Play "Advertising Slogans." This will be a competition between tables. Give them 10 minutes to complete as many as they can (see appendix pages 204-241).

2. Spring Poem Game

Give each table a numbered sheet of paper. Have them work together to write a four - or five-line poem about spring beginning with "spring is the season of the year..." They must use the words: tear, dear, peer, fear, smear, ear, and clear in their poems; collect and read to the group (see appendix pages 242-243).

Reading:

1. "The Truth about Nutrition"

Here is the final word on nutrition and health. It's a relief to know the truth after all those conflicting medical studies. The Japanese eat very little fat and suffer fewer heart attacks than do the British or Americans. The French eat a lot of fat and also suffer fewer heart attacks than the British or Americans. The Japanese drink very little red wine and suffer fewer heart attacks than the British or Americans. The Italians drink excessive amounts of red wine and also suffer fewer heart attacks than the British or Americans. The Germans drink a lot of beer and eat lots of sausages and fats and suffer fewer heart attacks than the British or Americans.

Conclusion: Eat and drink what you like. Speaking English is apparently what kills you.

2. "The Target"

A young lady named Sally relates an experience she had in a class at one of our Christian universities. The teacher was known for his elaborate object lessons. One particular day, Sally walked into class and knew they were in for another fun day. On the wall was a big target and on a nearby table were many darts. The instructor told the students to draw a picture of someone that they disliked or someone who had made them angry and he would allow them to throw darts at the person's picture.

Sally's friend (on her right), drew a picture of a girl who had stolen her boyfriend. Another friend (on her left), drew a picture of his older brother. Sally drew a picture of the teacher, putting a great deal of detail into her drawing. Sally was pleased at the overall effect she had achieved.

The class lined up and began throwing darts with much laughter and hilarity. Some of the students threw their darts with such force that their targets were ripping apart. Sally looked forward to her turn, and was filled with disappointment when the teacher, because of time limits, asked the students to return to their seats.

As Sally sat thinking about how angry she was because she didn't have a chance to throw any darts at her target, the instructor began removing the target from the wall. Underneath the target was a picture of Jesus. A complete hush fell over the room as each student viewed the mangled picture of Jesus; holes and jagged marks covered His face and His eyes were pierced out. The teacher then said only these words, "In as much as ye have done it unto the least of these my brethren, ye have done it unto Me."

No other words were necessary; tearful eyes of each student focused only on the picture of Christ. The students remained in their seats, even after the bell rang, then slowly left the classroom, tears streaming down their faces.

"And the King will answer and say to them, "Truly I say to you, to the extent that you did it to one of these brothers of mine, even the least of them, you did it to Me" (Matthew 25:40).

Sobering thoughts are sometimes the best way to keep us in check. Deal well with people you meet today.

3. "Ol' Spot" - A group of country friends from church wanted to get together on a regular basis, socialize, and play games. The lady of the house was to prepare the meal. When it came time for Al and Janet to be the hosts, Janet wanted to outdo all the others and have mushroom-smothered steak. But mushrooms were expensive, so her husband said, "Why don't you go down in the pasture and pick some of those mushrooms? There are plenty in the creek bed." Janet said, "No. Some wild mushrooms are poisonous." Al said, "Well, I see varmints eating them, and they're OK."

So Janet decided to give it a try. She picked a bunch of the mushrooms, washed, sliced, and diced them for her smothered steak. Then she went out on the back porch and gave Ol' Spot (the yard dog) a double handful. Ol' Spot ate every bite. All morning long, Janet watched Ol' Spot. The wild mushrooms didn't seem to affect him, so she decided to use them. She made her smothered steak and even hired a maid from a professional maid service to help her serve. The maid wore a white apron and a fancy little cap, and the meal was a great success.

After everyone had finished, they relaxed, socialized, and played 42 dominoes, the maid came in and whispered in Janet's ear. She said, "Mrs. Williams, Ol' Spot just died." Janet went into hysterics. After she finally calmed down, she called the doctor and told him what had happened. The doctor said, "That's bad, but I think we can take care of it. I will call for an ambulance and I will be there as quick as possible. We'll give everyone enemas and pump out everyone's stomach. Everything will be fine. Just keep them calm."

Soon they could hear the siren as the ambulance come down the road. The EMTs and the doctor had their suitcases, syringes, and a stomach pump. One by one, they took each person into the bathroom, gave them an enema, and pumped out their stomach. After the last one was finished, the doctor came out and said, "I think everything will be fine now" and left. They were all sitting around the living room looking pretty weak when the maid came in and said, "You know, that fellow that ran over Ol' Spot never even stopped."

Video/YouTube Clip:
Play several YouTube clips from the Smothers Brothers. They are funny and will be certain to bring back memories for the seniors!

Scripture for the Month: (Can put in newsletter to encourage memorization)
"Blessed is the one who does not walk in step with the wicked or stand in the way that sinners take or sit in the company of mockers, but whose delight is in the law of the Lord, and who meditates on his law day and night" (Psalms 1:1–2).

THE BEGINNER'S BOOK OF SENIOR ACTIVITIES

3. Mother's Day: Thrift/Resale Store Shopping Trip/Lunch

Most ladies are alike, in that they want to get a good deal! Celebrate Mother's Day by rewarding the ladies with a trip to the local thrift and resale stores with a lunch somewhere special prearranged in advance. For "Outings/Excursions Preparation" (see appendix page 244).

Quote for the Month/Event:
"Some people, no matter how old they get, never lose their beauty, they merely move it from their faces to their hearts." – Anonymous

Joke/Story for Lunchtime:
1. "Why I Want to Be a Bear"

If you're a bear, you get to hibernate. You do nothing but sleep for six months. I could deal with that. Before you hibernate, you're supposed to eat yourself stupid. I could deal with that, too. If you're a bear, you birth your children (who are the size of walnuts) while you're sleeping and wake to partially grown, cute cuddly cubs. I could definitely deal with that.

If you're a mama bear, everyone knows you mean business. You swat anyone who bothers your cubs. If your cubs get out of line, you swat them, too. If you're a bear, your mate EXPECTS you to wake up growling. He EXPECTS that you will have hairy legs and excess body fat. Yup. Now you see my point of why I want to be a bear.

2. "Was Jesus….?"

My Cajun friend had three good arguments that Jesus was a Cajun:
1. He liked to serve fish to his friends.
2. He could make his own wine.
3. He wasn't afraid of water.

My Italian friend gave his three equally good arguments that Jesus was Italian:
1. He talked with his hands.
2. He had wine with every meal.
3. He used olive oil.

My California friend also had three equally good arguments that Jesus was a Californian:
1. He never cut his hair.
2. He walked around barefoot all the time.
3. He started a new religion.

My Irish friend then gave his three equally good arguments that Jesus was Irish:
1. He never got married.
2. He was always telling stories.
3. He loved green pastures.

But my women friends have the most compelling evidence of all that Jesus was a woman:
1. He fed a crowd at a moment's notice when there was no food.
2. He kept trying to get a message across to a bunch of men who just didn't get it.
3. And even when he was dead, he had to get up because there was more work to do.
(Just kidding!)

3. Moms
You know you're a mother when you're up till 10:30 p.m., vacuuming, dusting, wiping, washing, drying, loading, unloading, shopping, cooking, driving, flushing, ironing, sweeping, picking up, changing sheets, changing diapers, bathing, helping with homework, paying bills, budgeting, clipping coupons, folding clothes, putting to bed, dragging out of bed, brushing, chasing, buckling, feeding, swinging, playing ball, bike riding, pushing trucks, cuddling dolls, roller blading, catching, blowing bubbles, running sprinklers, sliding, taking walks, coloring, jumping rope, raking, trimming, planting, edging, mowing, gardening, painting, and walking and feeding the dog.

You get up at 5:30 a.m., and you have no time to eat, sleep, drink, or go to the bathroom, and you still manage to gain ten pounds.

4. The BBQ Season Is Coming! (Since Mother's Day is in May, this is for the ladies.)
After four long months of cold and winter, we are finally coming up to summer and BBQ season. Therefore it is important to refresh your memory on the etiquette of this sublime outdoor cooking as it's the only type of cooking a real man will do, probably because there is an element of danger involved. When a man volunteers to do the BBQ, the following chain of events are put into motion:

Routine...
1. The woman buys the food.
2. The woman makes the salad, prepares the vegetables, and makes dessert.
3. The woman prepares the meat for cooking, places it on a tray along with the necessary cooking utensils and sauces, and takes it to the man who is lounging beside the grill.
Here comes the important part:
4. THE MAN PUTS THE MEAT ON THE GRILL.

5. The woman goes inside to organize the plates and cutlery.
6. The woman comes out to tell the man that the meat is burning. He thanks her and asks if she will bring him something to drink while he deals with the situation.
7. THE MAN TAKES THE MEAT OFF THE GRILL AND HANDS IT TO THE WOMAN.
8. The woman prepares the plates, salad, bread, utensils, napkins, sauces, and brings them to the table.
9. After eating, the woman clears the table and does the dishes.
And most important of all:
10. Everyone PRAISES the MAN and THANKS HIM for his cooking efforts.
11. The man asks the woman how she enjoyed "her night off." And, upon seeing her annoyed reaction, concludes that there's just no pleasing some women.

5. The Old Fisherman: A Priceless Story.

Our house was directly across the street from the clinic entrance of Johns Hopkins Hospital in Baltimore. We lived downstairs and rented the upstairs rooms to out-patients at the clinic. One summer evening as I was fixing supper, there was a knock at the door. I opened it to see a truly awful looking man. "Why he's hardly taller than my eight-year-old," I thought as I stared at the stooped, shriveled body. But the appalling thing was his face, lopsided from swelling, red and raw. Yet his voice was pleasant as he said, "Good evening. I've come to see if you've a room for just one night. I came for a treatment this morning from the eastern shore and there's no bus till morning. "He told me he'd been hunting for a room since noon but with no success. No one seemed to have a room. "I guess it's my face… I know it looks terrible, but my doctor says with a few more treatments…" For a moment I hesitated, but his next words convinced me: "I could sleep in this rocking chair on the porch. My bus leaves early in the morning." I told him we would find him a bed, but to rest on the porch. I went inside

and finished getting supper. When we were ready, I asked the old man if he would join us. "No, thank you. I have plenty." And he held up a brown paper bag. When I had finished the dishes, I went out on the porch to talk with him a few minutes.

It didn't take a long time to see that this old man had an oversized heart crowded into that tiny body. He told me he fished for a living to support his daughter, her five children, and her husband, who was hopelessly crippled from a back injury. He didn't tell it by way of complaint; in fact, every other sentence was prefaced with thanks to God for a blessing. He was grateful that no pain accompanied his disease, which was apparently a form of skin cancer. He thanked God for giving him the strength to keep going. At bedtime, we put a camp cot in the children's room for him. When I got up in the morning, the bed linens were neatly folded and the little man was out on the porch. He refused breakfast, but just before he left for his bus, haltingly, as if asking a great favor, he said, "Could I please come back and stay the next time I have treatment? I won't put you out a bit. I can sleep fine in a chair." He paused a moment and then added, "Your children made me feel at home. Grownups are bothered by my face, but children don't seem to mind. "I told him he was welcome to come again.

THE BEGINNER'S BOOK OF SENIOR ACTIVITIES | 93

On his next trip, he arrived a little after seven in the morning. As a gift, he brought a big fish and a quart of the largest oysters I had ever seen. He said he had shucked them that morning before he left so that they'd be nice and fresh. I knew his bus left at 4:00 a.m. and I wondered what time he had to get up in order to do this for us.

In the years he came to stay overnight with us, there was never a time that he did not bring us fish or oysters or vegetables from his garden. Other times we received packages in the mail, always by special delivery; fish and oysters packed in a box of fresh young spinach or kale, every leaf carefully washed. Knowing that he must walk three miles to mail these, and knowing how little money he had made the gifts doubly precious.

When I received these little remembrances, I often thought of a comment our next-door neighbor made after he left that first morning. "Did you keep that awful-looking man last night? I turned him away! You can lose roomers by putting up with such people!" Maybe we did lose roomers once or twice. But, oh! If only they could have known him, perhaps their illness would have been easier to bear. I know our family always will be grateful to have known him; from him we learned what it was to accept the bad without complaint and the good with gratitude to God.

Recently I was visiting a friend who has a greenhouse. As she showed me her flowers, we came to the most beautiful one of all, a golden chrysanthemum, bursting with blooms. But to my great surprise, it was growing in an old dented, rusty bucket. I thought to myself, "If this were my plant, I'd put it in the loveliest container I had!" My friend changed my mind. "I ran short of pots," she explained, "and knowing how beautiful this one would be, I thought it wouldn't mind starting out in this old pail. It's just for a little while, till I can put it out in the garden." She must have wondered why I laughed so delightedly, but I was imagining just such a scene in heaven. "Here's an especially beautiful one, God might have said when he came to the soul of the sweet old fisherman. "He won't mind starting in this small body."

"The Lord does not look at the things man looks at. Man looks at the outward appearance, but the Lord looks at the heart." (1 Samuel 16:7b)

Game/Activity: (For the Bus Ride or Lunch)
Play "Famous Women Quiz" then follow with "Famous Christian Women" (see appendix pages 245-246). Make the point that we know a lot about secular women but could use some studies on these amazing Christian women!

Reading:

"What I Want in a Man," Original List
1. Handsome
2. Charming
3. Financially Successful
4. A Caring Listener
5. Witty
6. In Good Shape
7. Dresses with Style
8. Appreciates the Finer Things
9. Full of Thoughtful Surprises
10. Very Romantic

"What I Want in a Man," Revised List
1. Not too ugly
2. Doesn't belch or scratch in public
3. Works steady
4. Doesn't nod off while I'm emoting
5. Usually remembers the punch lines of jokes
6. Is in good enough shape to rearrange the furniture
7. Usually wears matching socks and fresh underwear
8. Knows not to buy champagne with screw-top lids
9. Remembers to put the toilet seat lid down
10. Shaves on weekends

2. Read "Mom's Last Laugh," a very sweet and touching tribute to moms.

"Mom's Last Laugh"
Consumed by my loss, I didn't notice the hardness of the pew where I sat. I was at the funeral of my dearest friend, my mother. She had finally lost her long battle with cancer. The hurt was so intense; I found it hard to breathe at times. Always supportive, Mother clapped loudest at my school plays, held a box of tissues while listening to my first heartbreak, comforted me at my father's death, encouraged me in college, and prayed for me my entire life.

When Mother's illness was diagnosed, my sister had a new baby and my brother had recently married his childhood sweetheart, so it fell on me, the 27-year-old middle child without entanglements, to take care of her. I counted it an honor. "What now, Lord?" I asked sitting in the church. My life stretched out before me as an empty abyss. My brother sat stoically, staring at the casket while clutching his wife's hand. My sister sat slumped against her husband's shoulder, his arms around her as she cradled their child. All so deeply grieving, no one noticed I sat alone. My place had been with our mother, preparing her meals, helping her walk, taking her to the doctor, seeing to her medication, reading the Bible together. Now she was with the Lord. My work was finished and I was alone.

I heard the door open and slam shut at the back of the church. Quick footsteps hurried along the carpeted floor. An exasperated young man looked around briefly and then sat next to me. He folded his hands and placed them on his lap. His eyes were brimming with tears. He began to sniffle. "I'm late," he explained though no explanation was necessary.

After several eulogies, he leaned over and commented, "Why do they keep calling Mary by the name of Margaret?" "Because that was her name - no one called her "Mary," I whispered. I wondered why this person couldn't have sat on the other side of the church. He interrupted my grieving with his tears and fidgeting. Who was this stranger, anyway? "No, that isn't correct," he insisted, as several people glanced over at us. He whispered, "Her name is Mary, Mary Peters." "That isn't who this is!" I exclaimed. "Isn't this the Lutheran Church?" he asked. "No, the Lutheran Church is across the street." I explained. "Oh!" he replied. "I believe you're at the wrong funeral, sir."

The solemnity of the occasion mixed with the realization of the man's mistake bubbled up inside me and came out as laughter. I cupped my hands over my face, hoping it would be interpreted as sobs. The creaking pew gave me away. Sharp looks from other mourners only made the situation seem more hilarious. I peeked at the bewildered, misguided man seated beside me. He was laughing too, as he glanced around deciding it was too late for an uneventful exit! I imagined Mother laughing.

At the final amen, we darted out a door and into the parking lot. "I do believe we'll be the talk of the town," he smiled. He said his name was Rick and since he had missed his aunt's funeral, asked me out for a cup of coffee. That afternoon began a lifelong journey for me with this man who attended the wrong funeral, but was in the right place! A year after our meeting, we were married at a country church where he was the assistant pastor. This time we both arrived at the same church, right on time.

In my time of sorrow, God gave me laughter. In place of loneliness, God gave me love. This past June, we celebrated our twenty-second wedding anniversary. Whenever anyone asks how we met, Rick tells them, "Her mother and my Aunt Mary introduced us, and it's truly a match made in Heaven!"

3. Dust if you must, but wouldn't it be better to paint a picture or write a letter,
Bake a cake or plant a seed, ponder the difference between want and need?
Dust if you must, but there's not much time with rivers to swim and mountains to climb,
Music to hear and books to read, friends to cherish and life to lead.
Dust if you must, but the worlds out there with the sun in your eyes, the wind in your hair,
A flutter of snow, a shower of rain. This day will not come around again.
Dust if you must, but bear in mind, old age will come and it's not kind.
And when you go — and go you must — you, yourself, will make more dust!

Handout to take home:
Give the ladies the handout "Praying for My Husband" to take home. (see appendix pages 247-248)

Scripture for the Month: (Can put in newsletter to encourage memorization)
"Create in me a pure heart, O God, and renew a steadfast spirit within me" (Psalm 51:10).

JUNE
Monthly Ideas

June
Monthly Ideas

1. "Art is Ageless" Evening: Local Artist as Speaker; Art Competition

This event features a local artist coming to speak, artistic games to play, art to make, and an art competition. The local artist will be the judge and prizes should be awarded: first, second, third, and participant. Advertise this event three to four weeks in advance to give the participants time to finish their entries.

Pre-dinner Conversation Starter:
Have one or two of the games listed below for the people to do at the table, while waiting for the event to begin.

Advertising/game:
Have a funny/artsy hat night. Encourage (in advance) everyone who can to wear a hat. Prizes will be given for themes like:

Most artistic	Most Flamboyant	Most unusual
Classiest	Most indicative of the person's personality	

Decorations:
This night will have to have artsy flair. Vases with thin tree limbs/sticks (that have been spray painted) with paper flowers attached are very popular and give a trendy look. Another idea is to have a white paper covering for the center of the tables and crayons for people to decorate while waiting or use as an activity for "best table art."

Quote for the Month/Event:
"Youth is a gift of nature, but age is a work of art." – Stanislaw Lec

"Art is unquestionably one of the purest and highest elements in human happiness. It trains *the mind through the eye, and the eye through the mind. As the sun colors flowers, so does art color life."* – Sir John Lubbock, British biologist and politician

Joke/Story:

1. While eating at an outdoor cafe in the historic district, an art connoisseur noticed a mangy little kitten lapping up milk from a saucer. The saucer, he realized with a start, was a rare and precious piece. After finishing his meal, we went up to the owner and offered him two dollars for the cat. "It's not for sale," said the owner. "Now, now" said the collector, "that cat is just ugly and no one would want it, but I'm eccentric. I like to help out underprivileged animals. I'll raise my offer to five dollars." "It's a deal," said the proprietor with a smile, and pocketed the five on the spot. "For that amount I'm sure you won't mind throwing in the saucer," said the connoisseur. "The little kitten seems so content drinking from it." "No way," said the owner. "That's my lucky saucer. I've already sold 26 cats so far this week drinking from it!"

2. Mary goes to her first show at an art gallery and is looking at the paintings. One is a huge canvas that has black with yellow blobs of paint splattered all over it. The next painting is a murky gray color that has drips of purple paint streaked across it. Mary walks over to the artist and says, "I don't understand your paintings." "I paint what I feel inside me," explains the artist. Mary sweetly says "Have you ever tried Alka-Seltzer?"
(www.laughandlift.com Used by permission.)

3. Recently a guy in Paris nearly got away with stealing several paintings from the Louvre. However, after planning the crime, breaking in, evading security and escaping with the goods, he was captured only two blocks away when his rented van ran out of gas. When asked how he could mastermind such a crime and then make such an obvious error, he replied: "I had no Monet to buy Degas to make the Van Gogh."
(www.laughandlift.com Used by permission.)

Game/Activity:

1. Masterpiece Art: Give one 8 ½ x11 size or larger paper and a marker to every other person at the table. Game begins with each person drawing circles, lines or geometric shapes on the paper. After one minute the paper is passed to the person to their left who must draw a picture from the lines on that paper. Papers can be collected and displayed around the room.

2. Cut-Ups: Hide six numbers (1–6) somewhere at six seats/place settings (i.e., under a cup or chair) throughout the room. Then call up the six people, who have the numbers,

and give them a sheet of drawing paper and a pair of scissors. Have them hold both behind their backs and cut out, without looking, a tree, flower or shape. Have prizes for the best and runner up prizes for the others. Have the contestants close their eyes and have the crowd vote for the best by raised hands.

3. Playdough art: Each person has a small container of playdough in front of his place setting. Have the tables create a work of art out of their playdough and the top three win a prize (others get consolation prizes). Walmart carries the smaller individual size playdough.

4. Scratch Art: Have each individual do a scratch art piece (available at craft stores/online) just for fun. To cut down on costs, buy small craft sticks and sharpen them in a pencil sharpener, one for each person.

5. Cheetos Art: This will take a few easygoing men. Take several men who have agreed to this beforehand and have them sit in front of the group facing the group. The men then have a large trash bag placed over them, with their head sticking out. The individuals behind them will make the "artwork," the object to make the most artistic hairstyle. This is done with first spraying their heads with shaving cream and then using Cheetos to make a hair design.

6. Spray paint vases: This is an artistic option where old flower vases are collected in advance and are spray painted (in advance) with a light brown or white color. Purchase several different cans of spray paint, stones or marble (available at builder supply stores) for use at the dinner. Be sure and have paint tarps down on the floor and all areas protected from the paint. Individuals will choose a vase and label it on the bottom with their name (use a sharpie) and then spray paint, using the stone or marble paint, over the entire vase. The results are amazing, taking an old plain flower vase and turning it into a new modern-looking holder.

7. Splatter art: If the group is adventurous, hang a large splatter paint canvas (such as an old sheet) on a wall. Be sure to have paint tarps on the surrounding wall and floor. Workers are there to guide the individuals who simply take a small paint brush and choose a color of paint and then splatter it on the canvas! This can later be hung for display where the seniors can see it!

8. Balloon art: Balloons filled with helium, can be used as centerpieces and then for a game people will take magic markers and draw faces on each one. One balloon per person.

9. Soap carving: Everyone is given a bar of ivory soap (each will need a small knife) to carve out a "work of art." Make sure to place papers (can use sheets of wax paper) under each place setting for this game.

10. Group art: For art as a group, make a sculpture for the park or paint a mural downtown.

Reading:

1. Addressed to fellow painters, Michelangelo (1564)

"Why do you keep filling gallery after gallery with endless pictures of the one ever-reiterated theme of Christ in weakness, of Christ upon the cross, Christ dying, Christ hanging dead? Why do you stop there as if the curtain closed upon that horror? Keep the curtain open, and with the cross in the foreground, let us see beyond it to the Easter dawn with its beams streaming upon the risen Christ, Christ alive, Christ ruling, Christ triumphant.
For we should be ringing out over the world that Christ has won, that evil is toppling, that the end is sure, and that death is followed by victory. That is the tonic we need to keep us healthy, the trumpet blast to fire our blood and send us crowding in behind our Master, swinging happily upon our way, laughing and singing and recklessly unafraid, because the feel of victory is in the air, and our hearts thrill to it."

2. "I'm Fine"
I'm fine. I'm fine.
There's nothing whatever the matter with me,
I'm just as healthy as I can be.
I have arthritis in both of my knees
And when I talk, I talk with a wheeze.
My pulse is weak and my blood is thin,
But I'm awfully well for the shape I'm in.
My teeth eventually will have to come out
And I can't hear a word unless you shout.
I've overweight and I can't get thin
But I'm awfully well for the shape I'm in.
Arch supports I have for my feet
Or I wouldn't be able to walk down the street.
Sleep is denied me every night
And every morning I'm really a sight.
My memory is bad and my head's a-spin

And I practically live on aspirin.
But I'm awfully well for the shape I'm in.
The moral is, as this tale unfolds,
That for you and me, who are growing old,
It's better to say, "I'm fine," with a grin
Than to let people know the shape we're in!

Video/YouTube Clip:

A fun YouTube video to watch would be "TV Shows of the 1960s" compiled by Steve Forbes. Will be sure to bring back memories.

Scripture for the Month: (Can put in newsletter to encourage memorization)

"When the Lord takes pleasure in anyone's way, he causes their enemies to make peace with them" (Proverbs 16:7).

2. Lunch and Learn (with Beans and Greens)

Lunch can be provided by having something inexpensive like beans and greens. Many older people grew up with pinto or white beans and ham and turnips greens prepared with salted pork. Several informational topics can be addressed at different times (maybe once a month) such as:

1. Medical professionals on diabetes, arthritis treatments, etc.
2. Exercise and nutrition
3. Local travel agency on affordable senior bus trips.
4. How to use the latest techie devices.
5. Newspaper writer, politician, or university professor on current world news topics (the Middle East).

Pre-dinner Conversation Starter:

Play "The Quiz for those in the Know" (see appendix page 249).

Decorations:
Summertime is here and flowers abound. Put a bright colored bandana or napkin in the middle of the table and put a nice vase of summer flowers on it.

Quote for the Month/Event:
"No matter who you are or what your life has been like so far, the rest of your life's journey can be different. With God's help you can begin again." – Billy Graham

Joke/Story:
1. Since it is in the spirit of the event – you can tolerate a few blonde jokes…
A blonde & her husband are lying in bed listening to the next door neighbor's dog. It has been in the backyard barking for hours and hours. The blonde jumps up out of bed and says, "I've had enough of this". She goes downstairs. The blonde finally comes back up to bed and her husband says, "The dog is still barking, what have you been doing?" The blonde says, "I put the dog in our backyard … let's see how THEY like it!

2. Two Blondes with Hammers
Lisa & Judy were doing some carpenter work on a Habitat for Humanity House. Lisa was nailing down house siding, would reach into her nail pouch, pull out a nail and either toss it over her shoulder or nail it in.

Judy, figuring this was worth looking into, asked, "Why are you throwing those nails away?" Lisa explained, "When I pull a nail out of my pouch, about half of them have the head on the wrong end & I throw them away." Judy got completely upset and yelled, "You are so ignorant! Those nails aren't defective! They're for the other side of the house!"

3. A passerby asks a blonde: "Why do scuba divers always fall backwards off their boats?" To which the blond man replies: "If they fell forward, they'd still be in the boat."

4. Little Johnny and his family were having Sunday dinner at his Grandmother's house. Everyone was seated around the table as the food was being served. When Little Johnny received his plate, he started eating right away. "Johnny! Please wait until we say our prayer," said his mother. "I don't need to," the boy replied. "Of course, you do," his mother insisted. "We always say a prayer before eating at our house." "That's at our house." Johnny explained. "But this is Grandma's house and she knows how to cook."
(www.mikeysFunnies.com. Used by permission.)

5. Three students are leaving their last classes of the day.

The law student is thinking, "I'm tired and thirsty. I must have coffee."
The English student is thinking, "I'm tired and thirsty. I must have a latte."
The medical student is thinking, "I'm tired and thirsty. I must have diabetes."
(www.laughandlift.com. Used by permission.)

6. HAL 2000
For a computer programming class, I sat directly across from someone, and our computers were facing away from each other. A few minutes into the class, she got up to leave the room. I reached between our computers and switched the inputs for the keyboards. She came back and started typing and immediately got a distressed look on her face. She called the teacher over and explained that no matter what she typed, nothing would happen. The teacher tried everything.

By this time, I was hiding behind my monitor, quaking and red-faced. I typed, "Leave me alone!" They both jumped back, silenced. "What in the . . . " the teacher said. I typed, "I said, leave me alone!"

The kid got real upset. "I didn't do anything to it, I swear!" It was all I could do to keep from laughing out loud. The conversation between them and HAL 2000 went on for an amazing five minutes.

Me: "Don't touch me!"
Her: "I'm sorry; I didn't mean to hit your keys that hard."
Me: "Who do you think you are anyway?!"

Finally, I couldn't contain myself any longer and fell out of my chair laughing. After they had realized what I had done, they both turned beet red. Funny, I never got more than a C- in that class.
(www.laughandlift.com. Used by permission.)

Game/Activity:
1. "U.S. Geography": Quiz" (see appendix pages 250-251).

Reading:
1. He Gave His Only Son
There was once a big turntable bridge which spanned a large river. During most of the day, the bridge sat with the length running up and down the river parallel with the banks allowing ships to pass freely on both sides of the bridge. But at certain times of the day, a

certain train would come along and the bridge would be turned sideways across the river allowing the train to cross.

A switchman sat in a small shack on one side of the river where he operated the controls to turn the bridge and lock it into place when the train crossed. One evening when the switchman was waiting for the last train of the day to come, he looked off into the distance through the dimming twilight and caught sight of the train's light. He stepped to the controls and waited until the train was at a prescribed distance when he was to turn the bridge. He turned the bridge into position, but to his horror, he found that the locking control didn't work. If the bridge was not locked securely into position, it would wobble back and forth and end with the train jumping the track and go crashing into the river. This would be a passenger train with many people aboard.

He left the shack with the bridge turned across the river and hurried to the other side of the river where there was a lever which he could use to operate the lock manually. He could hear the rumble of the train now and leaned backward to apply his weight to it, locking the bridge. Many lives depended upon this man's strength.

Then, coming across the bridge from the other direction, he heard a sound that made his blood run cold. "Daddy, where are you?" His four-year-old son was crossing the bridge to look for him. His first instinct was to cry out to the child, "Run! Run!" But the train was too close. The tiny feet would never make it across the bridge in time. The man almost left the lever to run and snatch up his son and carry him to safety, but he realized he could not get back to the lever in time. Either the people on the train or his son must die. He took just a moment to make his decision.

The train sped swiftly and safely on its way and no one on board was even aware of the tiny, broken body thrown mercilessly into the river by the rushing train. Nor were they aware of the pitiful figure of a sobbing man still clinging tightly to the locking lever long after the train had passed. They didn't see him walking home more slowly than he had ever walked to tell his wife how he had sacrificed their son.

Now, if you can comprehend the emotions which went through this man's heart, you can begin to understand the feelings of our Heavenly Father when He sacrificed His Son to bridge the gap between us and eternal life. Can there be any wonder that He caused the earth to tremble and the skies to darken when His Son died? And how does it feel when we speed along life without giving a thought to what was done for us through Jesus Christ? When was the last time you thanked Him for the sacrifice of His Son?

(www.laughandlift.com Used by permission.)

2. The Smart Professor:

It was final exam week and two college seniors decided that instead of doing some much needed studying, they would to go to an "end of the year" party. So the next morning they decided to tell their professor that the night before their car had broken down due to a flat tire and that they needed a little more time to study. The professor, being a kindly sort, agreed and gave the boys one more day to study. The boys crammed all night until they felt they were ready to take the exam.

The next day, the boys came and were divided into two separate rooms for their final exam. They sat down and read the first question:
"For five points, name the parts of an atom."
"For 95 points, tell me which tire it was."

Video/YouTube Clip:
Pick a funny (if possible) YouTube video that deals with the chosen topic.

Scripture for the Month: (Can put in newsletter to encourage memorization)
"*A new command I give you: Love one another. As I have loved you, so you must love one another. By this everyone will know that you are my disciples, if you love one another*" (John 13:34-35).

3. Trip to a Botanical Garden (with lunch prearranged inside the Garden)

Who can resist a great trip to see the beauty of nature? A trip to a nearby botanical garden can be both an inspiration (appreciating the glory of God's creation) and a relaxing time of fellowship. If possible, arrange a pre-prepared lunch in the garden or garden café (most gardens will do this for a fee). Touring a botanical garden does require some walking, so try to arrange lunch halfway through the tour, ensuring a good rest break, before finishing the tour.

For "Outings/Excursions Preparation"
(see appendix page 244).

For en route travel games, play "Gardens Crossword" or "Fantastic Flora Facts: Quiz"
(see appendix pages 252-255). Be sure to take pencils along!

Quote for the Month/Event:

"The bee is more honored than other animals, not because she labors, but because she labors for others." – St. John Chrysostom

Joke/Story:

1. I heard a story of this couple who were having a terrible disagreement over a backyard patio that they wanted. The wife had very grand ideas, while the husband wanted costs kept to a minimum. The wife won out, and the construction bill climbed higher and higher.

The neighbor came over to see how the work was going as a workman was just smoothing out the final cement and the project was almost finished. Seeing the husband smiling from ear to ear, the neighbor asked why he was so happy since he had been against building such an elaborate patio. The husband said "You see where they're smoothing that cement?" he replied. "I just threw my wife's credit cards in there."

2. Unfortunately, getting a new passport required a new photo. As I handed my ten-year-old passport and the new picture to the clerk, I sighed.
"I like the original better," I told her.
"Trust me," she said. "Ten years from now, you'll like this one."

3. An older couple had just learned how to send text messages on their cell phones. The wife was a sweet romantic type person while the husband was a no nonsense guy.

One afternoon, the wife went out to a local restaurant to meet a friend for coffee. While waiting for her friend to arrive, she decided to send her husband a romantic text message. She said "If you are sleeping, send me your dreams. If you are laughing, send me your smile. If you

are eating, send me a bite. If you are drinking, send me a sip. If you are crying, send me your tears. I love you."

The husband texted back, "I am using the bathroom. Please advise."

4. A woman was out golfing one day when she hit the ball into the woods. She went into the woods to look for it and found a frog in a trap. The frog said to her, "If you release me from this trap, I will grant you three wishes." The woman freed the frog, and the frog said, "Thank you, but I failed to mention that there was a condition to your wishes. Whatever you wish for, your husband will get times ten!" The woman said, "That's okay."

For her first wish, she wanted to be the most beautiful woman in the world. The frog warned her, "You do realize that this wish will also make your husband the most handsome man in the world, an Adonis to whom women will flock." The woman replied, "That's okay, because I will be the most beautiful woman and he will have eyes only for me." So, KAZAM – she's the most beautiful woman in the world!

For her second wish, she wanted to be the richest woman in the world. The frog said, "That will make your husband the richest man in the world. And he will be ten times richer than you." The woman said, "That's okay, because what's mine is his and what's his is mine." So, KAZAM – she's the richest woman in the world! The frog then inquired about her third wish, and she answered, "I'd like a mild heart attack."

Moral of the story: Women are clever. Don't mess with them.

However, that is not the end of the story…
The man had a heart attack ten times milder than his wife. (Men get the last word on this one! Hey, it is Father's Day this month!)

Reading: (During the bus ride or lunch)

1. Tree Riddles

What tree is an insect? (Locust)

What tree reminds you of a couple? (Pear)

What tree is more respected than others? (Elder)

What tree keeps ladies warm? (Fir)

What tree is found after a fire? (Ash)

What tree makes clothes? (Cottonwood)

What tree longs after….? (Pine)

What tree has a color? (Redwood)

What tree do moths fear? (Cedar)

What tree is straight? (Plum)

What tree makes barrels? (Oak)

What tree is in your hand? (Palm)

What tree is round and fuzzy? (Peach)

What tree is chewable? (Gum)

2. "A Letter from a Mother to her Son"

Dear Son,

I am writing this slow, 'cause I know you can't read fast. We don't live where we did when you left. Your dad read in the paper where most accidents happen within twenty miles of home, so we moved. I won't be able to send you the address 'cause the last family who lived here took the number with them for their next house so they wouldn't have to change their address.

This place has a washing machine. The first day I put four shirts in it and pulled the chain and haven't seen them since. It only rained twice this week — three days the first time and four days the second time.

The coat you wanted me to send you, your Aunt Sue said it would be a little too heavy to send in the mail with them heavy buttons, so we cut the buttons off and put them in the pockets. We got a bill from the funeral home, said if we didn't make the last payment on Grandma's funeral bill, up she comes. About your father, he has a lovely new job with over 500 men under him. He is cutting grass at the cemetery.

About your sister, she had a baby this morning. I haven't found out whether it's a boy or a girl, so I don't know whether you're an aunt or an uncle.

Three of your friends went off the bridge in a pick-up. One was driving and the other two were in the back. The driver got out, rolled down his window, and swam to safety. The other two drowned. They couldn't get the tailgate down.

Your uncle John fell into the whiskey vat. Someone tried to pull him out, but he fought them off so he drowned. We cremated him. He burned for three days!

Love, Mom

P.S. I was going to send you some money, but the envelope was already sealed.

Scripture for the Month: (Can put in newsletter to encourage memorization)
"But blessed is the one who trusts in the Lord, whose confidence is in him. They will be like a tree planted by the water that sends out its roots by the stream. It does not fear when heat comes; its leaves are always green. It has no worries in a year of drought and never fails to bear fruit" (Jeremiah 17:7–8).

July
Monthly Ideas

1. Red, White and Blue BBQ: Veterans' Stories

It is amazing the wealth of information and stories there are in any group of people. Seniors especially have stories from war times, or can speak on what the war or life at home was like. If the leader could guide the conversation and ask the veterans to comment it could be a very interesting evening.

Topics such as:

What countries did you serve in?
What was the food like?
How did you do your laundry?
Did you make friends with any of the locals?
How was life different during war time?
Do you remember rationing?
What was rationed?
Most memorable memory from the war?
How do you see war as being different today?

Another idea would be to call the National Guard; they will usually provide a speaker for free!

*This would be a good meeting to have the youth of the church come, serve, and hear what these veterans have done for them — and to show their thanks and respect.

Dinner:
Find the best BBQ around and bless these precious people with a food most all like!

Pre-dinner Conversation Starter:
Place copies of "Theodore Roosevelt: How Much Do You Know?" at each place setting along with pencils (see appendix pages 256-257).

Decorations:
Go with the patriotic red, white, and blue theme. American flags for the center of the table can be purchased at United States Flag Store, 1-877-734-2458, www.united-states-flag.com which has stick flags 8x12 for 35 cents each.

Additional Idea:
Make a list of the individuals in your group who were in the service and what war/conflict they fought in and have that information on the tables as a tribute of thanks.

For military pictures to copy and scatter around, look on Google or Bing images on the Internet — but be sure to watch for trademark, registration or copyright information that may restrict the image usage.

Quote for the Month/Event:
You have to love our early president's wisdom:
"I hope I shall possess firmness and virtue to maintain what I consider the most enviable of all titles, the character of an honest man." – George Washington

"A veteran is someone who, at one point in their life, wrote a blank check made payable to The United States of America for an amount up to and including their life." – Anonymous

And lastly from a great comedian and American patriot:
"I have a scheme for stopping war. It's this — no nation is allowed to enter a war 'til they have paid for the last one." – Will Rogers

Joke/Story:
1. A cocky, newly promoted Army Colonel had just received a brand new office. His first morning in his new position, he was sitting behind his large desk when a sergeant knocked on the door and asked to speak to him. The colonel told him to come in. Then, feeling the need to impress the young sergeant in his new position, the colonel picked up his phone and said: "Yes, General, thank you. I understand and yes, I will pass that along to the president this afternoon. Yes, thank you and goodbye, sir." Then turning to the airman he gruffly said, "And what do you want?" "Nothing vital sir," said the sergeant. "I just came to install your telephone."

2. A minister and a congressman both arrived at the pearly gates at the same time. Saint Peter greeted both of them and gave them their room assignments. "Pastor, here are your keys; it's one of our nicest efficiency units. Then turning to the other gentleman, St. Peter said, "And for you, Mr. Congressman, here are the keys to our finest penthouse suite." "Hey — what is the deal here?" asked the minister. "This just doesn't seem right after I have spent my entire life working for the Lord!" "Listen," said Saint Peter, "ministers are a dime a dozen up here, but this is the first congressman we've ever seen."

3. The Pentagon once did a study on why so many American servicemen marry women in the countries where they're stationed. Contrary to popular belief, loneliness had nothing to do with it. Once the men rotated back to the U.S., all their in-laws were thousands of miles away.

4. There is a story of one Army recruiter who had just been assigned to Chicago. One morning he went to pick up a candidate at a crime-ridden high-rise building. When he stepped into the elevator, he was promptly joined by two tough-looking men who demanded money. His heart started pounding but immediately his training kicked in. Looking them directly eye to eye, he began his recruiter's pitch. "Hey, this could be your lucky day," he told them enthusiastically.

"I am an Army recruiter and we can use determined individuals like you in the Army. How would you like to serve your country?" When the elevator reached the candidate's floor and the doors opened, the bewildered thugs flew out and quickly disappeared.

5. Security Questions
I was scheduled to fly from North Carolina to Germany, where my husband was stationed in the military. As I checked in at the airport, the ticket agent asked me some standard security questions. "Has anyone given you any packages that you didn't pack yourself?" he asked. I told him that my mother-in-law had given me a parcel to take to her son. He paused for a second, looked at me very carefully and asked: "Does she like you?"
(www.GCFL.net, info@gcfl.net. Used by permission.)

Game/Activity:
1. "Who Am I?" Game
This game will require pre-made pieces of paper with a famous American patriot's name on it and a safety pin attached. The leader will need to pin one on each person's back upon arrival. Take a 15-minute break during the evening and ask people to mingle and ask each other yes or no questions to help each other guess who they are (the name on their back)!

(For example, Benjamin Franklin, Patrick Henry, Thomas Jefferson, George Washington, Thomas Paine, John Hancock, etc.)

Video/YouTube Clip:

Watch the video about Larry Eckhardt "The Flagman" that was aired on CBS Sunday Morning on May 27, 2012. It is the very touching story of how he honors military personnel in his own way.

Reading:

1. When we think of veterans, we think of giving of ourselves for others (God and Country). Here is a story of a "regular guy" who made an impact for the Kingdom. For "The Story of Carl" (see appendix pages 258-260).

Scripture for the Month: (Can put in newsletter to encourage memorization)

"So do not fear, for I am with you; do not be dismayed, for I am your God. I will strengthen you and help you; I will uphold you with my righteous right hand" (Isaiah 41:10).

2. A Night in Jolly Ol' England

This is a night of everything English!

Pre-dinner Conversation Starter:

At each seat have copies of "British Trivia" (see appendix page 261) to play. Be sure to have pencils at each seat as well.

Decorations:

Make this a proper dinner with white tablecloths (with lace on top) – flowers and fine china, if possible.

Quote for the Month/Event:

The famous English Baptist preacher, Charles Haddon Spurgeon (1834–1892) once advised young preachers: *"The horrors are a poor bait. The world will never be converted to God until Christians cry less and sing more."*

"Flee temptation and don't leave a forwarding address." – Anonymous

Joke/Story:

1. We all know how the English love fairy tale and rhymes – here is an update for today:
Fairy Tales and Technology
   - Little Bo Peep never loses sheep because of their embedded silicon identity chips.
   - Cinderella searches for her prince on Match.com and leases her pumpkin-colored SUV at Avis.com.
   - Hansel and Gretel use the GPS rather than bread crumbs but have reported problems stuffing the wicked witch into her microwave oven.
   - To avoid travel stress, Alice now plans her Wonder land vacation with travelocity.com.
   - A reformed Ebenezer Scrooge sends Bob Cratchett to update his certification for Excel and Quicken.
   - Jack's making a fortune on his beanstalk bioengineering breakthrough.
   - Old McDonald uses voice recognition to make ordering easy at his agricultural auction site, www.eieio.com.
   - Romeo and Juliet avoid tragic problems by keeping in touch through their cell phones.
   - With her early Web capabilities, Charlotte is now a motivational speaker at tech conferences around the world.
   - The Pied Piper switched career fields after his tunes were bootlegged on Napster.
   - King Arthur has replaced that expensive round table with satellite video conferencing.
   - Gulliver is on sabbatical using up all his frequent flyer miles.
   - Jack and Jill order their Evian on Amazon.

   (www.laughandlift.com. Used by permission.)

2. The Fourth of July was coming, so the kindergarten teacher decided to have a lesson on patriotism. "We have the best country on earth – one of the best things is that we are all free," the teacher said. One little boy came running up to the front of the room, stood with his hands on his hips and said "I'm not free, I'm four!"

3. Two kids are talking to each other. One says, "I'm really worried. My dad works twelve hours a day to give me a nice home and good food. My mom spends the whole day cleaning and cooking for me. I'm worried sick!" The other kid says, "What have you got to worry about? Sounds to me like you've got it made!" The first kid says, "What if they try to escape?"

4. Johnny's family was having the yearly 4th of July cookout where they invited all their family, including the "ornery" side of the family. The ornery group would always do something that aggravated Johnny's side, but they were family. Just before they were to arrive, Johnny's neighbor calls to say his plans had just fallen through and could they come along to the picnic – and they would bring steaks! "Sure, the more the merrier, Johnny's dad said."

The ornery family arrived and this year they brought fireworks (roman candles, bottle rockets, missile rockets, etc.) that they had bought just across the state line, as they were illegal here and gives them proudly to Johnny's dad. The father turns quickly and whispers to Johnny to take the bag of fireworks and hide them somewhere quickly.
Johnny disappears, and the father begins to chit chat about the weather and sports.

Their neighbor, the policeman, had treated them to steaks, so the father tells him the grill is set to go, just turn on the gas and push the ignition button with the lid down. The father hurries in to make sure Johnny had hidden those fireworks in a good place. "Did you hide them well?" the dad asks. "I sure did – nobody will ever think to look in the grill!"

Game/Activity:

1. For a table competition, play "Gents, Ladies and Language" (see appendix page 262).
Be sure to have a plate of British sugar cookies as a prize to the winning table.

2. Have a British Accent competition – whoever has the best British accent wins a prize! A panel of judges will have to be established before the contest begins!

Reading:

1. Travel Plans

I have been in many places, but I've never been in Cahoots. Apparently, you can't go alone.

I've also never been in Cognito. I hear no one recognizes you there.

I have, however, been in Sane. They don't have an airport; you have to be driven there. I have made several trips there, thanks to my children, friends, family and work.

I would like to go to Conclusions, but you have to jump, and I'm not too much on physical activity anymore.

I have also been in Doubt. That is a sad place to go, and I try not to visit there too often.

I've been in Flexible, but only when it was very important to stand firm.

Sometimes I'm in Capable, and I go there more often as I'm getting older.

One of my favorite places to be is in Suspense. It really gets the adrenalin flowing and pumps up the old heart! At my age I need all the stimuli I can get!

I may have been in Continent, but I don't remember what country I was in. It's an age thing. They tell me it is very wet and damp there.

Travel is very educational. I can now say "Kaopectate" in seven different languages.

(www.mikeysFunnies.com. Used by permission.)

2. The British love to play word games such as this clever reading.

How to Get On in Life

"Tell me how to get on in life," said the kettle.

"Take panes," said the window.

"Never be led," said the pencil.

"Do a driving business," said the hammer.

"Aspire to great things," said the nutmeg grater.

"Make light of everything," said the fire.

"Make much of small things," said the microscope.

"Never do anything offhand," said the glove.

"Just reflect," said the mirror.

"Be sharp," said the knife.

"Find a good thing and stick to it," said the glue.

And that's why the kettle sings as she works, and works as she sings.

(www.GCFL.net, info@gcfl.net. Used by permission.)

Video/YouTube Clip:
Show several YouTube videos from the British House of Commons – known for their crazy debating and arguing, search under funny house of common videos.

Scripture for the Month: (Can put in newsletter to encourage memorization)
"You will seek me and find me when you seek me with all your heart" (Jeremiah 29:13).

3. A USO Tribute to Bob Hope with "Patriotic Pictionary"

Watching Bob Hope and playing Pictionary can be such a fun time together! This night of Pictionary is tied to patriotic themes (presidents, important events in history, famous battles, etc.). Seniors will have fond memories of both Bob Hope and the USO and what it stood (and stands) for. Recognition of members who have served in the military followed by playing the national anthem would be appropriate at this meeting. Conclude the meeting with prayer for our nation and leaders.

Have dinner served first but not dessert until after the Pictionary game, as the desserts will be the prizes! Make sure to have special desserts planned for this evening.

Evening format:
For an introduction read "USO: Did You Know?" (see appendix page 263.
Recognize Military Veterans/Play the National Anthem
Dinner along with Bob Hope video part I
Pictionary
Hidden Flags Game
Bob Hope Video part II
Prayer for America
Pre-dinner Conversation Starter:
"Hope" Trivia (see appendix page 264).

Decorations:
Use a red, white, and blue patriotic theme. Pictures of Bob Hope downloaded and printed from the Internet can be scattered around the center of the table (downloadable from Google or Bing images – but be sure to watch for trademark, registration or copyright information that may restrict the image usage).

Quote for the Month/Event:
"The history of free men is never really written by chance but by choice, their choice!" – Dwight D. Eisenhower

"No arsenal, or no weapon in the arsenals of the world, is as formidable as the will and moral courage of free men and women." – Ronald Reagan

Joke/Story:
Bob Hope Jokes:
1. "I feel like my body has gotten totally out of shape, so I got my doctor's permission to join a fitness club and start exercising. I decided to take an aerobics class for seniors. I bent, twisted, gyrated, jumped up and down, and perspired for a whole hour. But, by the time I got my leotards on, the class was over."

2. Bob Hope milestones:
ON TURNING 70:
"You still chase women, but only downhill."

ON TURNING 80:
"That's the time of your life when even your birthday suit needs pressing."

ON TURNING 90:
"You know you're getting old when the candles cost more than the cake."

On TURNING 100:
"I don't feel old. In fact, I don't feel anything until noon. Then it's time for my nap!"

ON GIVING UP HIS EARLY CAREER, BOXING
"I ruined my hands in the ring. The referee kept stepping on them."

ON NEVER WINNING AN OSCAR
"Welcome to the Academy Awards! Or as it's called at my home, Passover."

ON GOLF
"Golf is my profession. Show business is just to pay the green fees."

ON WHY HE CHOSE SHOWBIZ FOR HIS CAREER
"When I was born, the doctor said to my mother, Congratulations, you have an eight-pound ham."

ON RECEIVING THE CONGRESSIONAL GOLD MEDAL
"I feel very humble, but I think I have the strength of character to fight it."

ON HIS FAMILY'S EARLY POVERTY
"Four of us slept in the one bed. When it got cold, mother threw on another brother."

ON HIS SIX BROTHERS
"That's how I learned to dance. Waiting for the bathroom."

ON HIS EARLY FAILURES
"I would not have had anything to eat if it wasn't for the stuff the audience threw at me."

3. For "Hope" jokes to use through the evening (see appendix page 265).

(Jokes taken from www.telegraph.uk.com, www.standupcomedyportal.com, www.jokes4us.com, www.brainyquote.com.)

Game/Activity:

1. Patriotic Pictionary (to play): The game will center on teams at each table where they will be playing rounds of Pictionary. There will be nine rounds. Encourage each person at the table to take a turn drawing, but if they are hesitant then allow them to "skip." Announce that there will be three rounds of each U.S. topic (presidents, important events in history, and famous battles). At the beginning of each round, the person leading the evening will give slips of the subject to be drawn to the person doing the drawing for the round. They all begin at the same time and have a minute to complete. Table members will try to guess what is being drawn — with the drawer using no words, only drawing. Tables will compete on how many they got correct. (The prizes will be dessert: the first place table gets to go get dessert first, then the second place table, and then third.)

Have the topics pre-cut (according to how many teams there will be) in nine different

envelopes labeled with the round number on it. For Patriotic Pictionary Topics have them ready to cut and a score sheet for each table (see appendix pages 266-267).

2. Hidden Flags: For a break in the evening have a game where people search the room for hidden patriotic objects (ex: small flags). For each one found there is a prize (candy bar or something small). This will be a good opportunity to stretch their legs.

Reading:

1. "For all those born before 1945 — we Are Survivors!"
Consider the changes we have witnessed:

We were born before television, before penicillin, before polio shots, frozen foods, Xerox, plastic, contact lenses, the Frisbee® disc, and the pill.
We were born before radar, credit cards, split atoms, laser beams, and ballpoint pens, before pantyhose, dishwashers, clothes dryers, electric blankets, air conditioners, drip-dry-clothes — and before man walked on the moon.

We got married first and then lived together. How quaint would that be? In our time, closets were for clothes, not for "coming out of." Bunnies were small rabbits and rabbits were not Volkswagens.

Designer jeans were scheming girls named Jean or Jeanne, and having a meaningful relationship meant getting along well with our cousins.
We were born before Bibles were taken from schools and condoms were introduced.

We thought fast food was what you ate during Lent. We were born before house husbands, gay rights, computer dating, dual careers, and computer marriages.

We were born before day care centers, group therapy, and nursing homes. We never heard of FM radio, tape decks, electric typewriters, artificial hearts, word processors, yogurt, and guys wearing earrings.

For us, time-sharing meant togetherness, not computers or condominiums. A "chip" meant a piece of wood, hardware meant hardware, and software wasn't even a word!

In 1940, "made in Japan" meant junk and the term "making out" referred to how you did on your exam. Pizza, "McDonald's" and instant coffee were unheard of.

We hit the scene when there were 5 and 10-cent stores, where you bought things for five and ten cents. Drugstores sold ice cream cones for a nickel or a dime. For one nickel you could ride a street car (trolley), make a phone call, and buy a Pepsi® or enough stamps to mail one letter and two postcards. You could buy a new Chevy Coupe for $600, but who could afford one; a pity too, because gas was 11 cents a gallon!

In our day, cigarette smoking was fashionable, grass was mowed, Coke® was a drink, and pot was something you cooked in. Rock music was Grandma's lullaby and AIDS were helpers in the principal's office.

We were certainly not born before the difference between the sexes was discovered but we were surely born before the sex change; we made do with what we had; and we were the last generation that was so dumb as to think you needed a husband to have a baby!
No wonder we are so confused and there is such a generation gap today! But somehow we survived! What better reason to celebrate?

Video/YouTube Clip:
The Department of Defense has made a compilation of USO performances by Bob Hope during 1967. It is 1 hour and 27 minutes long, so it will need to be split into parts during the evening. It is downloadable from YouTube.

Scripture for the Month: (Can put in newsletter to encourage memorization)
"He will yet fill your mouth with laughter and your lips with shouts of joy" (Job 8:21).

"A veteran is someone who, at one point in their life, wrote a blank check made payable to The United States of America for an amount up to and including their life."
— Anonymous

AUGUST
Monthly Ideas

August
Monthly Ideas

1. "Keep Your Mind Sharp with AARP" (Alzheimer's and Dementia prevention)

The title "Keep your mind sharp with AARP" presentation is a national program. Local AARP representatives can give presentations from this "Brain Smart" program and explain Dementia and Alzheimer's and why it is important for all seniors to incorporate the 5 core elements: work your mind, be fit, eat smart, socialize and stress less.

For more information visit: AARP.org/brainhealth

Pre-dinner Conversation Starter:
The brain health program has an excellent handout on the five core elements – have one copy at each place setting.

Decorations:
Decorations for this event should be bright and shiny, foil or sparkly. This needs to be a cheerful event – use brightly colored napkins and color matching centerpieces. Silver foil centerpieces can be purchased at most party or dollar stores. Sprinkle bright confetti around the center as well.

Quote for the Month/Event:
"To keep the heart unwrinkled, to be hopeful, kindly, cheerful, reverent--that is to triumph over old age." – Thomas Aldrich

"When you pray, your prayers are heard by the same God who answered Moses' prayer for water in the desert, the God who gave Abraham and his barren wife a son, and the God who made the slave Joseph second in power only to Pharaoh." – Francis Chan

"Too often we use petty little petitions, oratorical exercises, or the words of others rather than the cries of our inmost being. When you pray, pray!" – Billy Graham

Joke/Story:

1. What's for Dinner

I have my own system for labeling homemade freezer meals. Forget calling them "Veal Parmigianino" or "Turkey Loaf" or "Beef Pot Pie." If you look in my freezer you'll see "Whatever," "Anything," "I Don't Know," and, my favorite, "Food." That way when I ask my husband what he wants for dinner, I'm certain to have what he wants."
(www.laughandlift.com Used by permission.)

2. The End is Near

A local priest and pastor were fishing on the side of the road. They thoughtfully made a sign saying, "The end is near! Turn yourself around now before it's too late!" and showed it to each passing car. One driver who drove by didn't appreciate the sign and shouted at them: "Leave us alone, you religious nuts!" All of a sudden they heard a big SPLASH! The priest and the pastor looked at each other, and they said to each other. "Do you think we should just put up a sign that says 'bridge out' instead?'"
(www.laughandlift.com Used by permission.)

3. Silver Surfers

As we Silver Surfers know, sometimes we have trouble with our computers.
Yesterday, I had a problem, so I called Georgie, the 11-year-old next door, whose bedroom looks like Mission Control, and asked him to come over. Georgie clicked a couple of buttons and solved the problem. As he was walking away, I called after him, "So, what was wrong?"
He replied, "It was an ID ten T error."
I didn't want to appear stupid, but nonetheless inquired, "An ID ten T error? What's that? In case I need to fix it again."
Georgie grinned, "Haven't you ever heard of an ID ten T error before?"
"No," I replied.
"Write it down," he said, "and I think you'll figure it out."
So I wrote down: ID10T
I used to like Georgie.
(www.mikeysFunnies.com. Used by permission.)

4. Like a lot of husbands throughout history, Webster would sit down and try to talk to his wife. But as soon as he would start to say something, his wife said, "And what's that supposed to mean?" And thus, Webster's Dictionary was born.

Game/Activity:

1. Try to solve "Webster's Words" (see appendix page 268) by table – be sure to have prizes for most solved! Have a time limit such as ten minutes.

Reading:

1. GUIDELINES FOR LIFE

Pray not for things, but for wisdom and courage.
Compliment three people every day.
Watch a sunrise at least once a month.
Be the first to say hello.
Live beneath your means.
Treat everyone like you want to be treated.
Never give up on anybody; miracles happen.
Never deprive someone of hope; it may be all they have.
Be tough-minded, but tenderhearted.
Be kinder than necessary.
Keep your promises.
Learn to show cheerfulness, even when you don't feel like it.
Remember that overnight success usually takes about 15 years.
Never waste an opportunity to tell someone you love them.
(www.mikeysFunnies.com. Used by permission.)

2. What is life?
Life is an opportunity; benefit from it.
Life is a song; sing it.
Life is beauty; admire it.
Life is a challenge; meet it.
Life is a struggle; accept it.
Life is duty; complete it.
Life is sorrow; overcome it.
Life is an adventure; dare it.
Life is life; life it!
(Attributed by some sources to Mother Teresa).

Video/YouTube Clip:
Watch motivational speaker Karyn Buxman's FUNNY stress management techniques on YouTube video, then watch "Managing Stress – Brainsmart – BBC" on YouTube for a more sensible plan.

Scripture for the Month: (Can put in newsletter to encourage memorization)
"If any of you lacks wisdom, you should ask God, who gives generously to all without finding fault, and it will be given to you" (James 1:5).

2. Senior Fraud Protection: State Attorney General's Office Speaker

Invite a speaker from the state Attorney General's Office to come and speak. If a speaker cannot be found, then watch the YouTube video from AARP titled "Consumer Fraud Protection/AARP Live," Jan 23, 2014, which is an excellent informational one hour video. (Be sure to have paper and pens for people to take notes.)

Pre-dinner Conversation Starter:
Get handouts from the State or Federal Attorney General's Office on Fraud and place at each place setting.

Decorations:
Make this a very elegant evening with white tablecloths, nice napkins, candlelight and flowers in the center of the table. Individually wrapped chocolate mints or other chocolates can be placed at each place setting; disposable foil muffin liners make a good candy holder.

Quote for the Month/Event:
"Jesus said, 'I am the way, the truth, and the life; no man comes to the Father but by me.' On the surface, that seems the most intolerant of statements. Think of any man on the stage of human history claiming to be the supreme embodiment of all psychological, scientific, and religious truth! He was either an egomaniac, a liar, or He was what He claimed to be. By faith I accepted Him for what He claimed to be, the Son of the Living God. That simple decision changed my life - and I have seen it change the lives of countless others across the world." – Billy Graham

Joke/Story:

1. A lawyer phoned the governor's mansion shortly after midnight. "I need to talk to the governor – it's an emergency!" exclaimed the lawyer. After some cajoling, the governor's assistant agreed to wake him up. "So, what is it that's so important that it can't wait until morning?" grumbled the governor. Judge Pierson just died, and I want to take his place," begged the attorney. "Well, it's OK with me if it's OK with the funeral home," replied the governor. (www.GCFL.net, info@gcfl.net. Used by permission.)

2. A guy was in court charged with parking in a restricted area. The judge asked him if he had anything to say in his defense. "They shouldn't put up such misleading notices," said the guy. "It said `FINE FOR PARKING HERE`."

3. On Coast Guard Cutters, low-ranking crewmembers take turns in the galley helping the cooks. One young seaman aboard was always dropping dishes and spilling food. One day, alone in the galley, he noticed an unfrosted yellow sheet-cake cooling on a counter. Determined to rectify past errors, the seaman made chocolate icing and carefully decorated the cake with it. The seaman stood proudly by the dessert as the head

LAUGHTER is good for THE SOUL

cook returned to the galley. Frantically, the cook began to look around. "Where did my cornbread go?" he shouted.

4. ACTS 2:38 Concealed Carry & an Intruder

A woman had just returned to her home from an evening of church services, when she was startled by an intruder. She caught the man in the act of robbing her home of its valuables and yelled: "Stop! Acts 2:38!" (Repent and be baptized, in the name of Jesus Christ, so that your sins may be forgiven.) The burglar stopped in his tracks. The woman calmly called the police and explained what she had done. As the officer cuffed the man to take him in, he asked the burglar: "Why did you just stand there? All the old lady did was yell a scripture to you." "Scripture?" replied the burglar. "She said she had an Ax and Two 38's!"

5. CPR

A blonde lady had just completed a CPR course and was on the lookout for a chance to try it out. As she left a shopping center, she saw a man lying on the ground with a lot of people gathered around him. Screaming, "I know first aid!" she ran to the person, threw her bag down, loosened all his tight clothing, and got ready to start mouth-to-mouth. At this stage, a huge policeman tapped her on the shoulder and said, "Do you mind? I am trying to arrest this man." (http://www.GCFL.net, info@gcfl.net. Used by permission.)

Game/Activity:

1. Play "Crime Doesn't Pay" (see appendix page 269).

Reading:

1. The Most Important Discoveries
Man discovered weapons, invented hunting.
Woman discovered hunting, invented furs.
Man discovered colors, invented painting.
Woman discovered painting, invented make-up.
Man discovered speech, invented conversation.
Woman discovered conversation, invented gossip.
Man discovered agriculture, invented food.
Woman discovered food, invented diet.
Man discovered friendship, invented love.
Woman discovered love, invented marriage.
Man discovered trade, invented money.
Woman discovered money, man has never recovered.
(www.GCFL.net, info@gcfl.net. Used by permission.)

2. More Church Bulletin Bloopers

- Scouts are saving aluminum cans, bottles and other items to be recycled. Proceeds will be used to cripple children.

- The sermon this morning: 'Jesus Walks on the Water.' The sermon tonight: 'Searching for Jesus.'

- Don't let worry kill you off – let the church help.

- Miss Charlene sang 'I will not pass this way again,' giving obvious pleasure to the congregation.

- For those of you who have children and don't know it, we have a nursery downstairs.

- Next Thursday there will be try-outs for the choir. They need all the help they can get.

- A bean supper will be held on Tuesday evening in the church hall. Music will follow.

- At the evening service tonight, the sermon topic will be 'What Is Hell?' Come early and listen to our choir practice.

- Eight new choir robes are currently needed due to the addition of several new members and to the deterioration of some older ones.

- Please place your donation in the envelope along with the deceased person you want remembered.

- Low Self Esteem Support Group will meet Thursday at 7 PM. Please use the back door.

- The eighth-graders will be presenting Shakespeare's Hamlet in the church basement Friday at 7 PM. The congregation is invited to attend this tragedy.

- Weight Watchers will meet at 7 PM at the church. Please use large double door at the side entrance.

- Ladies, don't forget the rummage sale. It is a good chance to get rid of those things not worth keeping around the house. Bring your husbands.

- The peace-making meeting scheduled for today has been canceled due to a conflict.

- Now that Barbara is recovering from surgery in the hospital, she is having trouble sleeping and requests tapes of Pastor's sermons.

- The 'Over 60s Choir' will be disbanded for the summer with the thanks of the entire church.

- Announcement in a church bulletin for a National Prayer & Fasting Conference: "The cost for attending the Fasting & Prayer conference includes meals."

Video/YouTube Clip:
Watch videos on people who try to fake an injury – the YouTube video "Insurance Scammers are Awesome! (New 2015)" is an example.

Scripture for the Month: (Can put in newsletter to encourage memorization)
"I am sending you out like sheep among wolves. Therefore be as shrewd as snakes and as innocent as doves" (Matthew 10:16).

3. Rodeo/On the Trail Event/Backyard Chef Cook-off (Intergenerational: Kids/Youth)

If there is a nearby rodeo, then plan to attend! It will be a fun and an unusual outing for both seniors and grandkids/youth. If not, then try to arrange your own. This event will have to be out at a local park or rodeo arena. There are many areas that have Christian cowboy groups or rodeo associations that will put on a display of roping and riding. If needed, rent a local arena for several hours for the group to perform.

Have a cook-off of some type for lunch: "Steer Stew" and "Best Biscuits" competitions along with "Delectable Desserts." Have lunch, award prizes for the food competitions, and then watch the rodeo demonstrations. If time allows, a good bluegrass band would be the ending to a great event. For "Outings/Excursions Preparation" (see appendix page 244).

Decorations:
Use checkered tablecloths on tables if they are available; otherwise the food may have to be eaten picnic style on bleachers. Ask people to bring their own chairs if needed.

Quote for the Month/Event:
"Life begins when you do." – Hugh Downs

"I'd rather wear out than rust out." – Dan Rather

Game/Activity:
Play "Rodeo Lingo" en route to rodeo (see appendix page 261).

Scripture for the Month: (Can put in newsletter to encourage memorization)
"Come to me, all you who are weary and burdened, and I will give you rest. Take my yoke upon you and learn from me, for I am gentle and humble in heart, and you will find rest for your souls. For my yoke is easy and my burden is light" (Matthew 11:28–30).

SEPTEMBER
Monthly Ideas

September
Monthly Ideas

1. Political Debate/Speaker Dinner

This is the perfect time of the year to host a political debate/ speaker. Guests could be local or state candidates. Pick a moderator who could remain neutral. This would be an opportunity for voters to get to know the candidates before voting time. For an article that deals with religion and churches see "What can Pastors Say from the Pulpit about Candidates and Elections" (see appendix pages 272-273).

Pre-dinner Conversation Starter:
See www.wallbuilders.com for information that can be used as a handout.

Decorations:
This would be a good event to decorate with red, white and blue and elephants and donkeys - a patriotic and fun evening. Pictures can be downloaded from the internet to copy and paste on the parties, but be certain to watch for trademark, registration or copyright information that may restrict the image usage.

Quote for the Month/Event:
During World War II, President Franklin D. Roosevelt stated December 29, 1940:
"*No nation can appease the Nazis. No man can tame a tiger into a kitten by stroking it. There can be no appeasement with ruthlessness. There can be no reasoning with an incendiary bomb. We know now that a nation can have peace with the Nazis only at the price of total surrender... The American appeasers ignore the warning to be found in the fate of Austria, Czechoslovakia, Poland, Norway, Belgium, the Netherlands, Denmark, and France...They call it a 'negotiated peace.' Nonsense! Is it a negotiated peace if a gang of outlaws surrounds*

your community and on threat of extermination makes you pay tribute to save your own skins? Such a dictated peace would be no peace at all."

"No arsenal, or no weapon in the arsenals of the world, is as formidable as the will and moral courage of free men and women." – Ronald Reagan

"I've come to be familiarized with the PC (politically correct) culture and I'm willing to fight it. You know, somebody has to stand up for who we are." – Dr. Ben Carson

Joke/Story:

1. A preacher phoned the city's newspaper. "Thank you very much," said he, "for the error you made when you announced my sermon topic for last Sunday. The topic I sent you was 'What Jesus Saw in A Publican.' You printed it as 'What Jesus Saw in a Republican' I had the biggest crowd of the year!"

2. Outside a prominent hotel late one night, a mugger wearing a ski mask jumped into the path of a well-dressed man and stuck a gun in his ribs. "Give me all your money," he demanded. Indignant, the affluent man replied, "You can't do this! I am a United States congressman!" "In that case," replied the mugger, "then, give me MY money."

3. A man had just finished reading his book "Man Of The House" while making his commute home from work. When he reached home, he stormed into the house and walked directly up to his wife. Pointing his finger in her face, he said, "From now on I want you to know that I am the man of this house and my word is law! You are to prepare me a gourmet meal tonight, and when I'm finished eating my meal, I expect a sumptuous dessert afterward. Then, after dinner, you're going to draw my bath so I can relax. And when I'm finished with my bath, guess who's going to dress me and comb my hair?" His wife thought for a moment and responded, "The Funeral Director is my guess."

4. Giving a man his physical, a doctor noticed several dark, ugly bruises on his shins, so he asked, "Do you play hockey, soccer, or any physical sport?" "Not at all. I just play bridge with my wife."

Game/Activity:

1. Play "Elephants and Donkeys" (see appendix page 271) together by tables. Be sure to have copies and pencils at each place setting.

Reading:

1. Prayer for Outreach:

Today, I will live purposefully and honorably through my thoughts, actions and speech. I choose to be a follower of Jesus. I will love and not hate, I will give before I take and I will serve before being served. Today, I choose to make a difference in this world for the kingdom of God. I will put others higher than myself and commit to be not only a hearer of the Word but also a doer of the Word. Today I will live in such a way as to impact people for eternity, even if it is one person at a time. In this way, I will change the world!

2. Pearls of Wisdom:

- A mother can touch a whole generation just by loving her own child well.
- A veteran is someone who, at one point in their life, wrote a blank check made payable to The United States of America for an amount up to and including their life.
- After a fender-bender, the teenaged driver pointed to the damage and said: "Great news, Dad – you haven't been pouring those insurance payments down the drain after all!"
- Birthdays are good for you … the more you have the longer you live.
- Did Adam and Eve ever have a date? No, but they had an apple.
- Don't trust atoms…they make up everything.
- Farmer wisdom: Life is simpler when you plow around the stumps.
- I don't have gray hair. I have "wisdom highlights."
- I think your kids are like angels! (Of course, the Devil is an angel too.)
- I want one of those jobs where people ask, "Do you actually get paid to do this??"
- I'd like to be the ideal mother, but I'm too busy raising my kids.
- I've learned that even when I have pains, I don't have to be one.
- If it is not Valentine's day and you see a man in a flower shop, you can probably start up a conversation by asking, 'What did you do?'
- 33% say they won't have money to cover their holiday spending…Those people are called Congress.
- If you aim at nothing, you'll hit it every time.
- It's hard to gain a toehold if you're acting like a heel.
- Life isn't about how fast you run, or how high you climb; it's about how well you bounce.
- Men have feelings, too. For example, they feel hungry.
- On your birthday, send a thank you card to your mom.
- Quando Omni Flunkus Moritai (When all else fails, play dead)
- The best thing to spend on your children is time.
- The great thing about living in a small town is that when you don't know what you're doing, someone else does.
- The kids text me "plz" which is shorter than please. I text back "no" which is shorter than "yes."

- The older we get, the fewer things seem worth waiting in line for.
- We have 35 million laws to enforce the Ten Commandments.
- Wealthy people miss one of life's greatest thrills: Making the last car payment.
- When it rains, why don't sheep shrink?
- When you are dissatisfied and would like to go back to youth, think of algebra.
- With some people you spend an evening. With others you invest it.
- Wouldn't it be great if we could put ourselves in the dryer for ten minutes and come out wrinkle-free and three sizes smaller?
- You can tell a lot about a man by the way he handles these three things: a rainy day, lost luggage, and tangled Christmas tree lights.

(www.mikeysFunnies.com. Used by permission.)

3. Read "He Is!" for some energetic praising time! (see appendix pages 274-277).

Video/YouTube Clip:
Play a YouTube video of Kate Smith singing America the Beautiful, written by Irving Berlin.

Scripture for the Month: (Can put in newsletter to encourage memorization)
"He has shown you, O mortal, what is good. And what does the LORD require of you? To act justly and to love mercy and to walk humbly with your God" (Micah 6:8).

2. Farm (Fruit, Animal, or Dairy) Tour/Lunch Out

Having a farm tour followed by a lunch out is an educational and fun outing. There are so many options for this tour. For example the group could see how fruit or eggs are processed. If a dairy tour is arranged, make sure to have a time where those that want to milk a cow by hand can give it a try! For "Outings/Excursions Preparation" (see appendix page 244).

Quote for the Month/Event:

"*It helps to be humble*" a gushy reporter told Jack Nicklaus. "*You are spectacular! Your name is synonymous with the game of golf. You really know your way around the course. What's your secret?*" Nicklaus replied, "*The holes are numbered!*"

"The real voyage of discovery consists not in seeking new landscapes but in having new eyes."
– Marcel Proust

Joke/Story: (Can be read during lunch.)

1. Catching the Fish

Jim had an awful day fishing on the lake, sitting in the blazing sun all day without catching a single one. On his way home, he stopped at the supermarket and ordered four catfish. He told the fish salesman, "Pick four large ones out and throw them at me, will you?" "Why do you want me to throw them at you?" "Because I want to tell my wife that I caught them." "Okay, but I suggest that you take the orange roughy." "But why?" "Because your wife came in earlier today and said that if you came by, I should tell you to take orange roughy. She prefers that for supper tonight."

2. After being married, for fifty years, I took a careful look at my wife one day, and said, "Fifty years ago, we had a cheap house, a junk car, slept on a sofa bed, and watched a 10-inch TV. But then I got to sleep every night with a hot 23-year old girl. Now. . . I have a $750,000 home, a $45,000 car, a nice big bed, and a nice flat screen TV, but I am sleeping with a 73-year old woman. So I said to my wife, it seems to me that you are not holding up your side of things. My wife is a very reasonable woman. She told me to "go out and find a hot 23-year old girl and she would make sure that I would once again be living in a cheap house, driving a junk car, sleeping on a sofa bed and watching a 10-in black and white TV. Aren't older women great? They really know how to solve an old guy's problems!

Reading: (Can be read during lunch.)

1. A young woman went to her grandmother and told her about her life and how things were so hard for her – her husband had cheated on her and she was devastated. She did not know how she was going to make it and wanted to give up. She was tired of fighting and struggling. It seemed as soon as one problem was solved, a new one arose.

Her grandmother took her to the kitchen. She filled three pots with water and placed each on a high fire. Soon the pots came to boil. In the first she placed carrots, in the second she placed eggs, and in the last she placed ground coffee beans. She let them sit and boil; without saying a word.

In about twenty minutes she turned off the burners. She fished the carrots out and placed them in a bowl. She pulled the eggs out and placed them in a bowl. Then she ladled the coffee out and placed it in a bowl.

Turning to her granddaughter, she asked, 'Tell me what you see.'
'Carrots, eggs, and coffee,' she replied.

Her grandmother brought her closer and asked her to feel the carrots. She did and noted that they were soft. The grandmother then asked the granddaughter to take an egg and break it. After pulling off the shell, she observed the hardboiled egg.

Finally, the grandmother asked the granddaughter to sip the coffee. The granddaughter smiled as she tasted its rich aroma. The granddaughter then asked, 'What does it mean, grandmother?'
Her grandmother explained that each of these objects had faced the same adversity: boiling water. Each reacted differently. The carrots went in strong, hard, and unrelenting. However, after being subjected to the boiling water, they softened and became weak. The egg had been fragile. Its thin outer shell had protected its liquid interior, but after sitting through the boiling water, its inside became hardened. The ground coffee beans were unique, however. After they were in the boiling water, they had changed the water.

"Which are you?" she asked her granddaughter. "When adversity knocks on your door, how do you respond? Are you a carrot, an egg or a coffee bean?
Think of this: Which am I? Am I the carrot that seems strong; but with pain and adversity do I wilt and become soft and lose my strength?
Am I the egg that starts with a malleable heart, but changes with the heat? Did I have a fluid spirit, but after a death, a breakup, a financial hardship or some other trial, have I become hardened and stiff? Does my shell look the same, but on the inside am I bitter and tough with a stiff spirit and hardened heart?

Or am I like the coffee bean? The bean actually changes the hot water, the very circumstance that brings the pain. When the water gets hot, it releases the fragrance and flavor. If you are like the bean, when things are at their worst, you get better and change the situation around you. When the hour is the darkest and trials are their greatest, do you elevate yourself to another level?

How do you handle adversity? Are you a carrot, an egg or a coffee bean?

2. Seeing Jesus Face to Face
The hymn writer Fanny Crosby gave us more than 6,000 (yes, that's 6,000!) gospel songs throughout her life. Although blinded by an illness at the age of 6 weeks, she never became bitter.
One of Miss Crosby's hymns was so personal that for years she kept it to herself. Kenneth Osbeck, author of several books on hymnology, says its revelation to the public came about this way: "One day at the Bible conference in Northfield, Massachusetts, Miss

Crosby was asked by D.L. Moody to give a personal testimony. At first she hesitated, then quietly rose and said, 'There is one hymn I have written which has never been published. I call it my soul's poem. Sometimes when I am troubled, I repeat it to myself, for it brings comfort to my heart.'
She then recited while many wept:

"Someday the silver cord will break,
And I no more as now shall sing,
But, O, the joy when I awake
Within the palace of the King.

And I shall see Him face to face,
And tell the story saved by grace.
Some day my earthly house will fall,
I cannot tell how soon 'twill be,

But this I know, my All in All
Has now a place in heaven for me.
And I shall see Him face to face,
And tell the story saved by grace.

Some day, when fades the golden sun
Beneath the rosy-tinted West,
My blessed Lord will say, "Well done!"
And I shall enter into rest.

And I shall see Him face to face,
And tell the story saved by grace.
Some day - till then I'll watch and wait,
My lamp all trimmed and burning bright,

That when my Savior opens the gate,
My soul to Him may take its flight.
And I shall see Him face to face,
And tell the story saved by grace."
At the age of 95 Fanny Crosby passed into glory and saw the face of Jesus.
(www.laughandlift.com. Used by permission.)

Scripture for the Month:
(Can put in newsletter to encourage memorization)
"I am the vine; you are the branches. If you remain in me and I in you, you will bear much fruit; apart from me you can do nothing" (John 15:5).

3. Family Feud Game Night
(Intergenerational: Kids)

There is nothing more exciting than seeing a live competition, especially when there are two well-known families on stage competing against each other. Pick two large families (if possible) from the church or group with people who are willing to be laughed at and who will have a good time with it all.

The questions should be made up from people in the audience (with categories such as Bible knowledge, geography, and hodgepodge). At the beginning of the evening take some time for each table to compose and submit questions to be asked to the families in the contest. Have the moderator pick the top 45 questions to be asked.

There will need to be a moderator to read the questions and a timer/scorekeeper. The families will alternate having the questions asked

first; if they miss it, it goes to the other family. They will have 20 seconds to answer the question. For table question sheets and "Family Feud Game Night: Score Sheet" (see appendix pages 278-281).

Do two rounds (15 questions each) and then take a break either for a music performance or dessert time before doing the last round. Be sure to have different color T-shirts made for each team (for example, the blue team (Smiths) and the yellow team (Clarks).

Pre-dinner Conversation Starter:
Have copies of "Name That Game" at each place setting (see appendix page 282). As an opener, play the video below just before event begins.

Decorations:
Use young children's party games prizes from the dollar store to decorate the centers of the tables, such as cards, checkers, dice, pick-up sticks, and dominoes.

Divide the room (tables) up in half to support one team (family). Can have blue tablecloths or markers (Smiths team) on one side and yellow tablecloths or markers on the other (Clarks team).

Quote for the Month/Event:
Tonight's quote for the evening is appropriate for our contestants:

"One ought never to turn one's back on a threatened danger and try to run away from it. If you do that, you will double the danger. But if you meet it promptly and without flinching, you will reduce the danger by half. Never run away from anything. Never!"
– Winston Churchill

After the death of the great eighteenth-century Methodist evangelist, George Whitefield, a New York woman commented, *"Mr. Whitefield was so cheerful that it tempted me to be a Christian."*

Joke/Story:

1. A little boy is sitting in the bathroom trying to learn to use the potty. After some time his mother asks, "Johnny, are you OK?" He says, "Yes." More time passes and finally the mother's curiosity gets the best of her and she walks into the bathroom. He is red-faced and is slapping himself on the top of his head. The mother asks, "Johnny, what in the world are you doing?" He says, "Well, it works for the ketchup!"

2. In a certain suburban neighborhood, there were two brothers, eight and ten years old, who were exceedingly mischievous. Whatever went wrong in the neighborhood, it turned out they had had a hand in it. Their parents were at their wits end trying to control them. Hearing about a priest nearby who worked with delinquent boys, the mother suggested to the father that they ask the priest to talk with the boys. The father replied, "Sure, do that before I kill them!"

The mother went to the priest and made her request. He agreed, but said he wanted to see the younger boy first and alone. So the mother sent him to the priest. The priest sat the boy down in front of the huge, impressive desk he sat behind. For about five minutes they just sat and stared at each other. Finally, the priest pointed his forefinger at the boy and asked, "Where is God?"

The boy looked under the desk, in the corners of the room, all around, but said nothing. Again, louder, the priest pointed at the boy and asked, "Where is God?" Again the boy looked all around but said nothing. A third time, in a louder, firmer voice, the priest leaned far across the desk and put his forefinger almost to the boy's nose, and asked, "Where is God?"

The boy panicked and ran all the way home. Finding his older brother, he dragged him upstairs to their room and into the closet where they usually plotted their mischief. He finally said, "We are in BIG trouble!" The older boy asked, "What do you mean, BIG trouble?" His brother replied, "God is missing and they think we did it." (www.GCFL.net, info@gcfl.net)

3. A father brought home a backyard swing set for his children and immediately started to assemble it with all the neighborhood children anxiously waiting to play on it. After several hours of reading the directions, attempting to fit bolt A into slot B, etc., he finally

gave up and called upon old Joe, a carpenter working in a neighboring yard. Joe came over, threw the directions away, and in a short while had the set completely assembled. "It's beyond me," said the father, "how you got it together without even reading the instructions." "To tell the truth," replied the old-timer, "I can't read, and when you can't read, you've got to think."

Game/Activity:
Play "Word Puzzles" (see appendix pages 283-284).

Video/YouTube Clip:
Pre-record both families before the event at their homes with an interview about the contest, how they feel about the game, and who they think is going to win!

Reading:
1. Real Children's Letters to God

- Dear God, Are you really invisible or is that just a trick? —Lucy

- Dear God, Did you mean for giraffes to look like that or was it an accident? —Norma

- Dear God, I want to be just like my daddy when I get big, but not with so much hair all over. —Sam

- Dear God, Instead of letting people die and having to make new ones, why don't you just keep the ones you got now? —Jane

- Dear God, You don't have to worry about me, I always look both ways. —Dean

- Dear God, I went to this wedding and they kissed right in church. Is that okay? –Ned

- Dear God, I think the stapler is one of your greatest inventions. —Ruth

- Dear God, In the Bible times did they really talk that fancy? —Jennifer

- Dear God, I think about you sometimes even when I'm not praying. —Elliott

- Dear God, I'm American. What are you? —Robert

- Dear God, I bet it's very hard for you to love all of everybody in the whole world. There are only 4 people in our family and I never can do it. —Nan

- Dear God, Thank you for the baby brother, but what I prayed for was a puppy. —Joyce

- Dear God, Please put another holiday between Christmas and Easter. There is nothing good in there now. —Ginny

- Dear God, If you watch in church on Sunday, I will show you my new shoes. —Mickey

- Dear God, If we come back as something, please don't let me be Jennifer Horton because I hate her. —Denise

- Dear God, If you give me a genie lamp like Aladdin, I will give you anything you want except my money and my chess set. —Raphael

- Dear God, We read Thomas Edison made light, but in Sunday school they said you did it. So I bet he stole your idea. —Sincerely, Donna

2. Family
I ran into a stranger as he passed by,
"Oh excuse me, please," was my reply.
He said, "Please excuse me too;
I wasn't watching for you."
We were very polite, this stranger and I.
We went on our way saying goodbye.

But at home a difference is told,
How we treat our loved ones, young and old.
Later that day, cooking the evening meal,
My son stood beside me very still.
As I turned, I nearly knocked him down.
"Move out of the way," I said with a frown.
He walked away, his little heart, broken.
I didn't realize how harshly I'd spoken.

While I lay awake in bed,

God's still small voice came to me and said,
"While dealing with a stranger, common courtesy you use,
But the children you love, you seem to abuse.

Go and look on the kitchen floor,
You'll find some flowers there by the door.
Those are the flowers he brought for you.
He picked them himself: pink, yellow, and blue.
He stood very quietly not to spoil the surprise,
And you never saw the tears that filled his little eyes."

By this time, I felt very small,
And now my tears began to fall.
I quietly went and knelt by his bed;
"Wake up, little one, wake up," I said.
"Are these the flowers you picked for me?"
"I picked 'em because they're pretty like you.
I knew you'd like 'em, especially the blue."

I said, "Son, I'm very sorry for the way I acted today;
I shouldn't have yelled at you that way."
He said, "Oh, Mom, that's okay.
"I love you anyway."
I said, "Son, I love you too,
And I do like the flowers, especially the blue."

Scripture for the Month: (Can put in newsletter to encourage memorization)
"If you love me, keep my commands" (John 14:15).

OCTOBER
Monthly Ideas

October
Monthly Ideas

1. "What not to Wear" Fashion Show (by local shops)

Having a fun evening like this will be sure to provide a lot of laughs. The funnier the models the better; try to find well known members of the group who will be the models. Contact one or more local clothing shops to arrange for the models to come and pick out their outfits, which will be brought the day of the event.

Quote for the Month/Event:

"Everything you save is less you have to earn." – Herb Chapman

Speaking of weight control/dieting:

"Strength does not come from winning. Your struggles develop your strengths. When you go through hardships and decide not to surrender, that is strength." – Arnold Schwarzenegger

Joke/Story:

1. Speeding
A woman was driving down the highway about 75 miles per hour, when she noticed a cop following her. Instead of slowing down, she picked up speed. When she looked back again, there were 2 cops following her. She shot up to 90 miles per hour. The next time she looked around, there were 3 cops following her. Suddenly, she spotted a gas station looming ahead. She screeched to a stop and ran into the ladies' room. Ten minutes later, she innocently walked out. The 3 cops were standing there waiting for her. Without batting an eye, she said coyly, "I'll bet none of you thought I would make it."
(www.laughandlift.com Used by permission.)

2. Deer Season
The Wednesday night church service coincided with the last day of hunting season. Our pastor asked who had bagged a deer. No one raised a hand. Puzzled, the pastor said,

"I don't get it. Last Sunday many of you said you were missing because of hunting season. I had the whole congregation pray for your deer." One hunter groaned, "Well, it worked. They're all safe." (www.mikeysFunnies.com. Used by permission.)

3. Jeans
I spotted several pairs of men's Levi's jeans at a garage sale. They were sizes 30, 31, and 32, but I was looking for size 33. So I asked the owner if he had a pair. He shook his head. "I'm still wearing the 33s," he said. "Come back next year."

4. Near Death Experience
A middle-aged woman had a heart attack and was taken to the hospital. While on the operating table she had a near death experience. Seeing God, she asked, "Is my time up?" God said, "No, not yet, you have another 43 years, 2 hours and 8 days to live." Upon recovery, the woman decided to stay in the hospital and have a face lift, liposuction, and a tummy tuck. Since she had so much more time to live, she figured she might as well look even nicer. After her last operation, she was released from the hospital. While crossing the street on her way home, she was hit and killed by an ambulance. Arriving in the presence of God, she demanded, "I thought you said I had another 40 plus years? Why didn't you pull me out of the path of the ambulance?" God replied, "My child, I am sorry, but I didn't recognize you!"

Game/Activity:
1. Without prior notice (other than the need to attend), have the leaders or workers come up front. Have the audience vote on which one best fits each category (see appendix page 285).

a. The classiest shoes
b. The best hair design
c. The most comfortably dressed
d. Best color combination
e. The best legs
f. The most durable outfit

Reading:
1. "Senior Dress Code"
Many of us "Old Folks" (those over 50, WAY over 50, or hovering near 50) are unsure about the kind of image we are projecting and whether or not we are correct as we try to conform to current fashions. Despite what you may have seen on the streets, the following combinations DO NOT go together and should be avoided:

1. A nose ring and bifocals

2. Spiked hair and bald spots

3. A pierced tongue and dentures

4. Mini-skirts and support hose

5. Ankle bracelets and corn pads

6. Speedos and cellulite

7. A belly button ring and a gall bladder surgery scar

8. Unbuttoned disco shirts and a heart monitor

9. Midriff shirts and a midriff bulge

10. Bikinis and liver spots

11. Short shorts and varicose veins

12. Inline skates and a walker

And last, but not least:

13. Bikinis and Depends®

Video/YouTube Clip:

We have been seeing what not to wear now take a look at this real life success story of the prancercise exercise program – and see in our opinion "How not to exercise… Prancercise" Look up the YouTube video of Joanna Rohrback's newest video featuring horses and zebra print spandex.

Scripture for the Month: (Can put in newsletter to encourage memorization)
"People look at the outward appearance, but the LORD looks at the heart" (1 Samuel 16:7c).

2. National Quartet Competition/Creation Museum (Bus Trip)

The National Quartet competition is held yearly in Louisville, KY, from Monday–Saturday. The best gospel singers from all over the United States come to this event. Most seniors like good harmony and it doesn't get any better than this. For more information call 800-846-8499 or visit www.natqc.com. For "Outings/Excursions Preparation" (see appendix pages 244).

The Creation Museum located in Petersburg, KY (very close to Louisville) would be a perfect tandem trip. This new state-of-the-art 70,000 square-foot museum brings the Bible to life. Exhibits from a Christian worldview include The Stargazers Planetarium, Special Effects Theatre, Dinosaur Den, Natural Selection Truth Section, and A Walk Through History. There are various places to eat such as Noah's café, Palm café, and the Lakeside Grill outside. For more information call 1-888-582-4253 or visit creationmuseum.org

Travel games:

On a long trip it is necessary to have different types of entertainment for the bus riders. If possible, show a good movie or sermon. "Brain Games," as well, are fun to play en route. Be sure to have prizes. For games to use, go to:

Lumosity.com
brainteasers.org
billsgames.com/brain-teasers
twopaths.com/crossword

brainbashers.com
Incredibar.com/Sudoku
fillthevoid.org/games

brainden.com
braingle.com

Games can also be found in activity book form. Try different games such as picture puzzles, optical illusions, logic puzzles, crossword puzzles, and word puzzles. An excellent site is: www.pilbookstore.com. For a few examples of travel games to use see "Zaney Brainy: Words Ending in 'oat'," and "The Letter is T for Travel" (see appendix pages 286-287).

Quote for the Month/Event:
"With every rising of the sun, think of your life as just begun." – Anonymous

Scripture for the Month: (Can put in newsletter to encourage memorization)
"Shout for joy to the LORD, all the earth. Worship the LORD with gladness; come before Him with joyful songs. Know that the LORD is God. It is He who made us, and we are His; we are His people, the sheep of His pasture" (Psalm 100:103)

3. Apple or Pumpkin Picking/Sorghum Making/ Hayride and Bonfire (Intergenerational: Kids)

Getting out before the weather gets too cold will be a good fall activity. Going apple or pumpkin picking or observing sorghum making are very interesting activities to do during the day. Often local producers will have additional activities to do at harvest time as well. For "Outings/Excursions Preparation" (see appendix pages 244).

Often local Parks and Recreation offices plan hayrides in the fall and usually will have a bonfire ready at the end when requested. A great way to end the day would be hotdogs/

brats and s'mores by the fire. Prearrange to have someone play a guitar or banjo and lead in songs by the firelight.

Travel Game:
For a travel game play "Knowledge Challenge 2" Crossword (see appendix pages 288-289).

Quote for the Month/Event:
"It is neither wealth nor splendor, but tranquility and occupation, which give happiness."
– Thomas Jefferson

"Problems are only opportunities in work clothes." – Henry J. Kaiser

Scripture for the Month: (Can put in newsletter to encourage memorization)
"I am the vine; you are the branches. If you remain in me and I in you, you will bear much fruit; apart from me you can do nothing" (John 15:5).

NOVEMBER
Monthly Ideas

November
Monthly Ideas

1. A Charlie Brown Thanksgiving

Watching the Charlie Brown Thanksgiving show together will bring back a lot of memories for this generation. The theme song was tops for many years and is still a great song. A simple night of watching the show will be a lot of fun.

Pre-dinner Conversation Starter:
Play "Peanuts Trivia" (see appendix page 290). Be sure to have a copy and a pencil at each place setting. Snoopy stuffed animals could be given as prizes.

Decorations:
Fall is the theme, but also Charlie Brown. Brown napkins and plates would be fun. Peanuts in the shell and pictures of the characters, copied from the internet and scattered around the center of each table would be fun as well. Be sure to watch for trademark, registration or copyright information that may restrict the image usage.

Quote for the Month/Event:
"When everything seems to be going against you, remember that an airplane takes off against the wind, not with it." – Henry Ford

"I wish I could write the same letter to everybody: Wait patiently for the Lord. He will turn to you and hear your cry. It is amazing how clear things become when we are still before Him, not complaining, not insisting on quick answers, only seeking to hear His word in the stillness, and to see things in His light." – Elisabeth Elliot

Joke/Story:

1. Interest

Grandma Betty was visiting and explaining to her granddaughter, Holly that she hoped to win the lottery coming up on the weekend. Grandma told Holly that indeed if she won, she was going to put $500,000 into an account for each of her grandchildren, although they wouldn't be able to touch it until they were 25 years old. "Can you imagine all the interest there would be in it by then?" she said to Holly. "Oh Grandma," Holly said, "I'm already interested!"

2. Requirements

"What do you have to do to become a doctor?" my six-year-old granddaughter once asked. Her dad, seeing an opportunity, said, "You have to do extremely well in school, take a lot of math and science, get into an excellent college, make the highest grades possible, and then go to med school, and follow that with an internship. Then you can start your own practice. Honey, as smart as you are, you can be anything you want to be." Erin gave all this a moment's thought and then asked, "What do you have to do to be queen?"

3. Parenting

I'd had a pretty hectic day with my four-year-old. When bed-time finally came, I laid down the law: "We're putting on your p.j.'s, brushing your teeth, and reading ONE book. Then it's lights out!" Her arms went around my neck in a gentle embrace, and she said, "We learned in Sunday school about little boys and girls who don't have mommies and daddies." Even after I'd been such a grouch, I thought, she was still grateful to have me. I felt tears begin to well up in my eyes, and then she whispered, "Maybe you could go be THEIR mom?"

4. Dog Tired

An older, tired-looking dog wandered into my yard; I could tell from his collar and well-fed belly that he had a home and was taken care of. He calmly came over to me, I gave him a few pats on his head; he then followed me into my house, slowly walked down the hall, curled up in the corner of the sofa and fell asleep.

An hour later, he went to the door, and I let him out. The next day he was back, greeted me in my yard, walked inside and resumed his spot on the sofa and again slept for about an hour. This continued off and on for several weeks.

Curious, I pinned a note to his collar: 'I would like to find out who the owner of this wonderful sweet dog is and ask if you are aware that almost every afternoon your dog comes to my house for a nap.' The next day he arrived for his nap, with a different note pinned to his collar: 'He lives in a home with 6 children, 2 under the age of 3 - he's trying to catch up on his sleep. Can I come with him tomorrow?'

Reading:

1. Dear Mom,
I hope you are having a Happy Thanksgiving. This year we decided to do something a bit different and fry our turkey whole. I am in a newsgroup on the Internet that just could not say enough about how great they taste fried. I even got a recipe from one of the members. It went something like this:

1 turkey plucked and gutted - leave feet for holding turkey, and a 5 gal bucket peanut oil.
1 extra large deep fryer heated to 500 degrees. That didn't sound too complicated, and even though I've had several kitchen disasters in the past, I thought this would be a festive way to celebrate Thanksgiving.

Besides, we could do the deed outside on our wooden deck to avoid making a big mess in the kitchen. What could go wrong? I couldn't find a turkey with feet at the grocery store. The butcher thought I was crazy and suggested I try one of the nice frozen ones that was on sale. I figured a meat man should know, so I got one.

Have you ever tried to thaw out a frozen turkey? It's a week long job. I figured the hot grease would do the trick anyhow, so why worry?

Have you priced peanut oil lately? I decided some of the other stuff would work just as well. After all, cooking oil is cooking oil. I managed to get the oil in the pot just fine. Heating it was a bit tricky as it kept smoking and bubbling. But since we were outside, I thought the smoke wouldn't hurt anything.

Now this is the part you won't believe! I threw that sucker in the pot and when the thing thawed out the oil boiled over on the wooden deck and caught the deck on fire! We got the garden hose to put it out. Who would know not to put water on a grease fire? It didn't really matter anyhow. In all the excitement I forgot to watch the cooking thermometer and the grease must have become too hot. I was inside the house looking for the fire extinguisher when I heard the explosion. Have you ever seen a mushroom cloud? It was incredible!

After the fire department left, we decided to eat dinner out next year. Not only was our Thanksgiving dinner ruined, but the deck burned down and took half the garage with it. The dog will be just fine when his fur grows back. We've always wanted a Mexican hairless dog anyhow.

The fire department told us they make a lot of house calls about this time of the year from people frying turkeys who don't know what they are doing. Like, is it my fault that the grease was cheap and the stupid turkey wouldn't thaw out? They need to put consumer-warning labels on turkeys! Speaking of the turkey, we are still looking for it. I think it may have blown to bits as we've looked all over the neighborhood. If you see a turkey-shaped cloud of ash circling the earth, that's probably it.

By the way, you may see us on the evening news on TV. A lot of people thought it was a terrorist attack. I only hope we have not been reported to the FBI. Anyhow, I just want to let you know that we are all fine. I don't think the house will be fixed for a while since there is a lot of smoke damage. We are moving to a motel. Do you think we could come to your house for Christmas this year? You were not planning on frying a turkey, were you?

> "If you see a turkey-shaped cloud of ash circling the earth, that's probably it."

2. How to Observe Thanksgiving

Count your blessings instead of your crosses.
Count your gains instead of your losses.
Count your joys instead of your woes.
Count your friends instead of your foes.
Count your smiles instead of your tears.
Count your courage instead of your fears.
Count your full years instead of your lean.
Count your kind deeds instead of your mean.
Count your health instead of your wealth.
Count on God instead of yourself.
(www.GCFL.net, info@gcfl.net. Used by permission.)

Scripture for the Month: (Can put in newsletter to encourage memorization)
"Enter his gates with thanksgiving and his courts with praise; give thanks to him and praise his name" (Psalm 100:4)

2. Outlet Mall Shopping Trip: Beat the Christmas Rush

Beat the Christmas rush by doing a November shopping trip to assist your seniors with their Christmas shopping. For "Outings/Excursions Preparation" (see appendix page 244).

Travel Game:
During travel, try the "Christmas Songwriter/Composer" and "Musical Lyrics" games (see appendix pages 295-298). Be sure to have prizes for those participating.

Quote for the Month/Event:
"Whether we like it or not — all of us are engaged in a ceaseless war, the endless struggle between love and hate, good and evil, truth and lies, freedom and tyranny. Each of us has a thousand private battlefields. And the happiest people, it seems to me, are those who fight the hardest."
– Anonymous

"May this Thanksgiving help you to give thanks for all the turkeys in your life."
– Sr. Monique Rysavy

Scripture for the Month: (Can put in newsletter to encourage memorization)
"However, as it is written: 'What no eye has seen, what no ear has heard, and what no

human mind has conceived' — the things God has prepared for those who love him" (1 Corinthians 2:9).

3. Duck Dynasty Night

This is a redneck hillbilly night! A bluegrass group will need to be scheduled to play and the dinner menu will be the funny extra icing on the cake! Plan on some normal dishes like fried chicken, mashed potatoes, hominy, black eye peas, collard greens, corn bread, and bread pudding or rice pudding. If possible, just for fun, add some of the following:

Fried raccoon or opossum, squirrel or rabbit stew, fried frog legs, butter sautéed chitlins, pickled pig's feet, tripe and fried pork rinds. If alligator meat is available – try that and have a taste testing!

As people are coming in, give them a number, then put the matching number in a bag to be used later for the games.

Pre-dinner Conversation Starter:
Play "Duck Trivia" (see appendix pages 299-300).

Decorations:
A camouflage theme is perfect for this night. Scatter pictures of the Duck Dynasty family around the table (downloadable from Google or Bing images — but be sure to watch for trademark, registration or copyright information that may restrict the image usage). Save vegetable cans and place black eyed Susan's in them (with label still on cans). Place the cans on top of a camouflage napkin in the center of the table! Be sure to label the dishes on the serving table so people will know what they are eating!

Quote for the Month/Event:
"If your woman picks your ducks, and she cooks and carries her Bible…. Now that is a complete package of womanhood." – Phil Robertson

"Money can come and go, and fame comes and goes. Peace of mind and a relationship with God is far more important, so this is the precedent that we've set in our lives. The bottom line is we all die, so Jesus is the Answer." – Phil Robertson

Joke/Story:

1. Our minister announced that admission to a church social event would be six dollars per person. "However, if you're over 65," he said, "the price will be only $5.50." From the back of the congregation, a woman's voice rang out, "Do you really think I'd give you that information for only 50 cents?"

2. Three atheists were trying to bother a young minister at a local restaurant. "I think I will move to Nevada," said the first atheist, "Only 35 percent of the people are Baptist." "No, I think I would rather live in Colorado," said the second man, "only 20 percent of the people are Baptist." "Better yet," said the third atheist, "in New Mexico, only 15 percent there are Baptists." "I think the best place for you all is Hell," said the minister. "There are no Baptists there!"

3. I heard a funny story of a pastor who as he left his church began looking for his keys. He looked in his pockets, his coat, his office, in the sanctuary, and then he realized that he must have left them in the car. Frantically he headed to the parking lot. How his wife had repeatedly told him NOT to leave his keys in the car, which he did frequently. His thinking was that the ignition was the best place not to lose them. His wife's theory was that the car would be stolen. As he came through the doors of the church into the parking lot, he came to the conclusion that his wife was right — the parking lot was empty! He immediately called the police, gave them his name and location, and confessed that he had left his keys in the car and that it had been stolen.

Then, after putting it off as long as possible, he made that most difficult of calls… "Honey," he began (always calling her honey in times like these). "I left the keys in the car and it has been stolen." There was a prolonged period of silence. "Paul," she barked, "I dropped you off this morning!" Silence. Embarrassed, he said, "Well, would you come and get me?" His wife responded, "I will as soon as I can convince this policeman that I have not stolen your car!"

4. Read some excerpts from Jeff Foxworthy's "You Might Be a Redneck If…" available over the Internet.

Game/Activity:

Call the participants by number (drawn out of the hat) before each game is brought out in front of the audience! That will make it even funnier!

1. Toilet Paper Toss: A box will need to be prepared in advance with another smaller one on top to resemble a toilet. Paint a toilet lid (top and bottom) in a bright color on the box – with a hole in the middle of the seat. This will be where the contestants get three chances to throw the toilet paper rolls into the hole.

2. Pick the Chick: If you can find ducks to pick, then use them; if not, chickens will do. Have a competition to see who can do a better job of picking off the feathers in the fastest time – say two minutes! (You will need to get fresh birds then dip them in boiling water for a little while to get the feathers to release before the evening – then have them waiting!)

Be sure and have nice prizes for all the contestants for these games!

Reading:

1. Billy Graham's New Suit

Billy Graham is now 94 years-old, and has Parkinson's disease. In January, leaders in Charlotte, North Carolina, invited their favorite son, Billy Graham, to a luncheon in his honor. Billy initially hesitated to accept the invitation because he struggles with Parkinson's disease. But the Charlotte leaders said, We don't expect a major address. Just come and let us honor you. So he agreed.

After wonderful things were said about him, Dr. Graham stepped to the rostrum, looked at the crowd, and said: "I'm reminded today of Albert Einstein, the great physicist who this month has been honored by Time magazine as the Man of the Century. Einstein was once traveling from Princeton on a train, when the conductor came down the aisle, punching the tickets of every passenger. When he came to Einstein, Einstein reached in his vest pocket. He couldn't find his ticket, so he reached in his trouser pockets. It wasn't there. He looked in his briefcase but couldn't find it. Then he looked in the seat beside him. He still couldn't find it.

The conductor said, "Dr. Einstein, I know who you are. We all know who you are. I'm sure you bought a ticket. Don't worry about it." Einstein nodded appreciatively. The conductor continued down the aisle punching tickets. As he was ready to move to the next car, he turned around and saw the great physicist down on his hands and knees looking under his seat for his ticket.

The conductor rushed back and said, "Dr. Einstein, Dr. Einstein, don't worry, I know who you are; no problem. You don't need a ticket. I'm sure you bought one." Einstein looked at him and said, "Young man, I too, know who I am. What I don't know is where I'm going."

Having said that Billy Graham continued, "See the suit I'm wearing? It's a brand new suit. My children, and my grandchildren are telling me I've gotten a little slovenly in my old age. I used to be a bit more fastidious. So I went out and bought a new suit for this luncheon and one more occasion. You know what that occasion is? This is the suit in which I'll be buried. But when you hear I'm dead, I don't want

you to immediately remember the suit I'm wearing. I want you to remember this: "I not only know who I am. I also know where I'm going."

2. Tate Family

There is one family in your church that I bet you don't know how large it is! There is the old man Dic Tate who wants to run everything, while Uncle Ro Tate tries to change everything. Their sister, Agi Tate, stirs up plenty of trouble with help from her husband, Irri Tate.

Whenever new projects are suggested, Hesi Tate and his wife, Vegi Tate, want to wait until next year. Brother Facili Tate is quite helpful in church work though. Cousins, Cogi Tate and Medi Tate, always think things over and lend a helpful steady hand. And of course, there is the black sheep of the family, Ampu Tate, who has cut himself off completely from the Body of Christ. What a family!

Video/YouTube Clip:

There are several YouTube videos of the Robertsons – if there is time – the "I am second" videos are very eye opening, and Phil Robertson on Hannity about ISIS as well is interesting.

Scripture for the Month: (Can put in newsletter to encourage memorization)

"Very truly I tell you, whoever hears my word and believes him who sent me has eternal life and will not be judged but has crossed over from death to life" (John 5:24).

"I not only know who I am. I also know where I'm going."

– Billy Graham

DECEMBER
Monthly Ideas

December
Monthly Ideas

1. Animals for Alzheimers – (super soft stuffed animals to give to Alzheimer's patients)

Have a lunch where a collection of stuffed animals is collected for local Alzheimer's patients. Afterwards the group can go together to the nursing homes and deliver the animals or split up and go in teams to different ones (depending on how many animals were collected).

Pre-dinner Conversation Starter:
At each seat, have copies of "The Christmas Story: A to Z" (see appendix pages 291-292). Be sure to have pencils as well at each seat.

Decorations:
Have one stuffed animal sitting in the middle of the table as a centerpiece on top of a box wrapped in Christmas paper (the box will be filled with chocolates or a small gift for everyone and needs to be wrapped on the outside several times – at least 6 – this will be used for a game later).

Quote for the Month/Event:
"Who can add to Christmas? The perfect motive is that God so loved the world. The perfect gift is that He gave His only Son. The only requirement is to believe in Him. The reward of faith is that you shall have everlasting life." – Corrie ten Boom

Joke/Story:

1. The Top Ten Gifts Your Husband Doesn't Want for Christmas

10. Anne of Avonlea/Anne of Green Gables Collector's Edition with 74 minutes of extra footage
9. Any knick-knack
8. Tickets to the ballet
7. Another new tie
6. A Bath and Body Works Soap Basket
5. New teddy bear pajamas
4. Vacuum cleaner
3. A weekend seminar on "Getting in Touch With Your Feelings"
2. Pair of fuzzy bunny slippers
1. A nose and ear hair trimmer (OK, well maybe.)

(www.GCFL.net, info@gcfl.net. Used by Permission.)

2. The Top Ten Gifts Your Wife Doesn't Want for Christmas

10. A car wash kit
9. A table saw
8. Two all-day passes to Circuit City's Home Theatre Installation Seminar
7. A case of oil
6. Five-year subscription to Sports Illustrated
5. Custom engraved bowling ball
4. New outboard motor for fishing boat
3. Rambo Trilogy on DVD
2. New satellite dish with sports package
1. Three-year membership to Weight-Watchers Clinic

(www.GCFL.net, info@gcfl.net. Used by permission.)

3. Adam, a bright-eyed 3-year-old, had been told of his German heritage. After church in early December, he was asked if he had a part in the Sunday school Christmas pageant. "Yes," he replied, his eyes filling with joy. "I am going to be a German shepherd!"

4. As the little boy climbed onto Santa's lap, Santa asked the usual question: "And what would you like for Christmas?" The child stared at him open-mouthed, horrified, and then gasped, "Didn't you get my Snapchat?"

5. 21st Century Newspaper
I was visiting my daughter over Christmas when I asked if I could borrow a newspaper. "This is the 21st century," she said. "We don't waste money on newspapers. Here, use my iPad I got for Christmas." I can tell you this…that fly never knew what hit him…

Game/Activity:

1. For an audience participation game, try "Table Symphony Jingle Bells" (see appendix pages 293-294).

2. Cup Exchange: Advertise in advance for people to bring a wrapped coffee cup to exchange. These are collected at the door and at some point in the evening are distributed – it will be fun to open the packages and get a new cup. (Cups don't have to be new, but nice.)

3. Pass the box: Towards the end of the luncheon get the box out of the center of the table and pass around the table to music. When the music stops the person holding the package has to unwrap it. Then it continues again and again and again. When someone unwraps the last layer – then they get to open the box. Inside could be special chocolates or small gifts for everyone.

Reading:

1. The REAL Night Before Christmas

"Twas the night before Christmas when all through the house.
I searched for the tools, to hand to my spouse.
Instructions were studied, and we were inspired,
in hopes we could manage "Some Assembly Required."

The children were quiet (not asleep) in their beds,
while Dad and I faced the evening with dread:
a kitchen, two bikes, Barbie's townhouse to boot!
And now, thanks to Grandpa, a train with a toot!

We opened the boxes; my heart skipped a beat -
let no parts be missing or parts incomplete!
Too late for last-minute returns or replacement;
if we can't get it right, it goes straight to the basement!

When what to my worrying eyes should appear
but 50 sheets of directions, concise, but not clear.
With each part numbered and every slot named,
so if we failed, only we could be blamed.

More rapid than eagles the parts then fell out,
all over the carpet they were scattered about.
"Now bolt it! Now twist it! Attach it right there!
Slide on the seats, and staple the stair!

Hammer the shelves, and nail to the stand."
"Honey," said hubby, "you just glued my hand."
And then in a twinkling, I knew for a fact
that all the toy dealers had indeed made a pact;
to keep parents busy all Christmas Eve night
with "assembly required" till mornings first light.

We spoke not a word, but kept bent at our work,
till our eyes, they went blurry; our fingers all hurt.
The coffee went cold and the night, it wore thin
before we attached the last rod and last pin.

Then laying the tools away in the chest,
we fell into bed for a well-deserved rest.
But I said to my husband just before I passed out,
"This will be the best Christmas, without any doubt."

Tomorrow we'll cheer, let the holiday ring,
and not run to the store for one single thing!
"We did it! We did it! The toys are all set
for the perfect, most magical, Christmas, I bet!"

Then off to dreamland and sweet repose
I gratefully went, though I suppose
there's something to say for those self-deluded-
I'd forgotten that BATTERIES are never included!
(www.GCFL.net, info@gcfl.net. Used by permission.)

2. Did you Know…

John Wesley founded the Methodist movement and his brother Charles Wesley wrote over 6,000 hymns. Charles Wesley penned "Hark! how all the Welkin (Heaven) rings" but George Whitefield changed the first line to "Hark! The Herald Angels Sing." It was put to the music of Lutheran composer Felix Mendelssohn, grandson of the notable Jewish philosopher, Moses Mendelssohn.

3. A missionary who had served in a remote part of Central America for years was retiring and returning to the U.S., and word had gotten out to the people of the region. The nationals desired to honor her for all her years of service with a public celebration. News of the party went to all parts of the country that had been touched by the missionary's work.

One very old and very poor man walked to the ceremony, even though it was a four day journey over mountainous terrain. But he was determined to present a gift to this woman. The gift consisted of just two coconuts, but it was all the man could bring. The missionary recognized him and knew where he lived, and just how far he had traveled. "Brother," she said respectfully, "I cannot believe you would walk so far to present me with this gift." His response? "Long walk part of gift."

Video/YouTube Clip:
Watch several five minute YouTube videos of the Bob Hope Christmas with Marines at DaNang; USO Christmas Show – CuChi, Vietnam, 1966 and Bob Hope's Christmas Show at Show-Long Bing - which should bring back some sweet memories.

Scripture for the Month: (Can put in newsletter to encourage memorization)
"I keep my eyes always on the LORD. With him at my right hand, I will not be shaken" (Psalm 16:8)

2. Christmas Dinner with Local Orchestra/Group

A Christmas event should be something special, so find a special orchestra or singing group to come and do a dress up dinner/concert. Oftentimes local schools, universities or civic groups have singing groups that are looking for a venue to perform.

Pre-dinner Conversation Starter:
At each place setting, have a copy of a handout with information on the group and its members, and/or the game "Name That Christmas Tune" (see appendix pages 301-302).

Decorations:
Decorate the tables in the Christmas colors and with a large square of bright foil paper with a poinsettia placed on top.

Advertising/Game:
Advertise in advance for those who can, to wear their ugliest Christmas sweater or tie. Prizes will be given for "the ugliest" the "next to ugliest" and "honorable mention ugly"!

Quote for the Month/Event:
"Listen to the angel's song, all you who have a troubled heart! 'I bring you good tidings of great joy!' Jesus did not come to condemn you. If you want to define Christ rightly, then pay heed to how the angel defines Him, namely, 'a great joy!'" – Martin Luther

Joke/Story:

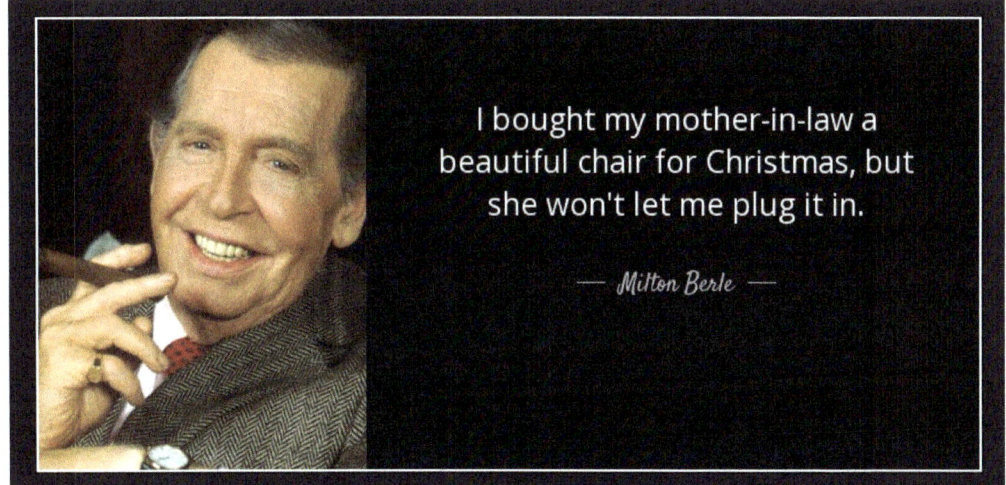

1. The holiday season was approaching and Advent was one week away so we thought we'd see what the children remembered from our family devotions the year before. "Who can tell me what the four candles in the Advent wreath represent?" I asked. Jake, shouted with seven-year-old wisdom and exuberance. "There's love, joy, peace, and. . . and. . ."I know!" four-year-old Sandy interrupted to finish her brother's sentence: "Peace and quiet!"

2. At Christmas sometimes we think of Scandinavian things. Here are a few jokes from the old country:
• Ole gets his first cell phone and Lena calls him up and says, "Ole! Ole! It just came in over da news dat der's one idiot driving down the interstate the wrong direction near to

where you are." Ole says, "Na, na! Ders hundreds of 'em!"

• Ole had been watching the news about man going to the moon. Ole suggests that they do something really spectacular, like taking a rocket to the sun. Sven says, "Ole, won't it burn up as it gets near the sun? Ole says, "No, we already thought of that. We're going at night."

• Ole and Svenya had really 'packed on the pounds' by over-eating during the Christmas holidays, so their doctor put them on the same diet. 'I want you to eat regularly for 2 days, then skip a day, and repeat this procedure for 2 weeks. The next time I see you, you should have lost at least 5 pounds.

When the Norwegians returned, they shocked their doctor by having lost nearly 25 POUNDS each. "Why, that's positively amazing!" the doctor said. "Did you follow my instructions?" Then Ole and Svenya nodded in unison and Ole said, "We vant to tell you though, we taut we was gonna drop dead dat 3rd day." "From hunger, you mean?" said the doctor. "No, yust from all dat skippin!" said Svenya.

• Ole got quite good at painting portraits. A very lovely woman came for a portrait and asked Ole if he would paint her in the nude. He said he'd have to ask his wife, Lena, if that was OK. A few minutes later he comes back, and says, "Yah, I paint in der nude, but Lena says I have to keep my socks on so I don't catch cold."

TEN COMMANDMENTS Ole STYLE
You betcha...
Der's only one God, ya know.
Don't make that fish on your mantle an idol.
Cussing ain't Minnesota nice.
Go to church even when you're up north.
Honor your folks.
Don't kill. Catch and release.
There is only one Lena for every Ole. No cheatin'.
If it ain't your lutefisk, don't take it.
Don't be braggin' about how much snow ya shoveled.
Keep your mind off your neighbor's hotdish.

3. A priest was invited to attend a Christmas party. Naturally, he was properly dressed and wearing his priest's collar. A little boy kept staring at him the entire evening. Finally, the priest asked the little boy what he was staring at. The little boy pointed to the priest's neck. When the priest finally realized what the boy was pointing at, he asked him, "Do you know why I am wearing that?" The boy nodded his head yes, and replied, "It kills fleas and ticks for up to three months." (www.mikeysFunnies.com. Used by permission.)

4. Help for Christmas: What to buy the man in your life!
Rule #1: When in doubt, buy him a cordless drill. It does not matter if he already has one. I have a friend who owns 17 and he has yet to complain. As a man, you can never have too many cordless drills. No one knows why.

Rule #2: If you cannot afford a cordless drill, buy him anything with the word ratchet or socket in it. Men love saying those two words. "Hey George, can I borrow your ratchet?" "OK. By the way, are you through with my 3/8-inch socket yet?" Again, no one knows why.

Rule #3: If you are really, really broke, buy him anything for his car, a 99-cent ice scraper, a small bottle of deicer or something to hang from his rearview mirror. Men love gifts for their cars. No one knows why.

Rule #4: Do not buy men socks. Do not buy men ties. And never buy men bathrobes. I was told that if God had wanted men to wear bathrobes, he wouldn't have invented briefs.

Rule #5: You can buy men new remote controls to replace the ones they have worn out. If you have a lot of money, buy your man a big-screen TV with the little picture in the corner. Watch him go wild as he flips, and flips, and flips.

Rule #6: Do not buy any man industrial-sized canisters of after-shave or deodorant. I'm told they do not stink — they are earthy.

Rule #7: Never buy a man anything that says "some assembly required" on the box. It will ruin his special day and he will always have parts left over.

Rule #8: Good places to shop for men include Lowes, Home Depot, John Deere, NAPA Auto Parts and Sears Clearance Centers. It doesn't matter if he doesn't know what it is. "From NAPA Auto, eh? Must be something I need. Hey! Isn't this a starter for a '68 Ford Fairlane? Wow! Thanks."

Rule #9: Men enjoy danger. That's why they never cook — but they will barbecue. Get him a monster barbecue with a 100-pound propane tank. Tell him the gas line leaks. "Oh the thrill! The challenge! Who wants a hamburger?"

Rule #10: Tickets to a football game are a smart gift. However, he will not appreciate tickets to "A Retrospective of 19th Century Quilts." Everyone knows why.

Rule #11: It's hard to beat a really good wheelbarrow or an aluminum extension ladder. Never buy a real man a stepladder. It must be an extension ladder.
Rule #13: Rope. Men love rope. It takes us back to our cowboy origins, or at least The Boy Scouts. Nothing says love like a hundred feet of 3/8" manila rope.

Game/Activity:
1. "Christmas Trivia" (see appendix page 303).

2. Human Christmas Trees. Choose five or six fellows and let each one select a woman to be his Christmas tree. Have on hand a large box of evergreens and Christmas decorations: balls, silver icicles, green and red crepe paper, tinsel, etc., and see which man can do the best job of trimming his "tree." He may take only one ornament from the box at a time. Have scissors and plenty of pins available. Judges will award first, second, and third place prizes (but also give away participation prizes). A very funny activity!

Video/YouTube Clip:
Play the YouTube video of Mark Lowry singing "Mary Did You Know?"

Reading:

1. The 12 days of Christmas

Have you ever wondered where the 12 days of Christmas originated? It is a very interesting story historically. In the Middle Ages, Western Europe celebrated Christmas on December 25th believing Jesus' birth was the holiest day. Eastern Europe celebrated Epiphany on January 6th believing the visit of the Wise Men and Jesus' baptism to be the holier.

It could not be decided which date was the holier, so at the council of Tours in 567 AD it was decided to make all 12 days from December 25 to January 6th "The Twelve Days of Christmas." They were called "holy days," which came to be pronounced "holidays.

2. One Solitary Life

Just one solitary life,
He grew up in a small village,
the son of a poor family.
He worked in a carpenter shop until he was 30.
Then for 3 years he was an itinerant preacher.
He never wrote a book,
He never held an office,
He never had a family or owned a home.
He didn't go to college,
He never visited a big city,
He never travelled two hundred miles from his hometown,
And He was only 33 when he was crucified.
While he was dying, the executioners gambled for his garments, the only property he had on earth.
When he was dead, his body was laid in a borrowed tomb, through the pity of a friend.
Yet no army, king, country or kingdom has ever affected life here on earth as much as this one solitary man.

Scripture for the Month: (Can put in newsletter to encourage memorization)
"Therefore the Lord himself will give you a sign: The virgin will conceive and give birth to a son, and will call him Immanuel" (Isaiah 7:14).

3. Dinner Theatre for the Holidays

Pick a good Christian play and have a group in your church act it out (youth or young adults). There are some good sites for Christian plays/skits such as:

>   howitiller.com   theaterministry.com
>   dramashare.org   crosspointscripts.com

Pre-dinner Conversation Starter:
Make a play bill with actors' names and information about them and/or have "Figure out THESE Holiday Songs!" at each place setting to play before dinner (see appendix pages 304-305).

Decorations:
Decorate the tables with gifts that the people can take home. Families can be encouraged, in advance, to donate Christmas decorations to the 50+. Cheap and pretty ball ornaments can be obtained as well from a dollar store. Gold and red are the colors for this dinner.

Quote for the Month/Event:
"People are like sticks of dynamite. The power's on the inside but nothing happens until the fuse gets lit." – Mac Anderson

"What is more joyful than the joy of a saint, what more happy than the happiness of a believer?" – Charles Spurgeon

Joke/Story:

1. Two boys were walking home from Sunday school after hearing a strong preaching on the devil. One said to the other, "What do you think about all this Satan stuff?" The other boy replied, "Well, you know how Santa Claus turned out. It's probably just your Dad."

2. There are three phases in a man's life: (1) When you believe there is a Santa Claus; (2) When you don't believe there is a Santa Claus; and (3) When you ARE Santa Claus!!!!

3. Steve Feldman's Christmas Jokes:
One Christmas morning, a husband gave his mother-in-law a tombstone as a gift. The next Christmas he didn't give his mother-in-law a gift, so the mother-in-law said to her son-in-law: "I see you didn't get me a gift this year." And the son-in law said: "What for? You still haven't used the one I got you last year."

The Jewish Christmas:
The teacher asked young Patrick Murphy, "What do you do at Christmas time?" Patrick addressed the class: "Well, Ms. Jones, I and my twelve brothers and sisters go to midnight mass and we sing hymns; then we come home very late and we put mince pies by the back door and hang up our stockings. Then all excited, we go to bed and wait for Father Christmas to come with all our toys. "Very nice, Patrick," she said.

"Now, Jimmy Brown, what do you do at Christmas?" "Well, Ms. Jones, me and my sister also go to church with mom and dad, and we sing carols, and we get home ever so late. We put cookies and milk by the chimney, and we hang up our stockings. We hardly sleep, waiting for Santa Claus to bring our presents."

Realizing there was a little Jewish boy in the class and not wanting to leave him out of the discussion, she asked, "Now, Isaac Cohen, what do you do at Christmas?" Isaac said, "Well, it's the same thing every year. Dad comes home from the office. We all pile into the Rolls Royce; and then we drive to dad's toy factory. When we get inside, we look at all the

empty shelves and begin to sing: "What a Friend We Have in Jesus!" Then we all go to the Bahamas."
(Steve Feldman. Used by permission.)

Game/Activity:

1. Christmas Charades: Have slips with numbered Christmas carols printed on them. Hand them out to individuals in the group, to act out by numerical order, in front of everyone. Very fun! For Christmas Charades Songs (see appendix page 306).

2. "Christmas Carol Matchup" (see appendix page 307).

Video/YouTube Clip:

1. To celebrate their 130th anniversary, the Spanish bank Banco Sabadell did an amazing video (on YouTube) in the town square of a child putting a coin in a musician's hat. The resulting flash mob concert of "Joyful, Joyful We Adore Thee" by both an orchestra and choir is amazing and uplifting. Search YouTube under Som Sabadell flash mob.

Reading:

1. (You will need to make two signs "Christmas Love" and "Christ Was Love" to hold up)

The "W" in Christmas
Each December, I vowed to make Christmas a calm and peaceful experience. I had cut back on nonessential obligations such as extensive card writing, endless baking, decorating, and even overspending. Yet still, I found myself exhausted, unable to appreciate the precious family moments, and of course, the true meaning of Christmas.

My son, Nicholas, was in kindergarten that year. It was an exciting season for a six-year-old. For weeks, he'd been memorizing songs for his school's Winter Pageant. I didn't have the heart to tell him I'd be working the night of the production. Unwilling to miss his shining moment, I spoke with his teacher. She assured me there'd be a dress rehearsal the morning of the presentation. All parents unable to attend that evening were welcome to come then. Fortunately, Nicholas seemed happy with the compromise.

So, the morning of the dress rehearsal, I filed in ten minutes early, found a spot on the cafeteria floor, and sat down. Around the room, I saw several other parents quietly scampering to their seats. As I waited, the students were led into the room. Each class accompanied by their teacher sat cross-legged on the floor. Then, each group, one by one, rose to perform their song. Because the public school system had long stopped referring to the holiday as "Christmas," I didn't expect anything other than fun, commercial entertainment: songs of reindeer, Santa Claus, snowflakes, and good cheer.

So, when my son's class rose to sing, "Christmas Love," I was slightly taken aback by its bold title. Nicholas was aglow, as were all of his classmates, adorned in fuzzy mittens, red sweaters, and bright snow caps upon their heads. Those in the front row — center stage — held up large letters, one by one, to spell out the title of the song. As the class would sing "C" is for Christmas, a child would hold up the letter C. Then "H" is for "Happy," and on and on until each child holding up his portion had presented the complete message, "Christmas Love." (Hold up "Christmas Love" sign)

The performance was going smoothly, until suddenly, we noticed her; a small quiet girl in the front row holding the letter "M" upside down — totally unaware her letter "M" appeared as a "W." The audience of first through sixth graders snickered at this little one's mistake. But she had no idea they were laughing at her, so she stood tall, proudly holding her "W." Although many teachers tried to shush the children, the laughter continued until the last letter was raised and we all saw it together.

A hush came over the audience and eyes began to widen. In that instant, we understood the reason we were there, why we celebrated the holiday in the first place, when even in the chaos there was a purpose for our festivities. For when the last letters held high, the message read loud and clear: (hold up "Christ Was Love" sign) "CHRIST WAS LOVE." And I believe He still is.

Scripture for the Month: (Can put in newsletter to encourage memorization)
"For to us a child is born, to us a son is given, and the government will be on his shoulders. And he will be called Wonderful Counselor, Mighty God, Everlasting Father, Prince of Peace" (Isaiah 9:6)

Appendix – Beginner
Activity Sheets to Print/Photocopy

Activity Sheet Index

1. Group Survey 192
2. Topics for Monthly Newsletters 193
3. Sign-up Sheet Example 194
4. Super Bowl Trivia 195
5. Coin Collecting: How Much Do You Know? 196-197
6. The Dementia Test 198-199
7. Tips for a Positive New Year 200-201
1. Tic Tac Toe and Dots Games 202
2. My Favorite Things to Do 203
3. Valentine Word Search 204
8. Famous Animals 205-206
9. Biblical Attributes to Pray for Your Grandchildren 207-208
10. Riddle Your Brain 209
11. Get to Know You Questions 210-211
12. Bible Pairs 212
13. Name That Couple 213
14. Photography Night Decorations 214
15. Heart Words 215
16. Valentine's Day Crossword 216-217
17. Awesome 218-219
4. Saint Patrick: How Much Do You Know? 220
5. "March Madness" Word Game 221
6. Square Dancing Trivia 222
7. "Take Your Foot out of Your Mouth!" 223
8. I Double Dog Dare You 224

9. Genealogy 101: How to Get Started 225
10. Favorite Websites 226
11. Get to Know Each Other. 227
12. Evolution vs. Creation: Where Do You Stand? 228-229
13. Science and the Bible: Parts 1 and 2 230-231
14. Blessings of the Lord 232-233
15. Scavenger Hunt Items 234
16. Old West Trivia. 235
17. Senior Student Exam 236
18. Homemade Sugar Scrubs and Lotion 237-238
19. Bible Testing Time 239
20. Advertising Slogans 240-241
21. Spring Poem Game 242-243
22. Outings/Excursions: Preparation. 244
23. Famous Women Quiz 245
24. Famous Christian Women 246
25. Praying for My Husband. 247-248
26. The Quiz for Those in the Know 249
27. U.S. Geography Quiz. 250-251
28. Gardens Crossword 252-253
29. Fantastic Flora Facts: Quiz 254-255
30. Theodore Roosevelt: How Much Do You Know? 256-257
31. The Story of Carl 258-260
32. British Trivia. 261
33. Gents, Ladies and Language. 262
34. USO: Did You Know? 263
35. Hope Trivia. 264
36. Hope Jokes 265
37. Patriotic Pictionary 266
38. Patriotic Pictionary: Score Sheet 267
39. Webster's Words. 268
40. Crime Doesn't Pay 269

41. Rodeo Lingo 270
42. Elephants and Donkeys. 271
43. What can Pastors Say from the Pulpit. 272-273
44. He Is. 274-277
45. Family Feud Game Night: Questions 278-280
46. Family Feud Game Night: Score Sheet 281
47. Name That Game 282
48. Word Puzzles 283-284
49. Voting Sheet 285
50. Zaney Brainy: Words Ending in "oat" 286
51. The Letter T is for Travel. 287
52. Knowledge Challenge 2 Crossword. 288-289
53. Peanuts Trivia 290
54. The Christmas Story: A to Z. 291-292
55. Table Symphony Jingle Bells. 293-294
56. Christmas Songwriter/Composer Game 295-296
57. Musical Lyrics. 297-298
58. Duck Trivia 299-300
59. Name That Christmas Tune 301-302
60. Christmas Trivia. 303
61. Figure out THESE Holiday Songs!. 304-305
62. Christmas Charades Songs 306
63. Christmas Carol Match-up. 307
64. Answers 308

We realize our responsibility to meet the needs of all ages that are part of our senior adult family. Our seniors are a vital part of our group, and we would like to better meet their needs and desires. Would you please take a minute to answer a few questions so that we may better serve you?

Name: _____

Address: _____

Phone: _____

Birthday: _____

1. Which of the following activities would you be interested in?

☐ Dinner Night held @ church once a month

      DAY: ☐ Tuesday OR ☐ Friday

      TIME: ☐ 5–7 p.m. OR ☐ 5:30–7:30 p.m.

☐ Outings (museums/shopping/points of interest)

☐ Missions/Outreach projects (hands-on project)

☐ Senior news/prayer newsletter

2. What else would you like to see happening with our seniors?

3. What can we do to better meet your needs?

Thank you for taking the time to fill out this form. Please return it to us after the service. Your opinions count!

Topics for Monthly Newsletters

Contact Information for 50+ Pastor

Monthly Meeting/Trip Topic and Cost (always include menu, very important to some seniors)

Birthdays of 50+ers

Local Christian Plays Info/Synopsis

Church Announcements

Church Needs (benevolence/workers)

Suggestions for Activities

Educational Opportunities

Medicare/Medicaid Info (such as the state phone number for info on plans/insurance/benefits)

Community Resources (can often be obtained from a hospital social worker)

Websites for Seniors

Christian Radio List of Stations/Times

Businesses with Senior Discounts

Scripture of the Month

Food/Financial/Transportation (assistance to seniors/amounts)

Local Senior Events (Council on Aging classes, etc.)

Legal Services

Support Groups

Coupons (arrange with local businesses)

Businesses that have drive-up or home delivery service (pharmacy/grocery)

VFW Info/Meetings

Tax Prep Assistance (AARP and VITA often provide)

Historical Society Meetings

Quotes (funny, inspirational)

Volunteer Opportunities

Cultural Events (within one-hour drive)

Senior Magazines (local and national)

Sign-up Sheet for 50+
Fellowship Dinner
Antique Road Show Evening

Super Bowl Trivia

1. What year did the Super Bowl start? _____

2. The Super Bowl is the annual championship game of what league?
   A. AFL (American Football League)   B. NFL (National Football League)
   C. NCAA (National Collegiate Athletic Association)

3. Super Bowl Sundays have been the second largest food consuming day of the year preceded only by Thanksgiving.
True   False

4. What team has won the most Super Bowl championships?
   A. Dallas Cowboys   B. San Francisco 49ers   C. Pittsburg Steelers

5. Which one of these performers did NOT perform in a Super Bowl?
   A. Michael Jackson   B. The Beatles   C. The Rolling Stones   D. The Who

6. The precursor game to the Super Bowl was the:
   A. Cotton Bowl   B. Rose Bowl   C. Yale Bowl   D. Sun Bowl

7. The winning team receives the Vince Lombardi Trophy, named after the coach of the:
   A. New Orleans's Saints   B. Pittsburg Steelers   C. Green Bay Packers

8. Since Super Bowl XIII in January 1979, the home team is given the choice of wearing their colored or white jerseys. Which has won more of the games played so far – 64%?
   A. Colored   B. White

9. Which state below has not hosted a Super Bowl?
   A. Florida   B. Montana   C. Texas   D. Michigan

THE BEGINNER'S BOOK OF SENIOR ACTIVITIES | 195

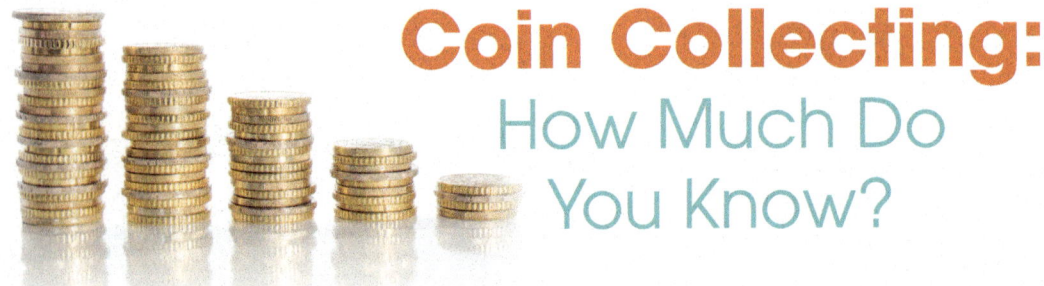

Coin Collecting: How Much Do You Know?

1. The study of coins is called:

a. Coinology   b. Numismatics   c. Monopoly   d. Moneyistics

2. George Washington was against putting any president's face on a coin, so Lady Liberty was used on almost every coin until the 20th century.

True   False

3. During the Renaissance, collecting coins was first called the hobby of _____ .

a. Kings   b. Queens   c. Knights   d. Noblemen

4. A coin is removed from circulation when:
   a. it cannot be run through coin sorters anymore
   b. the face becomes too worn
   c. a newer edition of the same coin is introduced
   d. it isn't shiny anymore

5. West Point mints bullion coins.   True   False

6. Coins were collected and catalogued by scholars and state treasuries as far back as Rome and _____
   a. Incas   b. Sumerians   c. Mesopotamia   d. Aztecs

7. Each quarter costs how much to make?
   a. ¼ of a cent   b. 3 cents   c. 5 cents   d. 25 cents

8. A coin should be cleaned and polished to increase its value.
    True   False

9. The Indian portrait on the Buffalo head nickel was a portrait of Sitting Bull, in commemoration of the last of the Indian revolts.
    True   False

10. Coins for circulation are made at the U.S. Mints in Philadelphia and
    a. Washington, D.C.   b. St. Louis, Mo.   c. Denver, Colo.

11. Caesar Augustus in the first century CE was known to present old and exotic coins to friends and visitors to the court on festivals and special occasions.
    True   False

12. Almost half of the new pennies made each year disappear from circulation within the first year. What is the explanation?
    a. coin collectors collect them
    b. they end up in pocket change bottles
    c. they are defective
    d. other nations use them to make their currency

13. Which of these famous people was not a coin collector?

    a. King Louis XIV   b. George Washington
    c. King of Farouk of Egypt   d. Emperor Maximilian
    e. Pope Boniface VIII

14. Although Benjamin Franklin is on our U.S. coins, he never held a government position higher than Postmaster General.
    True   False

15. A coin that is uncirculated and in a perfect state is called _____ condition.

The Dementia Test

Exercise of the brain is as important as exercise of the muscles. As we grow older, it's important to keep mentally alert. The saying, "If you don't use it, you will lose it" also applies to the brain. So below is a very private way to gauge your loss or non-loss of intelligence. Take the following test and determine if you are losing it or are still "with it." OK, relax, ready and let's begin…

1. What do you put in a toaster? (Pause)

Answer: "bread." If you said "toast" then give up now and go do something else. Try not to hurt yourself. If you said, "bread," go to Question 2.

2. Say "silk" five times. Now spell "silk." What do cows drink?

Answer: Cows drink water. If you said "milk" please do not attempt the next question. Your brain is obviously over stressed and may even overheat. It may be that you need to content yourself with reading something more appropriate, such as Children's World. If you said, "water," proceed to Question 3.

3. If a red house is made from red bricks, and a blue house is made from blue bricks, and a pink house is made from pink bricks, and a black house is made from black bricks, what is a greenhouse made from?

Answer: Greenhouses are made from glass. If you said "green bricks" what are you still doing reading these questions? If you said "glass" then go on to Question 4.

4. Twenty years ago, a plane was flying at 20,000 feet over Germany. If you recall, Germany at the time was politically

divided into West Germany and East Germany. Anyway, during the flight, two of the engines failed. The pilot, realizing that the last remaining engine is also failing, decides on a crash landing procedure. Unfortunately, the third engine fails before he has time to attempt an emergency landing, and the plane crashes smack in the middle of "no man's land" between East Germany and West Germany. Where would you bury the survivors, in East Germany or West Germany or in "no man's land?"

Answer: You don't, of course, bury survivors. If you said ANYTHING else, you are pretty slow and you must NEVER try to rescue anyone from a plane crash. Your efforts would not be appreciated. If you said, "Don't bury the survivors," proceed to the next question.

5. If the hour hand on a clock moves 1/60 of a degree every minute, how many degrees will the hour hand move in one hour?

Answer: One degree. If you said, "360 degrees" or anything other than "one degree," you are to be congratulated on getting this far, but you are obviously out of your league. Turn in your pencil and exit the room. (Just kidding!) Everyone else proceed to the final question.

6. Without using a calculator: You are driving a bus from London to Milford Haven in Wales. In London, 17 people get on the bus. In Reading, six people get off the bus, and nine people get on. In Swindon, two people get off and four get on. In Cardiff, 11 people get off and 16 people get on. In Swansea, three people get off and five people get on. In Carmarthen, six people get off and three get on. You then arrive at Milford Haven. What was the name of the bus driver?

Answer: Oh, for crying out loud! Don't you remember? It was YOU!!"

Tips for a Positive New Year

1. **Have a positive outlook.** We serve a great God, and He is for us not against us. So much of our life is determined by our thoughts.

2. **Have a good sense of humor.** Laughter is a natural anti-depressant and a medicine that helps us deal with the hard issues of life.

3. **Eat healthily.** Losing those unwanted pounds will make you feel so much better about yourself and life!

4. **Exercise.** Even if it is a short walk, exercise makes us feel better physically and mentally.

5. **Be thankful.** Attitude directs how we see our world and affects our personalities. Make a choice to be thankful for what you have.

6. **Get enough sleep.** Caffeine may keep you going, but it should be used only in moderation; there is no substitute for sleep.

7. **Find something you enjoy and do it!**

8. **Volunteer in an area where you are gifted in.** We all need to feel like we are useful.

9. **Feed your spirit.** A daily time for Bible reading and prayer is the most important aspect of your day.

10. Don't be a person who looks to the past. Be a forward-looking person. You are still alive! God has you here for a reason.

11. Self-improvement: take a course. We all need to be learning or we stagnate. New ideas are invigorating and motivating to us. Photography, cooking, sewing, pottery, piano, painting, genealogy, computer courses, etc., — something you have always wanted to do but didn't have the opportunity. Some community colleges and universities will waive tuition if the individual is over 65 years of age.

12. Read. Books can take you to places (and thoughts) that you never knew existed.

13. Look at life as "I get to…" rather than "I have to…." Life is made up of your choices, not a list that you have to do.

14. Travel: Seeing new sites is both fun and motivating.

15. Carpe Diem: Seize the DAY!

Tic Tac Toe

Tic Tac Toe

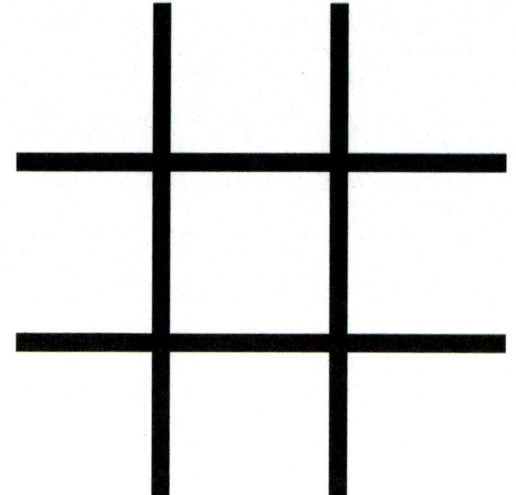

Dots

Dots

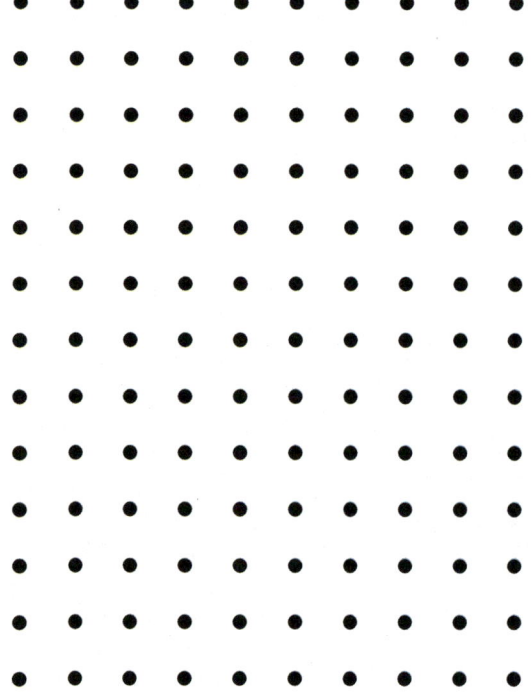

My Favorite Things to Do

Get to know your grandchildren better and let them get to know you better by each one listing what they think are your favorite things to do! It is sure to be a conversation starter.

1. For Grandchild:

What do you think are your grandparent's favorite things to do? Make a list below:

2. For Grandparent:

What do you think are your grandchild's favorite things to do? Make a list below:

Valentine Word Search

```
E N I T N E L A V Y R
C L O J Q S E S O R C
A O H W P S K B G A U
N V U Z K T I J R U Q
D E R P O R S D C R H
Y J I U L A S O P B U
V N N S W E E T I E S
K J A G U H S Z O F J
```

CANDY **HUGS** **ROSES**
CARDS **KISSES** **SWEETIES**
PINK **COUPLES** **LOVE**
FEBRUARY **HEARTS** **VALENTINE**
　　　　　RED

Famous Animals
See how many of these famous animals you remember.

1. The most famous collie dog in history. _____

2. Known for saying "What's up, Doc?" _____

3. A pig and the spider that saved his life. _____ and _____

4. Walt Disney's male & female mouse team. _____ and _____

5. The panther from the movie, "The Jungle Book." _____

6. The performing Orca whale. _____

7. Named for a planet, this cartoon dog was ever faithful. _____

8. Pinocchio's pal. _____

9. This little dog had several movies named for him. _____

10. The most depressed donkey ever made. _____

11. The ever-bouncing _____ whose "tops are made out of rubber and their bottoms are made out of springs."

12. Christopher Robin's ever-faithful friend. _____

13. The infamous huge whale with a book named for him. _____

14. The singing purple dinosaur. _____

15. The Lion King's son. _____

16. The little elephant with the large ears. _____

17. The jungle bear, who only needed the "bare necessities." _____

18. The little orphan fawn who had great forest friends. _____

19. Anna Sewell character named after a horse that was mistreated. _____
_____

20. This duck appears on "Looney Tunes" and "Merrie Melodies." _____
_____

21. The famous talking pig who herds sheep. _____

22. A lasagna-loving animal and his best buddy/rival _____ and
_____

23. This "Looney Tunes" duo never gives up the chase or the cunning contraptions. _____ and the _____

24. Uncle Remus' southern trickster character. _____

25. The Triple Crown race horse champion from 1973. _____

26. The forest bunny with a big foot. _____

206 | DEUTSCH

Biblical Attributes to Pray for Your Grandchildren

1. **Salvation:** "For the wages of sin is death, but the gift of God is eternal life in Christ Jesus our Lord" (Romans 6:23).

2. **Love for God's Word:** "Jesus answered, 'It is written: Man shall not live on bread alone, but on every word that comes from the mouth of God" (Matthew 4:4).

3. **Love for Others:** "A new command I give you: Love one another. As I have loved you, so you must love one another. By this everyone will know that you are my disciples, if you love one another" (John 13:34–35).

4. **Faithful in Prayer:** "The prayer of a righteous person is powerful and effective" (James 5:16).

5. **Sensitive to the Holy Spirit:** "And I will ask the Father, and he will give you another advocate to help you and be with you forever, the Spirit of truth" (John 14:16–17a).

6. **To Have a Servant's Heart:** "He has shown you, O mortal, what is good. And what does the LORD require of you? To act justly and to love mercy and to walk humbly with your God" (Micah 6:8).

7. **For a Believing Spouse:** "Do not be yoked together with unbelievers. For what do righteousness and wickedness have in common? Or what fellowship can light have with darkness?" (2 Corinthians 6:14)?

8. **A Pure Heart:** "Create in me a pure heart, O God, and renew a steadfast spirit within me" (Psalms 51:10).

9. **Obedient:** "If you love me, keep my commands" (John 14:15).

10. **To Be Grateful:** "Rejoice always, pray continually, give thanks in all circumstances; for this is God's will for you in Christ Jesus" (1 Thes. 5:16–18).

11. Generous: "Give and it will be given to you. A good measure, pressed down, shaken together and running over, will be poured into your lap. For with the measure you use, it will be measured to you" (Luke 6:38).

12. To Be a Person of Praise: "Therefore I will praise you, LORD, among the nations; I will sing the praises of your name" (2 Samuel 22:50).

13. Desire for God's Will for Their Lives: "Therefore, since we are surrounded by such a great cloud of witnesses, let us throw off everything that hinders, and the sin that so easily entangles. And let us run with perseverance the race marked out for us" (Hebrews 12:1).

14. An Eternal Perspective: "Do not store up for yourselves treasures on earth, where moths and vermin destroy, and where thieves break in and steal. But store up for yourselves treasure in heaven...For where your treasure is, there your heart will be also" (Matthew 6:19–21).

15. A Heart for the Lost: "For I am not ashamed of the Gospel, because it is the power of God that brings salvation to everyone who believes: first to the Jew, then to the Gentile" (Romans 1:16).

16. Contentment: "Therefore, since we have been justified through faith, we have peace with God through our Lord Jesus Christ" (Romans 5:1).

17. Willingness to Work: "Whatever you do, work at it with all your heart, as working for the Lord, not for human masters, since you know that you will receive an inheritance from the Lord as a reward. It is the Lord Christ you are serving" (Colossians 3:23–24).

18. Childlike Faith: "And he said: 'Truly I tell you, unless you change and become like little children, you will never enter the kingdom of heaven'" (Matthew 18:3).

19. Humility: "Pride goes before destruction, a haughty spirit before a fall" (Proverbs 16:18).

20. Full of Hope: "Show me your ways, LORD, teach me your paths. Guide me in your truth and teach me, for you are God my Savior, and my hope is in you all day long" (Psalm 25:4-5).

Riddle Your Brain

Here are some riddles to sharpen your brain. This can be played by individuals or by tables.

1. A murderer is condemned to death. He has to choose between three rooms. The first is full of raging fires, the second is full of assassins with loaded guns, and the third is full of lions that haven't eaten in 3 years. Which room is safest for him?

2. A woman shoots her husband. Then she holds him under water for over 5 minutes. Finally, she hangs him. But 5 minutes later they both go out together and enjoy a wonderful dinner together. How can this be?

3. What is black when you buy it, red when you use it, and grey when you throw it away?

4. Can you name three consecutive days without using the words Wednesday, Friday, or Sunday?

5. This is an unusual paragraph. I'm curious as to just how quickly you can find out what is so unusual about it. It looks so ordinary and plain that you would think nothing was wrong with it. In fact, nothing is wrong with it! It is highly unusual though. Study it and think about it, but you still may not find anything odd but if you work at it a bit, you might find out. Try to do so without any coaching!

Photo by Freepik

Get to Know You Questions

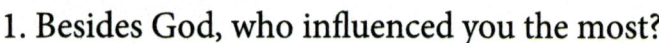

1. Besides God, who influenced you the most?

2. If you could go anywhere in the world, where would you go?

3. What animal would you most like to be?

4. What animal would you be the most afraid of head to head?

5. What is the best movie you have ever seen?

6. Besides the Bible, what is the best book you have ever read?

7. If you inherited a million dollars, what would you do with it?

8. If money was not an issue, what would your dream home look like?

9. What makes the world go around for you?

10. What is the worst gift you ever received?

11. What is the best gift you ever received?

12. What is the bravest thing you have ever done?

13. If money were no object, where would you like to go on vacation?

14. What special gift have you received that you will treasure forever?

15. If you could be granted three wishes what would they be?

16. What was your most embarrassing moment in high school?

17. How did your husband propose?

18. What is the one thing you would do for the world if you could?

19. When you were a child, what did you want to be when you grew up?

20. What is the worst thing your mother-in-law ever did to/for you?

21. What is your favorite ice cream flavor?

22. If you could go back in time, what time period would you go to?

23. If money were no object, would you have a maid?

24. If you could go back in time, who would you like to meet?

25. If you could go forward in time, what would you like to know?

26. What was the worst advice you ever received about marriage or parenting?

27. If you could trade places with someone for one day, who would it be?

28. If you could only have one food to eat for the rest of your life, what would it be?

29. If you could meet one famous person, who would it be?

30. If money were no object, would you still be driving the same car?

Bible Pairs
Find the Biblical pairs that go together.

1. Peter & _____

2. Noah & _____

3. Priscilla & _____

4. Jacob & _____

5. Mary & _____

6. Elijah & _____

7. James & _____

8. Ananias & _____

9. Hophni & _____

10. Manasseh & _____

11. Ruth & _____

12. Adam & _____

13. Cain & _____

14. Mary & _____

15. David & _____

16. Isaac & _____

17. Eli & _____

18. Moses & _____

19. Paul & _____

A. Jonathan

B. Michael

C. Elizabeth

D. Nabal

E. Barnabas

F. Ephraim

G. Rebecca

H. Samuel

I. Aquilla

K. Sapphira

L. Phinehas

M. Naomi

N. Animals

O. Mordecai

P. Esau

Q. Joseph

R. Eve

S. John

T. Elisha

Carol Holem. Used by permission.

Name That Couple

Look over the photos of the couples and write in their names in the space provided below for you.

Couple #1 _____

Couple #2 _____

Couple #3 _____

Couple #4 _____

Couple #5 _____

Couple #6 _____

Couple #7 _____

Couple #8 _____

Couple #9 _____

Couple #10 _____

Photography Night Decorations

Cut out below note and put onto cameras at tables.

> **Please use this camera to take pictures of people at your table. We will get copies to all attending.**

"Heart" Words
See how many of these "heart" words you can come up with!

1. Intense emotional pain.

2. Having or showing a kind and gentle nature.

3. Emotion, said to "pull on one's _____."

4. Unenthusiastic, unconcerned, only partially attempted.

5. Romantic pair.

6. An unfeeling way sometimes used as a description of a murderer.

7. Indigestion.

8. United States military award to those wounded or killed in battle.

9. Common problem with dogs.

10. Vigorous, dynamic, exuberant.

11. Richard I, King of England was called Richard the _____.

12. In the 1950s sometimes teen singing idols were called _____.

13. Giving, generous, kind.

14. Timid, lacking courage … "This is not for the _____."

15. Separated into pieces from hurtful feelings.

16. Touching, moving, uplifting.

17. Carefree, cheerful, happy.

18. Unconditional commitment, devotion, unreserved enthusiasm.

ACROSS

1. a couple
4. a special time out
6. delicate trimming
8. sweet favorites
11. love month
12. thorny buds
13. love symbol
14. a favorite color

DOWN

2. valentine couple
3. cherish
5. be mine
7. item for many occasions
9. a sweet of many flavors
10. an expected item on this day
11. a fragrant bouquet

Nancy Jahnke. Used by permission.

ACROSS

1. a couple
4. a special time out
6. delicate trimming
8. sweet favorites
11. love month
12. thorny buds
13. love symbol
14. a favorite color

DOWN

2. valentine couple
3. cherish
5. be mine
7. item for many occasions
9. a sweet of many flavors
10. an expected item on this day
11. a fragrant bouquet

Nancy Jahnke. Used by permission.

"Awesome"

He is the first and the last, the beginning and the end!

He is the keeper of creation and the creator of all!

He is the architect of the universe and the manager of all times.

He always was, he always is and he always will be…

Unmoved, unchanged, undefeated, and never undone!

He was bruised and brought healing! He was pierced and eased pain!

He was persecuted and brought freedom! He was dead and brought life!

He is risen and brings power! He reigns and brings peace!

The world can't understand him, armies can't defeat him.

The schools can't explain him and the leaders can't ignore him.

Herod couldn't kill him, the Pharisees couldn't confuse him, and the people couldn't hold him!

Nero couldn't crush him and Hitler couldn't silence him!

He is light, love, longevity, and Lord.

He is goodness, kindness, gentleness and God.

He is bold, righteous, mighty, and pure.

His ways are right, his word eternal, his will is unchanging, and his mind is on me.

He is my redeemer, he is my savior, he is my guide, and he is my peace!

He is my joy, he is my comfort, he is Lord, and rules my life!

I serve him because his bond is love.

His burden is light and his goal for me is abundant life.

I follow him because he is the wisdom of the wise, the power of the powerful, the Ancient of Days, the leader of all leaders, the overseer of overcomers, and the sovereign Lord of all that was and is to come.

And if that seems impressive to you, try this on for size: his goal is a relationship with me!

He will never leave me, never forsake me, never mislead me, never forget me, never overlook me, and never cancel me in his appointment book!

When I fall, he lifts me up. When I fail, he forgives me!

When I am weak, he is strong! When I am lost, he is the way!

When I am afraid, he is my courage! When I stumble, he steadies me!

When I am hurt, he heals me! When I am broken, he mends me!

When I am blind, he leads me! When I am hungry, he feeds me!

When I face trials, he is with me! When I face persecution, he shields me!

When I face problems, he comforts me!

When I face loss, he provides for me!

When I face death, he carries me home!

He is everything for everybody, everywhere, every time and every way.

He is God, he is faithful. I am his and he is mine! So if you are wondering why I feel so secure, understand this...

He said it and that settles it!

God is in control, I am on his side, and that means all is well with my soul; every day is a blessing for God IS!

He is my source of existence and my Savior.

He keeps me functioning each and every day.

Saint Patrick
How Much Do You Know?

1. St. Patrick is the patron saint of what country?
    a. England   b. Scotland   c. Ireland   d. Israel

2. St. Patrick's real name was?
    a. Sean Connery   b. Maewyn Succat   c. Peter O'Toole   d. Ian Fleming

3. St. Patrick originally came to Ireland as?
    a. an apprentice to a printer   b. a potato farmer   c. a slave   d. a Baptist

4. The name of St. Patrick's disciple was?
    a. Ian   b. Judas   c. Mochta   d. Scottie

5. St. Patrick lived to the ripe old age of?
    a. 120   b. 35   c. 96   d. 65

6. After conversion, many of the wealthy women converts became?
    a. nuns   b. teachers   c. movie stars with John Wayne   d. deaconesses

7. St. Patrick was born in?
    a. Ireland   b. Britain   c. Iceland   d. Rhode Island

8. During his trial, St. Patrick was charged with?
    a. selling "lucky charms"   b. financial impropriety   c. flirting with women

9. St. Patrick refused to do what?
    a. accept gifts from kings   b. mop monastery floors
    c. travel on a boat   d. wear green

10. St. Patrick tells of having a vision of what?
    a. leprechauns   b. Heaven
    c. the system of monastic hierarchy   d. a man calling him to come to his country

March Madness Word Game

**How many words can you make up out of "March Madness"?
The table with the most wins a prize!**

1.
2.
3.
4.
5.
6.
7.
8.
9.
10.
11.
12.
13.
14.
15.
16.
17.
18.
19.
20.
21.
22.

Square Dancing Trivia

1. **What president of the U.S. made square dancing the National Folk Dance?**
   a. Ronald Reagan   b. Richard Nixon   c. Thomas Jefferson
2. **True or false: the "Two-Step" dance move is actually three steps.**
   a. True   b. False
3. **What famous inventor made the first square dance record?**
   a. Eli Whitney   b. Alexander Graham Bell   c. Thomas Edison
4. **Which of these is NOT a square dance call?**
   a. Promenade   b. Spin the Top   c. Half Sashay   d. Do-si-do
   e. Weave the Ring   f. Spare the Rod   g. Back Track
5. **What great businessman is credited with preserving square dancing in America?**
   a. Bill Gates   b. Henry Ford   c. Lee Iacocca
6. **Which TV cartoon show has NOT had square dancing on it at one time?**
   a. Bugs Bunny   b. Bob the Builder   c. Peanuts
7. **The Salt Lake City Olympic Games featured Square Dancing and Break Dancing in their opening ceremony in 2002. True or False?**
   a. True   b. False
8. **Which TV show(s) had a square dancing episode?**
   a. "The Brady Bunch"   b. "Lassie"   c. "The Waltons"
9. **What famous 1950s comic strip put out a square dance book?**
   a. "Peanuts"   b. "Scooby Doo"
   c. "Li'l Abner"
10. **What is another name for a square dance?**

Take your Foot out of Your Mouth!

See how many of these common "foot" words you can come up with!

1. To stumble is to lose your _____
2. A novice _____
3. Used by the shorter segment of the population _____
4. Strange game where pigskin is fought after _____
5. A good dancer is said to have fancy _____
6. One said to be quick _____
7. Storage container _____
8. These are poured not built _____
9. Runners-up to mountains _____
10. Mysterious American creature _____
11. In poetry, a group of two or three syllables _____
12. With not a care in the world, free _____
13. A birth defect _____
14. Something to cross over _____
15. Must climb to reach the top _____
16. A marked way to go _____
17. The title of a famous poem about God's care for us _____
18. These are shot _____
19. Husbands love to play this with their wives _____
20. To give proper credit to _____

I Double Dog Dare You
(See how many you remember)

Candy cigarettes
Wax colored and shaped bottles with colored sugar water inside
Soda pop machines that dispensed glass bottles
Coffee shops with tableside jukeboxes
Blackjack, Clove and Teaberry chewing gum
Home milk delivery in glass bottles with cardboard stoppers
Party lines
Newsreels before the movies
P. F. Flyers
Butch wax
Telephone numbers with a word prefix (Drexel-5505)
Peashooters
45-rpm Records
Green Stamps
Hi-fi's
Metal ice cube trays with levers
Mimeograph paper
Blue flash bulbs
Beanie and Cecil
Roller skate keys
Cork popguns
Drive-ins
Wringer washtubs
The Fuller Brush man
Reel-to-reel tape recorders
Tinker toys
The Fort Apache play set
Lincoln Logs
15-cent McDonald's hamburgers
Packs of baseball cards…with that awful pink slab of bubblegum
Penny candy

Genealogy 101: How to Get Started
Forms – Document – Organize

Forms – Main forms needed to start: (available from www.familysearch.org)

 1. **Four Generation Form**, you're #1, Father is #2, and Mother is #3. Document information. Make copies if at all possible.

 2. **Family Group Record** – Start with you! One sheet for each family. You'll end up needing a lot of these. Add all dates known or partial dates. If not known, indicate with a question mark (?) and try to verify as many as possible.

 Start with what you know! Research: personal knowledge, family Bibles, birth certificates, marriage licenses, death certificates, marriage records from county library, grave headstones, etc. Write down all the information about your parents, grandparents, aunts, uncles, and cousins using the forms listed above. Connect with as much of the family as you can especially older relatives. Ask about any relatives who may be working on the same family. Just remember to use a tape recorder if they will allow it and encourage family stories. Pictures are a huge bonus, but remember to identify who is in the picture. (Hint: if your family has a family reunion, they're gold mines.)

 Library Search – Each county has a source of genealogy information. Your city librarian can advise what the county/city will have and where it's located. Each state will have a state archives that will have a wealth of information about most if not all counties in the state. (Hint: write names of books, author, and a short note, particularly if you find something you copy. This will keep you from duplicating efforts.)

 Web Search for Genealogy –The Internet is an amazing resource that will turn up volumes of resources. See the sheet "Favorite Websites" for the ones most commonly used. Check the Secretary of State for your individual state for birth and death certificates and the state genealogical society for information.

 Genealogy programs are available for free, or you may purchase one. If you're going to get serious about searching your family tree, using a computer program is recommended; if only doing basic research then paper will probably serve you well. (Carol Shoemaker. Used by permission.)

Favorite Websites

- **www.familysearch.org** – This website has a free downloadable genealogy database AND the individual forms. Information can just be typed directly onto the program where it puts the info directly onto a pre-prepared form. This is the database I recommend as it prints out very nice reports on your data.

- **www.Rootsweb.com** – you can search for your family name as well as search from other families' databases.

- **www.mcpl.org** – Mid-Continent Genealogy in Independence Mo. This is a huge library with documents and books from around the world. They also have an online site that you can search.

- **www.findagrave.com** – This is a work in progress, and it's updated often. You can find pictures of the cemetery, the person, and the headstones on some of the entries. I have found stories added as well. I have found errors there but it's usually a story that is added into this record rather than the stone.

- **www.usgenweb.org** – You can find each state listed on this website. Some are more developed than others, but all are good resources.

- **www.censusfinder.com** – this is the website to find census data for all states and counties.

- **www.familytree.com** – This is the popular website for the magazine by that title.

- **$$$ www.ancestry.com** – is a popular website, but there is a charge for it. This is a good one for someone who will use it often such as the retired. It costs approximately $30 a month, depending on discounts available.

- **www.Mocavo.com** – the world's largest genealogy search engine with more than six billion names in the index. It is a centralized and free resource.

- **www.EllisIsland.org** – tracks immigrants who came in through Ellis Island.

- **www.cyndislist.com** – This is a popular site.

Carol Shoemaker. Used by permission.

Get to Know Each Other

Pick out four people you do not know well if possible and ask the following questions…

1. Add everyone's age together. _____

2. Total the number of grandchildren for each person. _____

3. How many pieces of jewelry are there? _____

4. How many pets are owned? _____

5. How many great-grandchildren for each person? _____

6. How many states have been lived in? _____

7. Total the number of pocketbooks and wallets. _____

8. How many homemade items do the people have with them? _____

9. How many different professions are represented? _____

10. How many different hobbies are there per person? _____

Total _____

Evolution vs. Creation:
Where Do You Stand?

Ten Best Evidences for a Young Earth and Universe
(4.5 Million years vs. 6,000 years)

1. Very Little Sediment on the Sea Floor -
If sediments have been accumulating on the sea floor for three billion years, the sea floor should be choked with sediments many miles deep. Yet the average thickness of all these sediments globally over the whole sea floor is not even 1300 feet. Considering the effects of the Flood and type of sediment and faster rates of deposit supports a young Earth.

2. Bent Rock Layers - In many mountainous areas, rock layers thousands of feet thick have been bent and folded without fracturing. Hardened rock layers are brittle. The Earth's layers must have been deposited and bent before hardening, not over 460 million years. The Grand Canyon is a great example of rapid sedimentation and bending before natural cements have a chance to harden them.

3. Soft Tissue in Fossils - If dinosaurs lived over 65 million years ago, why do some dinosaur fossils still contain well-preserved soft tissues such as bone marrow and blood cells with nuclei? The idea that biological tissues preserved and present might be only 3000–4000 years old is supported by historically known studies of mummies of that age. It is implausible that soft tissue could be preserved for the estimated 65 million years!

4. Faint Sun Paradox - Astronomers believe that the sun's power comes from the fusion of hydrogen into helium deep in the sun's core. As the hydrogen fuses, it should change the composition of the sun's core, increasing the sun's temperature and brightness. Calculations in reverse show that the sun would be 25 percent less bright and only warm the earth to a temperature still below freezing when life supposedly evolved. There is no scientific evidence for a less bright sun and cooler earth.

5. Rapidly Decaying Magnetic Field - The earth's magnetic field, which protects living things from solar radiation, is wearing down so quickly that the field and thus the earth could not be more than 20,000 years old. Further consideration to fluctuation that would occur during the Flood cataclysm points to a closer estimate of 6,000 years old.

6. Helium in Radioactive Rocks
During the radioactive decay of uranium and thorium in rocks, helium is produced and diffuses so rapidly that all the helium should have leaked out of rocks in less than 100,000 years. So why can rocks be found still full of helium atoms? Calculation using the measured rate of helium diffusion support a 6,000-year-old age of such rocks.

7. Carbon-14 in Fossils, Coal, and Diamonds
If Radiocarbon (Carbon-14) decays consistently and measurably, one would expect that none would be present in fossils, coal, and diamonds after just a few hundred thousand years. Why is it found in ALL the earth's diamonds dated at billions of years old? Even in such calculations using Carbon 14, there is an assumption that the earth's magnetic field has always been constant. This assumption is not true, however, as the magnetic field is actually declining, supporting much younger ages in calculations to the 5,000-6,000 year time frame.

8. Short Lived Comets
Comets spend most of their time in the deep freeze of space. Once during each its orbit, they come close to the sun, which evaporates the comet's ice and dislodges dust to form the tail. Comets have little mass, so each pass by the sun reduces the size and they fade away. They cannot survive billions of years, so wouldn't be present for an "old earth."

9. Very Little Salt in the Sea
If oceans have been around for three billion years or more, one would expect to see 70 times more salt in the ocean than we see today. A biblical timescale of about six thousand years is more plausible.

10. DNA in "Ancient" Bacteria
DNA normally breaks down quickly even in ideal conditions. Even evolutionists agree that DNA in bacterial spores (a dormant state) should not last more than a million years, yet it is being found today in items thought to be 250 million years old! "Their quandary is quite substantial."

(From "10 Best Evidences from Science That Confirm a Young Earth," Answers Magazine, Vol. 7, no. 4, Oct–Dec 2012. pp 44–57. Used by permission.)

Science and the Bible - 1
(Find the Match)

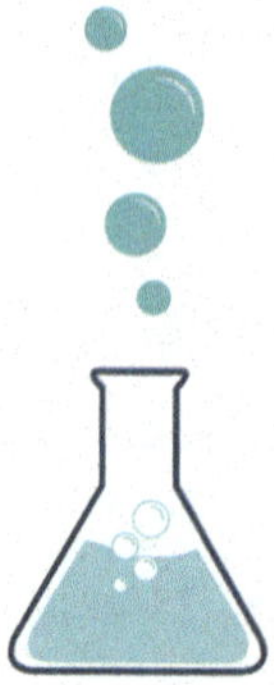

___ Java man   A. Critical interpretation of Scripture

___ Radioisotope Dating   B. One who rejects the Bible

___ Paleontologist   C. Short period of warming between glacier growth

___ Stellar Evolution   D. Creationist and author

___ Archaeology   E. The first fossil specimen of Homo erectus

___ Edward Blyth   F. A process that determines the age of the earth

___ Interglacial   G. The Big Bang

___ Atheist   H. Studies forms of life existing in previous times

___ Humanism   I. Digging to uncover past time period

___ Charles Darwin   J. Systematic study of the structure of the universe

___ Gap theory   K. Jewish historian around A.D. 90

___ Clone   L. An extinct people of Europe and Eastern Asia

___ Cosmology   M. A belief in mankind as the measure of all things

___ Artifact   N. A compromise belief that a vast period of time exists between Genesis 1:1 and 1:2

___ Josephus   O. Organism that is genetically identical to its parent

___ Cro-Magnon man   P. Evolutionist

___ Exegesis   Q. An item or its remains produced in the past by humans

(Taken from the *New Answers Book 1: Over 25 Questions on Creation/Evolution and the Bible*. ed. Ken Ham. Green Forest, AR: AIG Master Books, 2006. Used by permission.)

Science and the Bible – 2
(Find the Match)

_____ Meshech

_____ Jesus

_____ Materialism

_____ Septuagint

_____ Mutation

_____ Sir Isaac Newton

_____ Pentateuch

_____ Apocrypha

_____ Mizraim

_____ Tarsus

_____ Cush

_____ Canon

_____ Methuselah

A. 66 books found in the Bible

B. Ancient name of Ethiopia

C. A mountain range in Turkey

D. The "Last Adam"

E. Lived to be 969 years old

F. A group of about 14 books written between the close of the Old Testament and beginning of the New

G. The assumption that all that exists is mass and energy; there are no supernatural forces

H. The Hebrew name for Egypt

I. Is the old name for Moscow, Russia

J. The translation of the Old Testament into Greek during the third century B.C. The word itself means 70

K. Invented calculus, law of gravity, and law of motion

L. Any change in the sequence of DNA

M. Known as "The Law," the first five books of the Bible

(Taken from the *New Answers Book 2: Over 30 Questions on Creation/Evolution and the Bible.* ed. Ken Ham. Green Forest, AR: AIG Master Books, 2006. Used by permission.)

Proverbs 10:22 –
"The Blessing of the Lord brings wealth, without painful toil for it."

Acts 20:23	"Now I commit you to God and to the word of His grace—which can build you up—and give you an inheritance among all those who are sanctified."
Numbers 6:24–26	May "the Lord bless you and keep you; the Lord make His face shine upon you and be gracious to you, the Lord turn His face toward you and give you peace."
Deuteronomy 28 (Selection)	May the Lord your God set you high above all nations on earth, and may all these blessing come upon you as you obey the Lord your God. May you be blessed in the city and blessed in the country. May you be blessed when you come in and when you go out. May the Lord cause the enemies who rise up against you to be defeated before you and to flee from you in seven directions. May the Lord send a blessing on everything you put our hand to. May the Lord establish you as His holy people as you walk in His ways. May all the peoples on earth see that you are called by the name of the Lord. May the Lord grant you abundant prosperity. May the Lord open the heavens, the storehouse of His bounty, to bless all the work of your hands. May the Lord make you the head and not the tail, and may He cause you to be at the top, never at the bottom. May the God of patience and consolation grant you to be likeminded one toward another according to Christ Jesus, that you may with one mind and one mouth glorify God, even the Father of our Lord Jesus Christ. May the God of hope fill you with all joy and peace in believing, that you may abound in hope through the power of the Holy Ghost.

2 Corinthians 13:14	"May the grace of the Lord Jesus Christ, and the love of God, and the fellowship of the Holy Spirit be with you all."
2 Thessalonians 2:16-17	"May our Lord Jesus Christ himself and God our Father who loved us and by His grace gave us eternal encouragement and good hope, encourage your hearts and strengthen you in every good deed and word."
Hebrews 13:20-21a (Selection)	May the God of peace, who through the blood of the eternal covenant brought back from the dead our Lord Jesus Christ, that great Shepherd of the sheep, equip you with everything good for doing His will, and may He work in you what is pleasing to him.
Psalm 20:1-5 (Selection)	May the Lord answer you when you are in distress; may the name of the God of Jacob protect you. May He send you help from the sanctuary and grant you support from Zion. May He remember all your sacrifices and accept your offerings. May He grant all your requests. May He give you the desires of your heart and make all your plans succeed. We will shout for joy when you are victorious and will lift up our banners in the name of our God.
2 Thessalonians 3:18 (Selection)	The grace of the Lord Jesus Christ be with God's people.

These blessings we pronounce upon you today by the authority of the Word of God and in the name of our Lord Jesus Christ. Amen.

(Rev. Lowell S. Perkins, Used by permission.)

Scavenger Hunt Items

Indoor Hunt

Pencil	Paperclip	Tissue	note paper
Pen	Lipstick	Comb	Safety pin
Keys	Mirror	Lotion	Fingernail file
Credit card	Driver's license	Candy	Cough drop
Chewing gum	Brush	Photograph	Earring
Coin	Hairpin	Piece of tape	Cup
Match	Lighter	Piece of string	Utensil

Indoor Hunt

Pencil	Paperclip	Tissue	note paper
Pen	Lipstick	Comb	Safety pin
Keys	Mirror	Lotion	Fingernail file
Credit card	Driver's license	Candy	Cough Drop
Chewing gum	Brush	Photograph	Earring
Coin	Hairpin	Piece of tape	Cup
Match	Lighter	Piece of string	Utensil

Old West Trivia

1. See if you can name these popular Old West songs:
"Home on the _____," "Red _____ Valley," "_____ Rose of _____," and "Get along Little _____"

2. Where is a cowboy if the shout goes out "man at the pot"?

   a. Around the campfire   b. At the outhouse door   c. At a branding

3. The old adage "well heeled" comes from the preference of horsemen to wear _____.

4. In the 1890s, former cowboys formed the famous _____ under Lt. Theodore Roosevelt and fought in the war against Spain and Cuba in 1898.

5. About how many miles did a herd cover in a day on a drive?
   a. 5   b. 10   c. 15   d. 20

6. One of the greatest contributions the Spanish brought to North America was the _____ cattle.

7. Can cows see color? _____

8. How many gallons of milk does it take to make one gallon of ice cream?
   a. ¾   b. 1   c. 1 ¼   d. 1 ½

9. Why did cowboys sing? _____

10. What Western movie was named after the shoot-out between lawmen Wyatt Earp and Doc Holliday and outlaws Frank and Tom McLaury and Bill Clanton? _____

11. A maverick is:
    a. An especially wild cowboy   b. A cow that escaped
    c. A brand used by ranchers on stolen cattle

12. A cow can detect odors up to: a. 10 feet   b. 50 feet   c. 1 mile   d. 5 miles

Senior Student Exam

You only need 4 correct out of 10 questions to pass. WARNING: These are tricky!

1. How long did the Hundred Years' War last?

2. Which country makes Panama hats?

3. From which animal do we get cat gut?

4. In which month do Russians celebrate the October Revolution?

5. What is a camel's hair brush made of?

6. The Canary Islands in the Pacific are named after what animal?

7. What was King George VI's first name?

8. What color is a purple finch?

9. Where are Chinese gooseberries from?

10. What is the color of the black box in a commercial airplane?

Homemade Sugar Scrubs and Lotion

Sugar Scrubs
These can be put in small jars with little spoons with ribbon wrapped around the top. Can use for face or by a sink for a hand scrub.

Christmas

1. Peppermint

1 1/3 cups granulated sugar
2 drops peppermint essential oil
1/3 cup almond oil
Food coloring to make it pink

Mix together and store in airtight container.

2. Gingerbread

1 cup granulated sugar
¼ cup almond oil
½ teaspoon vanilla extract
½ teaspoon nutmeg
½ teaspoon ginger
1 cup brown sugar
½ cup coconut oil
½ teaspoon cinnamon
½ teaspoon allspice

Mix together and store in airtight container.

Thanksgiving:

1. Pumpkin Spice

2 cups brown sugar
2 tablespoons pumpkin pie spice
1 teaspoon nutmeg
1 cup granulated sugar
½ cup coconut oil
1 teaspoon cinnamon

Mix together and store in airtight container.

(cont.)

Homemade Sugar Scrubs and Lotion

Handmade Hand Cream

16 ounces baby lotion
8 ounces Vaseline
8 ounces Vitamin E cream

Mix together well with a mixer until it resembles icing. Put in containers as desired.

Use Dollar General Brand ingredients and it makes a BIG mixer bowlful, so you should be prepared with some empty jars/containers.

(Terry Mitchell. Used by permission)

"Bible Testing" Time

Here are 20 questions. See how well you do on them. Give yourself 5 points for each correct answer.

1. How many of each clean animal did Moses take with him into the ark? _____
2. Is the book of Hezekiah in the Old Testament or the New Testament? _____
3. Which Bible verse is sometimes referred to as "The gospel in a nutshell"? _____
4. Matthew, Mark, Luke, and John are known as the four _____
5. How many books of the Bible did John write? _____
6. How many books are in the Old Testament? _____
7. How many books are in the New Testament? _____
8. _____ marched around the city of Jericho and the walls fell down.
9. Upon which mountain did Moses receive the 10 Commandments? _____
10. Complete this verse, "Blessed are the _____ in heart for they shall see_____."
11. Jesus said, "Behold, I stand at the _____ and _____."
12. Abraham came from the land of _____
13. John 10:35, "Jesus wept," is known as _____.
14. Does the Bible say, "Charity begins at home" _____
15. Which Old Testament prophet challenged the prophets of Baal on Mount Carmel? _____

True or False

16. True or False: The word, "Gospel" means "Faithfulness" _____
17. Jesus ascended into heaven from Mt. Sinai _____
18. The Jerusalem Council met in Bethlehem _____
19. Jesus prayed in the Garden of Eden _____
20. The disciples were called "Christians" first at Ephesus _____

Score yourself:

18–20 correct ** Excellent   12–17 correct ** Good
5–11 correct ** Fair   1–4 correct ** Not the sharpest knife in the drawer

THE BEGINNER'S BOOK OF SENIOR ACTIVITIES | 239

Advertising Slogans
See how many of these advertising slogans you can remember!

1. "It's finger lickin' good."

2. "Impossible is nothing."

3. "You're in good hands…"

4. "Good to the last drop."

5. "The choice of a new generation."

6. "Reach out and touch someone."

7. "Melts in your mouth, not in your hand."

8. "Think small."

9. "Kills bugs dead."

10. "Snap, crackle, pop."

11. "Think outside the bun."

12. "Let your fingers do the walking."

13. Where "taste is king."

14. "The worldwide leader in sports."

15. "Takes a licking and keeps on ticking."

16. "Always low prices. Always."

"Fly the friendly skies!"

17. "We try harder."

18. "It's the real thing."

19. "The ultimate driving machine."

20. "The copper top battery."

21. "Fly the friendly skies."

22. "Just do it."

23. "Because you're worth it."

24. "15 minutes can save you 15% or more…"

25. "Nothing runs like a Deere."

26. "Every kiss begins with Kay."

27. "We bring good things to life."

28. "Share moments. Share life."

29. "They're Gr-r-eat!"

30. "I'm lovin' it!"

31. "When it absolutely has to be there overnight."

32. "The quicker picker-upper."

33. "The breakfast of champions."

Spring Poem Game

In olden days, rhyming was a popular game.
See how your skills of prose are today!
Make a short poem using the words:
dear, tear, peer, fear, smear, ear, clear and
beginning with …
"Spring is the season of the year,

Outings/Excursions: Preparation

A. Preparation for trips:
Good planning is essential for smooth trips and outings.

1. Games:
If the trip is more than 45 minutes, have a game, such as a word search game, to play along the way. Bring small prizes to add to the fun.

2. Snacks:
It is a good idea to have snacks for the trip if a meal is not within a couple of hours. Walmart has little clear treat bags that a napkin and a prepackaged snack can be put in. (Some of the members might like to volunteer to bake cookies for one trip.)

3. Drinks:
ALWAYS give each person a disposable bottle of water for each trip. Sam's and Walmart have inexpensive small bottles. If the trip is early in the morning, then coffee and donuts are also a treat.

4. Bathroom Stops/Accessibility:
This is a very important aspect to some seniors. Before departing, announce when the next bathroom stop will be, and schedule these in at least once every two hours. This helps reassure anxious minds.

5. Trip duration:
Announce in the newsletter the length of the trip beforehand. Day trips can be challenging for some seniors. Try to end the trip before dark, if possible, to make traveling home safer.

6. First Aid Kit and Wet Wipes/Hand Sanitizers:
Having a good first aid kit for an emergency injury is mandatory. Also it is a good idea to have wet wipes or hand sanitizers to cut down on the transmission of germs.

Note: Check with your administrator to see if your church or organization requires participants to sign a "Waiver of Liability Form" for bus trips to avoid legal issues should something unforeseen happen during the trip.

Famous Women Quiz
See How Many You Know!

1. Best-known lady chef on TV. _____

2. This woman, known for being a talk show host and champion of current causes, is the fifteenth weathiest woman in America as of 2013. _____

3. Actress known for her love of jewelry and husbands. _____

4. This famous actress who wooed a U.S. president was known for her blonde hair and voluptuous figure. _____

5. Beloved female prime minister of Israel . _____

6. Female pilot who disappeared in her attempt to fly around the world. _____

7. Former U.S. Secretary of State. _____

8. Alaskan governor who ran for Vice-President of the United States. _____

9. The lady who began the "home" business empire. _____

10. Actress who married Prince Rainier of Monaco. _____

11. The "Iron Lady" of Britian. _____

12. Daughter and heir to a famous Arkansas businessman's U.S. empire. _____

13. Prime Minister of India who was assassinated in office. _____

14. American novelist and fourth bestselling author of all time. Known for writing fictional love stories. _____

Famous Christian Women:
Giving All to the Lord

1. Known as the Queen of Calabar. This Scottish missionary was one of the first missionaries to Nigeria. _____

2. South American missionary. Husband was killed by a tribe in Ecuador. She and her daughter returned back to minister to the people who killed her husband. _____

3. Helped Jews escape Nazi capture in WWII. Arrested and sent to Ravensbruck concentration camp. Author of The Hiding Place. _____

4. Christian Songwriter. Dove award winner. _____

5. British missionary to China, famous for saving orphans during WWI. Ingrid Bergman starred in "The Inn of Sixth Happiness" about her life. _____

6. Blind lyricist and composer. She wrote over 8,000 hymns. _____

7. The Lord raised her from the dead in response to her evangelist husband's prayers! _____

8. Evangelist who held healing crusades. _____

9. Bible teacher, author, and speaker known for her wit. _____

10. Early missionary and orphanage founder in Egypt. _____

11. She and her husband were missionaries and orphanage founders in India. _____

12. Evangelist who travelled with her two children preaching and founded the Foursquare Church. _____

13. Christian comedian and speaker. _____

A. Lillian Trasher
B. Joyce Meyer
C. Huldah Buntain
D. Kathryn Kulhman
E. Anita Renfroe
F. Mary Slessor
G. Amee Simple McPherson
H. Gloria Gaither
I. Fanny Crosby
J. Elisabeth Elliott
K. Corrie Ten Boom
L. Gladys Alyward
M. Mrs. Smith Wigglesworth

Praying for My Husband

1. That he might be a righteous man, a man of prayer, mature in the Lord, growing in his knowledge of the Lord.
Ephesians 1:18–19

2. That he might speak the truth, saying no slander of anyone, be kind to his neighbor, keep his word, honor what is right but despise evil, lend money without interest, take no bribe, to claim the promise that he will not be shaken. Psalm 15

3. That he might be a man of contentment. 1 Timothy 6:6–8

4. That he would have a thankful heart and be filled with the joy of the Lord.
Nehemiah 8:10; 1 Thessalonians 5:18

5. That he might daily seek God with all his heart, walking in the Spirit moment by moment, growing in his dependence on Him. Psalms 119:1–2; Proverbs 3:5–6

6. That he would ever be captivated by my love. Proverbs 5:18–19

7. That the Lord might give him wisdom to lead his family physically, emotionally, mentally, and spiritually. Ephesians 1:17–19

8. That he would accomplish God's will for his life.
Proverbs 16:9; Hebrews 12:1

9. That he might stand firm against the schemes of the devil and resist Satan in all circumstances. John 17:15; Ephesians 6:10–18; James 4:7

10. That he would learn to not depend on his circumstances for happiness but on God alone. Philippians 4:12; Habakkuk 3:17–19

11. That the Lord would give him His strength for his work.
Ephesians 3:14–19

12. **That he might have a burden to see lost people come to know Jesus Christ as Lord and Savior.** Matthew 28:19–20

13. **That he might learn to be thoughtful of how he lives and manage his time well.** Ephesians 5:15-16

14. **That he might learn to take every thought captive, to not be conformed to the world's thinking and think scripturally.** Romans 12:2; 2 Corinthians 10:5; 1Timothy 6:11

15. **That his self-image might be a reflection of the Lord's thoughts toward him.**
Ephesians 1:17–19; Romans 12:3; Psalm 139

16. **That he might learn to love as God has commanded.**
1 Corinthians 13:4–7; Ephesians 5:25

17. **That he would be a man of courage, knowing that God will protect him and guard his course.**
Deuteronomy 31:6; Proverbs 2:8

18. **That the fruit of the Spirit might be exhibited more and more in his life.**
Galatians 5:22–23; John 15:8

19. **That he might grow daily in character.**
1 Peter 5:5–8

20. **That he might have a pure heart, a steadfast spirit, and a clear conscience.**
1Thessalonians 5:23; Psalm 51:10; 1 Peter 3:16–18

21. **That he may have a holy fear of God.**
Psalms 34:11 and 111:10; Proverbs 9:10

22. **That he would be a man of the Word, reading and studying the Bible daily.** Psalm 119:11

The Quiz for Those in the Know

This is a quiz for people who think they know everything!
These are not trick questions – but are straight-forward questions with straight-forward answers.

1. Name the one sport in which neither the spectators nor the participants know the score or the leader until the contest ends.
   _____

2. What famous North American landmark is constantly moving backward?
   _____

3. Of all vegetables, only two can live to produce on their own for several growing seasons. All other vegetables must be replanted every year. What are the only two perennial vegetables? _____ and _____

4. What fruit has its seeds on the outside? _____

5. Only three words in standard English begin with the letters 'dw' and they are all common words. Name two of them. _____ and
   _____

6. There are 14 punctuation marks in English grammar. Can you name at least half of them?
   _____

7. Name the only vegetable AND fruit that is never sold frozen, canned, processed, cooked, or in any other form except fresh. _____

8. Name 6 or more things that you can wear on your feet beginning with the letter 'S.' _____
   _____

(www.mikeysFunnies.com. Used by permission.)

U.S. Geography Quiz

1. Which state only borders one additional state?_____

2. The city of Oatman gets so hot that it hosts an egg-frying contest on its streets every July. What state is it in? _____

3. This state is home to the "Chocolate Capital." _____

4. "Carlsbad Caverns" are found in this state. _____

5. This state has a half a million earthquakes and tremors each year. _____

6. Which state had the first English colony in America? _____

7. The Hoover Dam is found in this state. _____

8. This state has the lowest point of elevation at 282 feet below sea level! It is so low it is called "Death Valley!" _____

9. Residents in this state are allowed to hunt more fish and game than residents in other U.S. states. _____

10. The colors in this state's flag are said to represent natural elements: red soil, white snow-capped mountains, blue skies, and golden sunshine.
_____

11. Which state has the lowest population? _____

12. This is the only state that has a unicameral legislature, meaning that it has only one house of government, the Senate. All other states have both the House and the Senate. _____

13. What is the southernmost point in the United States?_____

14. Coffee is grown in this state. _____

15. The famous Corn Palace dating from 1892 is located in the city of Mitchell. The palace is known for its murals made out of corn! What state is it in? _____

16. Which state (other than Alaska) has the most shoreline? _____

17. This state is famous for one thing, crabs! Each year they host the National Hard Crab Derby and crown a Miss Crustacean!
_____

18. Which is the largest state? _____

19. Which is the smallest state? _____

20. What state was the first to declare independence from England? _____
_____

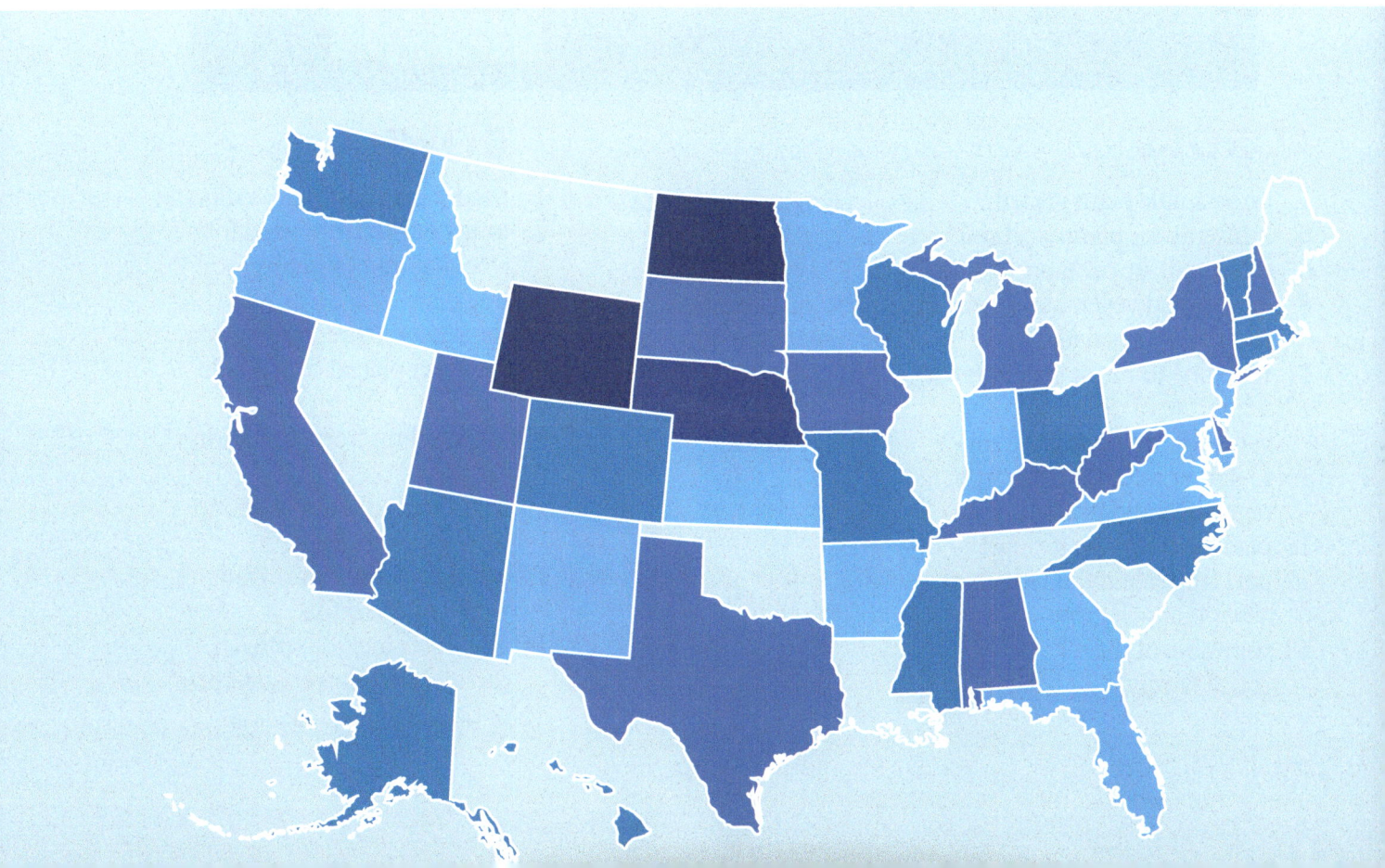

Gardens

ACROSS

1. undesirable plant growth
5. nutrients for plants and soil
6. fertile soil, upper layer of soil
8. long, green vegetable, sliced and mixed in salads
11. machine to break up the earth
12. a mixture of decxomposing plants for fertilizing the soil
15. to gather in the mature fruit, vegetables and grain
16. place seeds in the ground
17. part from a plant in which a new plant will grow
18. vegetable of the gourd family, varieties include yellow, acorn or zucchini
19. long handled tool with teeth or prongs used to gather leaves, grass, etc.

DOWN

1. used to haul dirt and rocks
2. long handled tool used for weeding and loosening soil
3. bugs
4. the season to begin planting
7. an object placed on poles in a garden to frighten birds
9. water falling from the sky in droplets
10. main ingredient of ketchup and spaghetti sauce
13. animal excrement mixed with soil to fertilize it.
14. examples include spinach, carrots, cauliflower and corn

(Nancy Jahnke. Used by permission.)

Gardens

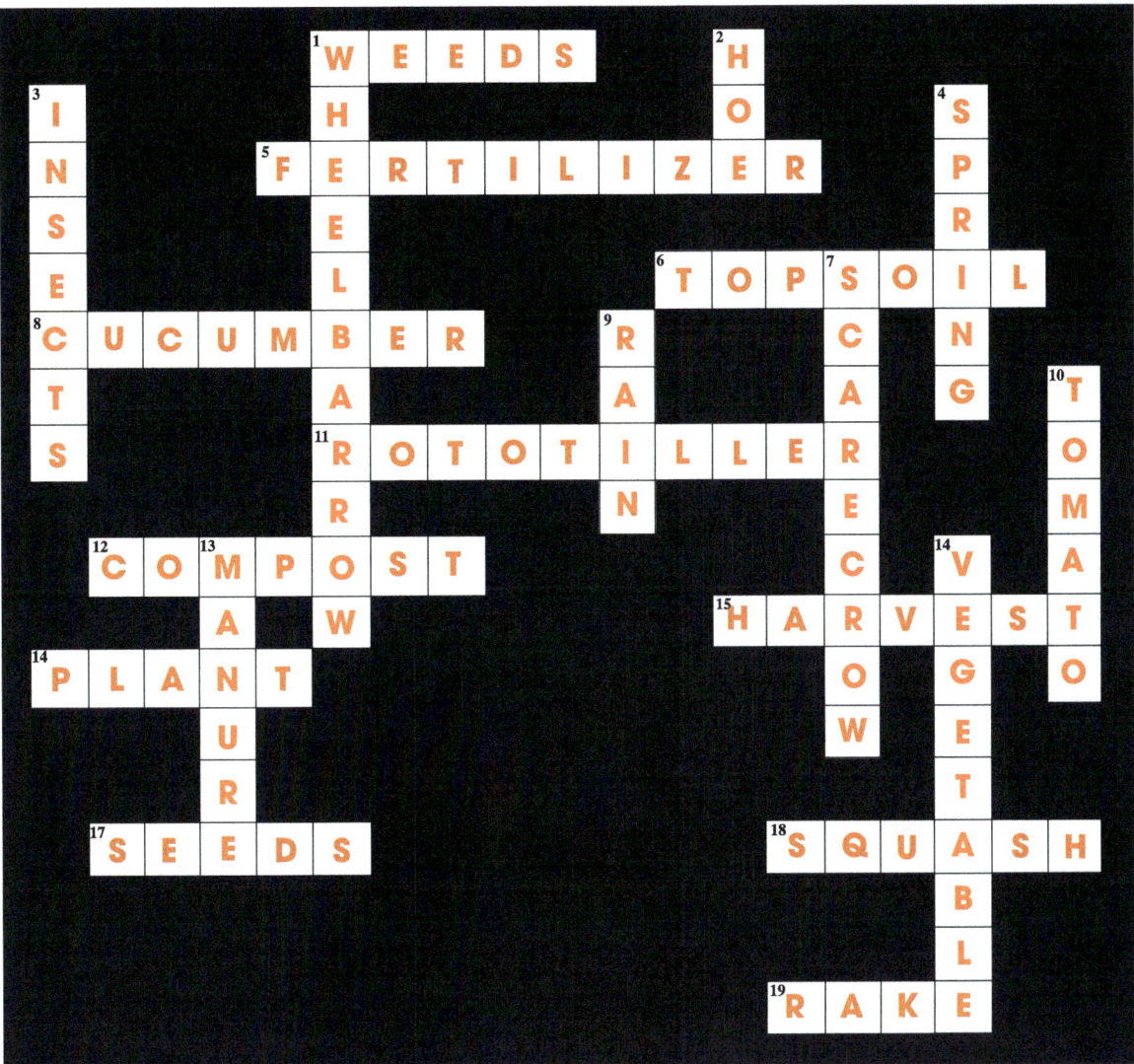

ACROSS

1. undesirable plant growth
5. nutrients for plants and soil
6. fertile soil, upper layer of soil
8. long, green vegetable, sliced and mixed in salads
11. machine to break up the earth
12. a mixture of decomposing plants for fertilizing the soil
15. to gather in the mature fruit, vegetables and grain
16. place seeds in the ground
17. part from a plant in which a new plant will grow
18. vegetable of the gourd family, varieties include yellow, acorn or zucchini
19. long handled tool with teeth or prongs used to gather leaves, grass, etc.

DOWN

1. used to haul dirt and rocks
2. long handled tool used for weeding and loosening soil
3. bugs
4. the season to begin planting
7. an object placed on poles in a garden to frighten birds
9. water falling from the sky in droplets
10. main ingredient of ketchup and spaghetti sauce
13. animal excrement mixed with soil to fertilize it.
14. examples include spinach, carrots, cauliflower and corn

(Nancy Jahnke. Used by permission.)

Fantastic Flora Facts: Quiz

Match the fact with the flora.

1. What is the largest living organism in the world? _____

2. This plant is now being used to make crayons for kids that are safer, brighter in color, and less expensive. _____

3. What is the oldest living thing in existence? _____

4. This vegetable contains a mild antibiotic that fights infection, soothes burns, and Redwood trees helps with stings and itches. _____

5. One bushel of this can sweeten 400 cans of pop. _____

6. This fruit tree can be grafted onto the nectarine tree and still produce its own kind. _____

A. Bananas
B. Asparagus
C. Bamboo
D. California Bristlecones pine
E. Pineapples
F. Onions
G. White Potatoes
H. Saffron
I. Strawberry
J. Peach
K. California
L. Grapes
M. Broccoli
N. Orchid
O. Corn
P. Soybeans

7. California produces almost all of this vegetable in the U.S. _____

8. Vanilla comes from this plant. _____

9. This member of the lily family can produce food annually for up to 25 years. _____

10. Archaeologists have found 8,000-year-old evidence of these in Mesopotamia and Egypt. _____

11. This plant can grow up to 3.28 feet in one day! _____

12. These were first cultivated by local Indians in the mountains of South America. _____

13. The stigmas of this blooming flower are used in cooking. _____

14. The only fruit to bear its seeds on the outside of it. _____

15. What is the most popular fruit in America? _____

16. This sweet fruit is often cooked upside down. _____

Theodore Roosevelt:
How Much Do You Know?

1. **What relationship was Eleanor Roosevelt to T.R?**
   a. His wife
   b. His niece
   c. His daughter
   d. No blood relation

2. **Roosevelt disliked the name Teddy (even after the bear was named after him). Close friends and family never dared to address him that way.**
   True or False

3. **T.R. selected his "Rough Riders" from a pool of over 23,000 volunteers, taking a large number from which of the following groups?**
   a. Cowboys, Native Americans, and athletes
   b. Calvary, Civil War veterans and "Buffalo Soldiers"
   c. Circus Riders, West Point graduates, and sharpshooters
   d. Immigrants, factory workers, and retired soldiers

4. **Roosevelt's Brazilian expedition of 1913 was fraught with trouble. Which of the following did NOT happen?**
   a. Roosevelt almost died from malaria and dysentery.
   b. One member of the expedition drowned.
   c. One member went insane, killed another member, and then disappeared into the jungle.
   d. His son Kermit broke his arm.

5. **What condition did T.R. suffer from in his youth that caused him to push for a "fit" life?**
   a. Polio
   b. Asthma
   c. Anemia
   d. Diabetes

6. **While boxing with a sparring partner at the gym at the White House, T.R. was blinded in one eye and permanently lost the use of his left eye.**
   True or False

7. **Which of the following is NOT a T.R. quote?**
   a. "No president has ever enjoyed himself as much as I."
   b. "Keep your eyes on the stars, and your feet on the ground."
   c. "Great victories require great sacrifices."
   d. "Speak softly and carry a big stick."

8. **T.R. graduated from which one of the following universities?**
   a. Princeton
   b. University of New York
   c. Harvard
   d. Georgetown

9. **T.R. was the first American president to accept which honor?**
   a. A Purple Heart
   b. The Pulitzer Prize
   c. The Nobel Peace Prize
   d. The Congressional Medal of Honor

10. **Which of the following expressions did Roosevelt NOT come up with?**
    a. The lunatic fringe
    b. Muckrakers
    c. Second rate …
    d. My hat is in the ring

11. **Who were Jonathan Edwards, Bishop Doane, and Eli Yale?**
    a. Rough Riders
    b. T.R.'s children's pets
    c. Travel assistants on his many trips
    d. T.R.'s household help

12. **T.R. drank about a gallon of what a day?**
    a. Water
    b. Milk
    c. Iced Tea
    d. Coffee

The Story of Carl

Carl was a quiet man. He didn't talk much. He would always greet you with a big smile and a firm handshake. Even after living in our neighborhood for over 50 years, no one could really say they knew him very well. Before his retirement, he took the bus to work each morning. The sight of him walking alone down the street often made us worry about his safety.

He had a slight limp from a bullet wound received in WWII. Watching him, we worried that although he had survived WWII, he may not make it through our changing uptown neighborhood with its ever-increasing random violence, gangs, and drug activity.

When he saw the flyer at our local church asking for volunteers for caring for the gardens behind the minister's residence, he responded in his characteristically unassuming manner. Without fanfare, he just signed up.

He was well into his 87th year when the very thing we had always feared finally happened. He was just finishing his watering for the day when three gang members approached him. Ignoring their attempt to intimidate him, he simply asked, "Would you like a drink from the hose?" The tallest and toughest looking of the three said, "Yeah, sure," with a malevolent little smile. As Carl offered the hose to him, the other two grabbed Carl's arms and threw him down. As the hose snaked crazily over the ground, dousing everything in its way, Carl's assailants stole his retirement watch and his wallet, and then fled.

Carl tried to get himself up, but he had been thrown down on his bad leg. He lay there trying to gather himself as the minister came running to help him. Although the minister had witnessed the attack from his window, he couldn't get there fast enough to stop it. "Carl, are you OK? Are you hurt?" the minister kept asking as he helped Carl to his feet. Carl just passed a hand over his brow and sighed, shaking his head. "Just some punk kids; I hope they'll wise up someday."

His wet clothes clung to his slight frame as he bent to pick up the hose. He adjusted the nozzle again and started to water. Confused and a little concerned, the minister asked, "Carl, what are you doing?" "I've got to finish my watering. It's been very dry lately," came the response. Satisfying himself that Carl really was all right, the minister could only marvel. Carl was a man from a different time and place.

A few weeks later the three returned. Just as before their threat was unchallenged. Carl again offered them a drink from his hose. This time they didn't rob him. They wrenched the hose from his hand and drenched him head to foot in the icy water. When they had finished their humiliation of him, they sauntered off down the street, throwing catcalls and curses, falling over one another laughing at the hilarity of what they had just done. Carl just watched them. Then he turned toward the warmth of the sun, picked up his hose, and went on with his watering.

The summer was quickly fading into fall. Carl was doing some tilling when he was startled by the sudden approach of someone behind him. Caught off guard, he stumbled and fell into some evergreen branches. As he struggled to regain his footing, he turned to see the tall leader of his summer tormentors reaching down for him. He braced himself for the expected attack. "Don't worry, old man, I'm not gonna hurt you."

The young man spoke softly, still offering the tattooed and scarred hand to Carl. As he helped Carl get up, the man pulled a crumpled bag from his pocket and handed it to Carl. "What's this?" Carl asked. "It's your stuff," the man explained. "It's your stuff back, even the money in your wallet." "I don't understand." Carl said. "Why would you help me now?"

The man shifted his feet, seeming embarrassed and ill at ease. "I learned something from you," he said. "I ran with that gang and hurt people like you. We picked you because you were old and we knew we could do it but every time we came and did something to you, instead of yelling and fighting back, you tried to give us a drink. You didn't hate us for hating you. You kept showing love for our hate."

He stopped for a moment. "I couldn't sleep after we stole your stuff, so here it is back." He paused for another awkward moment, not knowing what more to say. "That bag's my way of saying thanks for straightening me out, I guess." And with that he walked off down the street.

Carl looked down at the sack in his hands and gingerly opened it. He took out his retirement watch and put it back on his wrist. Opening his wallet, he checked for his wedding photo. He gazed for a moment at the young bride that still smiled back at him from all those years ago.

He died that winter, the day after Christmas. Many people attended his funeral in spite of the weather. In particular the minister noticed a tall young man that looked vaguely familiar quietly sitting in a distant corner of the church. The minister spoke of Carl's garden as a lesson in life. In a voice made thick with unshed tears, he said "Do your best and make your garden as beautiful as you can. We will never forget Carl and his garden."

The following spring another flyer went up. It read: "Person needed to care for Carl's garden." The flyer went unnoticed by the busy parishioners until one day when a knock was heard at the minister's office door. Opening the door, the minister saw a pair of scarred and tattooed hands holding the flyer. "I believe this is my job, if you'll have me," the young man said. The minster recognized him as the same young man who had returned the stolen watch and wallet to Carl.

He knew that Carl's kindness had turned this man's life around. As the minister handed him the keys to the garden shed, he said, "Yes, go take care of Carl's garden and honor him." The man went to work, and over the next several years he tended the flowers and vegetables just as Carl had done. During that time, he went to college, got married, and became a prominent member of the community. But he never forgot his promise to Carl's memory and kept the garden as beautiful as he thought Carl would have kept it.

One day he approached the new minister and told him that he couldn't care for the garden any longer. He explained with a shy and happy smile. "My wife just had a baby boy last night, and she's bringing him home on Saturday." "Well, congratulations!" said the minister, as he was handed the garden shed keys. "That's wonderful! What's the baby's name?" "Carl," the man replied.

(That's the gospel message simply stated.)

British Trivia

See how much you know of the English!

1. The United Kingdom is made up of what four areas: _____, _____, _____ _____, and _____.

2. The capital of Britain is what city? _____

3. The British are known for making what popular pie? _____

4. Who was known as the "Virgin Queen?" _____

5. What member of the United Kingdom held a vote to become an independent country in 2015? _____ (The vote failed.)

6. The British are known for the love of _____ hunting.

7. She was the queen of England and Ireland the only surviving child of Henry 8th and Catherine, the first of his six wives. She became known as "Bloody _____" because of her executions of Protestants.

8. What are the colors of the British flag? _____

9. What is the British National Anthem? _____ The melody was used for America's "My Country, Tis of Thee."

10. Prior to this queen's wedding, wedding dresses were usually made of colored heavy silk satin, however, after her choice of the unusual color of white – it became a standard! _____

11. Used as the one of the Queen's official residences. It is the largest occupied castle in the world. _____

Gents, Ladies and Language

1. The famous wife of Prince Charles, now deceased.

2. One of the oldest known British actors and writer.

3. A cookie, often had with tea.

4. The British actress known for her love of jewelry

5. This comedian portrays the character "Mr. Bean"

6. The British word for truck.

7. The very thin model of the 60's.

8. James Bond character

9. French Fries

10. An actress, known for her lovely singing voice.

11. Prime Minister during WWII

12. An elevator

13. Known for her beautiful big eyes and movies such as Breakfast at Tiffany's and Roman Holiday.

14. Soccer

15. Known for such films as Wuthering Heights and Hamlet.

A. Chips

B. Lorry

C. Julie Andrews

D. Sir. Lawrence Olivier and Richard Burton.

E. Lift

F. Audrey Hepburn

G. Princess Diana

H. Elizabeth Taylor

I. Biscuit

J. Football

K. Sir Winston Churchill

L. Rowan Atkinson

M. William Shakespeare

N. Twiggy

O. Roger Moore

USO: Did You Know?

- USO stands for United Service Organizations

- The USO is a nonprofit, congressionally chartered, private organization; it is NOT part of the U.S. Government.

- The President of the United States serves as Honorary Chairman of the USO.

- Mission Statement: The USO lifts the spirits of America's troops and their families.

- Supporting America's troops was the first mission of the USO.

- In 1941, as the nation was heading into World War II, several organizations mobilized to support the growing U.S. military: The Salvation Army, Young Men's Christian Association, Young Women's Christian Association, National Catholic Community Services, National Travelers Aid Association, and the National Jewish Welfare Board.

- President Franklin D. Roosevelt, seeing the need for a centralized place for service organizations, formed the United Service Organization, with the objective of providing the emotional support the troops needed.

- Today, the USO continues to lift the spirits of America's troops and their families, and will continue to be there for them "until everyone comes home."

"Hope" Trivia

1. Bob was born in:
    a. USA   b. England   c. Ireland   d. Israel

2. Coming from a modest background (immigrant parents), he had various jobs which included:
    a. selling newspapers   b. shoe salesman
    c. a delivery boy for a meat market   d. all the above

3. After a gig in the "Ziegfeld Follies" with Fanny Brice, he had a role in "Red, Hot, and Blue" with Ethel _____ and Jimmy _____.

4. What was Bob Hope's wife's name? _____.

5. Bob broke into stardom with his "road pictures" with Bing Crosby and Dorothy Lamour in "The Road to _____.

6. Bob's career lasted 60 years working with what network?
    a. ABC   b. NBC   c. CBS   d. Fox network

7. Bob golfed with many U.S. presidents including all but:
    a. Harry Truman   b. Richard Nixon
    c. Ronald Reagan   d. Bill Clinton

8. Known as "G.I. Bob" he entertained troops during all but one:
    a. World war I   b. World War II   c. Korean conflict
    d. Vietnam war   e. Operation Desert Storm

9. Was Bob a knight? _____.

"Hope" Jokes

1. "The only thing chicken about Israel is their soup."

2. "You know you're getting old when the candles cost more than the cake."

3. "You never get tired unless you stop and take time for it."

4. "The trees in Siberia are miles apart; that is why the dogs are so fast."

5. "A bank is a place that will loan you money, if you can prove that you don't need it."

6. "Middle Age is when your age starts to show around your middle."

7. "I love to go to Washington, if only to be nearer my money."

8. "I grew up with six brothers. That's how I learned to dance, waiting for the bathroom."

9. "I don't feel old. I don't feel anything until noon. That's when it's time for my nap."

10. "I have a wonderful make-up crew. They're the same people restoring the Statue of Liberty."

11. "Kids are wonderful, but I like mine barbecued."

12. "People who throw kisses are hopelessly lazy."

13. "Most of the people who came for dancing lessons had rumba ambitions and minuet bodies."

14. "I'll tell ya' how to stay young: hang around with older people."

15. "It's so cold here in Washington, D.C. that politicians have their hands in their own pockets."

Jokes taken from www.telegraph.uk.com, www.standupcomedyportal.com, www.jokes4us.com, www.brainyquote.com

Patriotic Pictionary:
Topics to Use (cut individually)

Presidents:

Richard M. Nixon

Ronald Reagan

George Bush

Important Events in History:

Assassination of John F. Kennedy

Bombing of Pearl Harbor

Attack on the Twin Towers in New York

Famous Battles:

Iwo Jima (WWII)

Gettysburg (Civil War)

Saratoga (Revolutionary War)

Patriotic Pictionary: Score Sheet

Presidents:

Round 1:

Round 2:

Round 3:

Important Events in History:

Round 4:

Round 5:

Round 6:

Famous Battles:

Round 7:

Round 8:

Round 9:

Webster's Words
Match the word with the correct definition.

1. Something that is strict, severe or hard

2. Information that provides data about other data.

3. A forceful warning or scolding

4. Behavior that is irreverent toward the sacred

5. Favoritism based on family ties

6. Great strength and vigor

7. Someone who is careful about how they use their resources

8. Something that is an indication a lead or a trend

9. Very delicate, difficult or light

10. A book of words similar to others

11. Unruly, full of uncontrolled energy

12. A person who is unbothered by morals or tradition

13. Having knowledge that is limited to a small group

14. An unskilled laborer especially in an oil field or shipyard

15. A jail

A. Stalwart

B. Sacrilegious

C. Frugal

D. Thesaurus

E. Stringent

F. Libertine

G. Rambunctious

H. Nepotism

I. Hoosegow

J. Gossamer

K. Metadata

L. Roustabout

M. Esoteric

N. Riot act

O. Bellwether

Crime Doesn't Pay

1. The most famous Male and Female Robber Team

2. The deadliest U.S. High School massacre

3. Accused of axing her parents to death.

4. Distrustful of technology; for 18 years he used packages and letters to harm.

5. Known for robbing banks and trains, in the Old West and had a movie made about them.

6. He bombed the federal building in Oklahoma

7. Who shot JFK?

8. Prohibition Gangster from Chicago who ruled an empire.

9. Known for killing actress Sharon Tate

10. Leader of a cult that fled to Guyana, where all died from cyanide poisoning.

11. Two brothers who robbed trains and banks often scalped captive Union soldiers during the Civil war.

12. Accused of murdering his x-wife and her boyfriend.

A. Frank and Jessie James

B. Lizzy Borden

C. Charles Manson

D. Al Capone

E. Jim Jones

F. O.J. Simpson

G. Columbine High School

H. Unabomber

I. Lee Harvey Oswald

J. Bonnie and Clyde

K. Timothy McVeigh

L. Butch Cassidy and the Sundance Kid

Rodeo Lingo

A. Wrangler
B. Judges
C. Mark out
D. Box
E. Barrier
F. Covered
G. Rank

1. The area a horse and rider back into before making a run, in a timed event. ____

2. Term for when a cowboy makes a full eight-second ride. ____

3. The line at the end of the box that the contestant and his horse cannot cross over until the calf or steer has gotten a head start. ____

4. Term of respect to describe stock especially tough and difficult to ride. ____

5. Trained professionals who score the events and ensure all the rules are followed by contestants. ____

6. The term for how a cowboy's feet must be above a bucking horse's shoulder when the horse makes its first move out of the chute. ____

7. A person in charge of horses or other livestock. ____

Elephants & Donkeys

1. The Democratic Party's symbol was taken from the toughness of one presidential candidate who was called a jackass by the opponents. Which one?

    A. Ulysses S. Grant   B. Andrew Jackson   C. Robert E. Lee

2. The Republican Party's symbol was drawn as a political cartoon initially.
    True or False

3. Who was the first Republican president?

    A. Abraham Lincoln   B. Howard Taft   C. William McKinley

4. Who was the first Democratic president?

    A. James Madison   B. Woodrow Wilson   C. Andrew Jackson

5. The Republican Party emerged to combat the Kansas-Nebraska act, which threatened to extend slavery into the territories.   True or False

6. Which party came first the republican or the democratic?

7. The Democratic Party was formed by Federalists in the 1700's. True or False

8. There was only one party initially in the United States. Which one?

    A. Democratic-Republican   B. The Whigs   C. The Federalists

A Special Message for Pastors, Churches, and Concerned Christian Citizens

What Can Pastors Say from the Pulpit About Candidates and Elections?

Guidelines Concerning Political Activity

Recently, many pastors and churches across Missouri received a letter from the group Americans United for Separation of Church and State. This letter is a regular intimidation tactic by this atheist organization designed to silence the voice of pastors and churches prior to a presidential election.

The letter suggests that pastors may not legally make any statements that could be construed to influence the outcome of an election. The letter also strongly insinuates that pastors may not allow the distribution of voter guides without the possible loss of their church's tax-exempt status. These statements are false.

Here are the central legal guidelines concerning the activity of pastors and churches relating to candidates and elections:

• Churches may not support or oppose political candidates, nor may pastors endorse or oppose political candidates on behalf of the churches they pastor.

• Pastors may speak about the issues of the day, the actions of government, and the actions of public officials in the government.

• Pastors may speak about the stands of candidates on issues of concern to the church and the community of faith, as long as they do not encourage a vote for or against any particular candidate.

• Pastors may speak about the platforms of the political parties on issues of concern to the church and the community of faith, as long as they do not encourage a vote for or against a political party.

• Churches can sponsor voter registration activities and voter turnout activities.

• Pastors can encourage members of their congregation to vote for candidates who respect and reflect Biblical values, so long as they do not mention any particular candidates by name.

• Churches can distribute voter guides so long as the guides are neutral and have been approved for use by 501(c)3 organizations. Such guides can list responses of candidates to questionnaires, or the voting records and stands of candidates for office, so long as the guides do not indicate agreement or disagreement with those responses, stands, or records.

• Pastors can support and oppose candidates publicly as private citizens so long as their political activity does not occur within the church or in the name of the church.

An issue that often arises during election times is the distribution of political literature on church parking lots. While churches have every right to prohibit the distribution of political flyers on their premises, they have no obligation to halt or prevent the placement of flyers on cars parked on their premises. Churches are not legally responsible for literature distributed without their permission or consent.

The Alliance Defending Freedom has prepared an excellent overview on the subject of churches and political activity. The paper is entitled "Guidelines for Political Activities by Churches and Pastors." You can find the guide by clicking the link "Guidelines for Pastors."
Once you reach the website, go to the section which reads "Churches and Politics." Under that section, click the menu item that reads "General Resources," and then choose the item "Guidelines for Political Activities."

Should you have any questions about your legal rights as a pastor or church leader, please contact us at 636-536-0014.

We encourage every pastor and ministry leader to challenge your congregation to vote in accordance with God's Word and Biblical values in this critical election.
10/18/12

Joe Ortwerth

(Reprinted from Missouri Family Policy Council, October 18, 2012 Email update. Used by permission.)

He Is!

He is the First and Last,
the Beginning and the End!
He is the keeper of Creation
and the Creator of all!

He is the Architect of the Universe
and the Manager of all times.
He always was,
He always is,
and He always will be . . .
Unmoved,
Unchanged,
Undefeated,
and never Undone!

He was bruised and brought healing!
He was pierced and eased pain!
He was persecuted and brought freedom!
He was dead and brought life!
He is risen and brings power!
He reigns and brings peace!

The world can't understand him,
The armies can't defeat Him,
The schools can't explain Him,
and the leaders can't ignore Him.

Herod couldn't kill Him,
The Pharisees couldn't confuse Him, and
The people couldn't hold Him!

Nero couldn't crush Him,

Hitler couldn't silence Him,
The New Age can't replace Him,
and non-believers can't explain Him away!

He is Light,
Love,
Longevity,
and Lord.

He is Goodness,
Kindness,
Gentleness,
and God.

He is Holy,
Righteous,
Mighty,
Powerful,
and Pure.

His ways are right,
His Word is eternal,
His will is unchanging,
and His mind is on me!

He is my Redeemer,
He is my Savior,
He is my Guide, and
He is my Peace!

He is my Joy,
He is my Comfort,
He is my Lord, and
He rules my life!

I serve Him because His bond is love,

His burden is light,
and His goal for me is abundant life.

I follow Him because He is the Wisdom of the wise,
the Power of the powerful, the Ancient of Days,
the Ruler of rulers,
the Leader of leaders,
the Overseer of the overcomers,
and the Sovereign Lord of all that was, and is and is to come.

And if that seems impressive to you, try this for size . . .
His goal is a relationship with me!

He will NEVER leave me,
NEVER forsake me,
NEVER mislead me,
NEVER forget me,
NEVER overlook me,
and NEVER cancel my appointment in His appointment book!

When I fall, He lifts me up!
When I fail, He forgives!
When I am weak, He is strong!
When I am lost, He is the way!
When I am afraid, He is my courage!
When I stumble, He steadies me!

When I am hurt, He heals me!
When I am broken, He mends me!
When I am blind, He leads me!
When I am hungry, He feeds me!
When I face trials, He is with me!
When I face persecution, He shields me!
When I face loss, He provides for me!
When I face Death, He carries me Home!

He is God!
He is Faithful.
I am His,
and He is mine!

My Father in Heaven can whip the father of this world.
So, if you're wondering why I feel so secure, understand this . . .
He said it and that settles it.

God is in control,
I am on His side,
and that means all is well with my soul.
Everyday is a blessing, for GOD Is!

May Grace and Peace be multiplied unto you.

(www.laughandlift.com. Used by permission.)

Family Feud Game Night: Questions
Category: Bible Knowledge

1.

Answer:

2.

Answer:

3.

Answer:

4.

Answer:

5.

Answer:

Category: Geography

1.

Answer:

2.

Answer:

3.

Answer:

4.

Answer:

5.

Answer:

Category: Hodge Podge

1.

Answer:

2.

Answer:

3.

Answer:

4.

Answer:

5.

Answer:

Family Feud Game Night: Score Sheet

Question   _____ Family   _____

Category: Bible Knowledge

1. ____ ____
2. ____ ____
3. ____ ____
4. ____ ____
5. ____ ____

         Sub-totals   ____   ____

Category: Geography

1. ____ ____
2. ____ ____
3. ____ ____
4. ____ ____
5. ____ ____

         Sub-totals   ____   ____

Category: Hodge Podge

1. ____ ____
2. ____ ____
3. ____ ____
4. ____ ____
5. ____ ____

         Sub-totals   ____   ____

         TOTALS   ____   ____

Name That Game

1. "Colonel Mustard" and "Mrs. Peacock" ____

2. Pink peg = a girl, blue peg = a boy ____

3. Oh No! You sunk my … ____

4. Game that originated in India ____

5. Racecar, shoe ____

6. Four – "go back 4 squares" ____

7. Queen Frostine and Gramma Nutt ____

8. "Draw 4" ____

9. A "rooster" of a game ____

10. "Right hand blue" ____

11. Knight, King, and Queen ____

12. Pop a lot in this game ____

13. Black and red pieces ____

14. Double word square ____

15. Diagonal, Horizontal ____

16. Play in a circle ____

17. Created by an English poet ____

18. North/South/East/West ____

19. Fivestones, Knucklebones or Snobs ____

A. Trouble
B. Twister
C. Cribbage
D. Checkers
E. Connect 4
F. Marbles
G. Chess
H. Bridge
I. Scrabble
J. Parcheesi
K. Battleship
L. Jacks
M. Uno
N. Clue
O. Monopoly
P. Sorry
Q. Rook
R. Life
S. Candyland

Word Puzzles

Game One

Think of a single word that goes with each to form a compound word. (Helpful hint: can be at the front or the back of each word.)

Answer: bread

1. ginger, corn, crumbs _____
2. work, pile, worm _____
3. man, place, proof _____
4. light, ache, master _____
5. bags, castle, paper _____
6. bell, step, way _____

Game Two

Use the pairs of letters to complete the words.

7. po_ _ e _ _ ive _____
8. a _ _ e _ _ _____
9. mi _ _ i _ _ ippi _____
10. o_ _ u _ _ ing _____
11. dum_ _ e _ _ _____
12. ra_ _ _ _ n _____

Game Three

Try to figure out the garbled proverb where each word has had one letter replaced.

13. I twitch is lime paves mine. _____

14. Wetter fate that lever. _____

15. Fake bay white she sin whines. _____

16. To is a pay, dot is a to. _____

17. Taste sot pant sot. _____

18. Won't try oven spilt mild. _____

Game Four

These words begin and end with the same letter...

19. _luf_   _____

20. _hrif_   _____

21. _otato_   _____

22. _ividen_   _____

23. _rus_   _____

24. _urpas_   _____

Voting Sheet

Place the person's name next to the category that they best fit.

1. The classiest shoes _____

2. The best hair design _____

3. The most comfortably dressed _____

4. Best color combination _____

5. The best legs _____

6. The most durable outfit _____

Others:

7.

8.

9.

Zaney Brainy: Words Ending in "oat"
How Many Can You Think of?

Got your Goat?

The Letter is T for Travel

See how many words you can come up with that begin with the letter T for the following:

1. Seven letter word _____

2. Something in mall_____

3. Item in a hospital _____

4. Something in a school_____

5. Pet's Name_____

6. Something stored in a garage_____

7. Relative's name_____

8. Name of a tool _____

9. Friend's name_____

10. Something in a home_____

Number _____

knowledge challenge #2

ACROSS

5. worn by kings

6. in Revelation, John writes Jesus' eyes appearing like this

9. word of God

10. unjustly imprisoned but then used by God to deliver his family from severe famine

11. went to heaven in chariot of fire

12. decorative wood or stone around a fireplace

DOWN

1. method used to locate a person or building using signals from a gps or cell phone

2. symbol or trademark

3. drawn out of the Nile by Pharaoh's daughter

4. used to hold clothes, term can also be applied to failed efforts to do something

5. to tighten a belt or rope, term can also be applied to a simple task

7. goes before humility and also a fall

8. person in the Bible who was told he/she was there for "such a time as this"

(Nancy Jahnke. Used by permission.)

knowledge challenge #2

ACROSS

5. worn by kings

6. in Revelation, John writes Jesus' eyes appearing like this

9. word of God

10. unjustly imprisoned but then used by God to deliver his family from severe famine

11. went to heaven in chariot of fire

12. decorative wood or stone around a fireplace

DOWN

1. method used to locate a person or building using signals from a gps or cell phone

2. symbol or trademark

3. drawn out of the Nile by Pharaoh's daughter

4. used to hold clothes, term can also be applied to failed efforts to do something

5. to tighten a belt or rope, term can also be applied to a simple task

7. goes before humility and also a fall

8. person in the Bible who was told he/she was there for "such a time as this"

(Nancy Jahnke. Used by permission.)

Peanut's Trivia

1. Charlie Brown's faithful dog is _____.

2. What is Charlie Brown's neighbor's cat's name? _____

3. The self proclaimed grumpy psychologist is _____.

4. A trail of dust follows Charlie's friend named _____.

5. Which character always has his blanket? _____

6. What character plays Beethoven on his piano? _____

7. Who is Charlie's younger sister? _____

8. The bird who is best friends with Snoopy is _____.

9. A freckle faced tomboy who loves Charlie Brown _____

10. Who illustrated the comic strip, Peanuts? _____

11. What does Snoopy like to pretend he is, when on top of his doghouse?

_____

The Christmas Story: A to Z

A. is for _____ shining and bright, telling of Jesus that first Christmas night. (Luke 2:13)

B. is for _____ crowded and old, birthplace of Jesus by prophets foretold. (Micah 5:2)

C. is for _____, their manger, His bed, there in a stable where he laid His head. (Luke 2:7)

D. is for _____ and his ancient throne, promised forever to Jesus alone. (Luke 1:32)

E. is for _____ where men saw the star, and rode away quickly to follow it far. (Matt. 2:1–2)

F. is for _____ with myrrh and fine gold, brought by the Wise Men, as Matthew has told. (Matt. 2:11)

G. Is for _____ who from heaven above sent down to mankind the Son of His love. (John 3:16)

H. is for _____ murderous schemes were told to the wise men and Joseph in dreams. (Matt. 2:12–13)

I. is for _____ taken by night down into Egypt from the wicked king's sight. (Matt. 2:13)

J. is for _____ noble and just obeying God's orders with absolute trust. (Matt. 1:24)

K. is for _____ a true King was He, coming to rule in great majesty. (Zech. 9:9)

L. is for _____ Jesus brought down to earth that night in a stable in lowly birth. (I John 4:9)

M. is for _____ his mother so brave, counting God faithful and mighty to save. (Luke 1:47)

N. is for _____ when the Savior was born for nations of earth and people forlorn. (Luke 2:8)

O. is for _____ meaning "the last"; He's eternal, present, future, and past. (Rev 22:13)

P. is for _____ who foretold Jesus' story in visions of Bethlehem, Calvary, and glory. (Num. 24:17)

Q. is for _____ as shepherds who heard hastened to act on that heavenly word. (Luke 2:16)

R. is for _____ the sorrow of sin is banished forever when Jesus comes in. (Luke 1:14)

S. is for _____ to be this He came, the angel of God assigned Him His name. (Matt. 1:21)

T. is for _____ related to all, telling of Him who was born in a stall. (Luke 2:10)

U. is for _____ to whom Jesus was given; to show us the way and take us to heaven. (Luke 2:11)

V. is for _____ foretold by the sage, God's revelation on prophecy's page. (Isaiah 7:14)

W. is for _____ that's the Lord's name; with wonderful words and works He came. (Isaiah 9:6)

Y. is for _____ to all of God's ways, like Mary whose "yes" filled her spirit with praise. (Luke 1:38)

Z. is for _____ that burned in God's Son from His childhood year till His life's work was done.

(John 2:17)

Table Symphony Jingle Bells

Assign a phrase to each table and have them follow the directions before each phrase as you sing the song.

Copy and cut

(Knife on Fork) — "Dashing thru' the snow in a one-horse open sleigh…"

(Clap Hands) — "O'er the fields we go, laughing all the way…"

(Snap Fingers) — "Bells on bob-tail ring, making spirits bright…"

(Knife on Fork) — "Oh what fun it is to ride and sing a sleighing song tonight…"

(Knife on Glass) — "Jingle bells, jingle bells, jingle all the way…"

(Clap and Whistle) — "Oh what fun it is to ride in a one-horse open sleigh…"

(Knife on glass) — "Jingle bells, jingle bells, jingle all the way."

(Snap Fingers and Whistle) — "Oh what fun it is to ride in a one-horse open sleigh…"

Christmas Songwriter or Composer

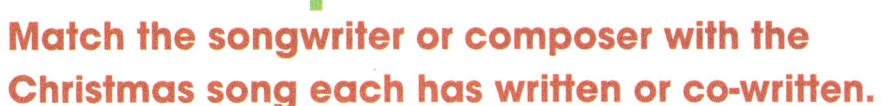

Match the songwriter or composer with the Christmas song each has written or co-written.

___ Gene Autry   A. "Away in a Manger"

___ Irving Berlin   B. "The Christmas Song"

___ George Frederick Handel   C. "Dance of the Sugar Plum Fairy"

___ Martin Luther   D. "Hark! The Herald Angels Sing"

___ Felix Mendelssohn   E. "Here Comes Santa Claus"

___ Peter Ilyich Tchaikovsky   F. "Joy to the World"

___ Mel Torme   G. "White Christmas"

WHO SAID IT?
Who said the following?

1. "Blessed are you among women, and blessed is the child you will bear." Luke 1:42 _____

2. "My soul glorifies the Lord." Luke 1:46 _____

3. "In Bethlehem of Judea; they replied, for this is what the prophet has written." Matthew 2:5 _____

4. "He will be great and will be called the Son of the Most High." Luke 1:32a
   _____

5. "His name is John." Luke 1:63b _____

6. "Sovereign Lord, as you have promised, you may now dismiss your servant in peace. For my eyes have seen your salvation." Luke 2:29–30
   _____

7. "Where is the one who has been born King of the Jews?" Matthew 2:2a
   _____

8. "Glory to God in the highest heaven, and on earth, peace to those on whom his favor rests." Luke 2:13-14 _____

9. "Go, and search carefully for the child." Matthew 2:8a
   _____

10. "Let's go to Bethlehem and see this thing that has happened, which the Lord has told us about." Luke 2:15b _____

Musical Lyrics

1. All I want for Christmas…

   _____

2. I saw Mommy….

   _____

3. When the weather outside is frightful, but the fire is so delightful, what should we do?

   _____

4. Where are we walking if, in the lane, snow is glistening?

   _____

5. He was a jolly, happy soul, even if his eyes were made of coal.

   _____

6. What am I dreaming of with every card I write?

   _____

7. What do we sing while waiting for the chestnuts to roast?

   _____

(OVER)

11. Where will you be if there is snow and mistletoe and presents on the tree?

_____

12. Where can you hang your stocking "on a great big coconut tree?"

_____

13. Do you know why you'd better not pout or cry?

_____

14. "Take a look in the five-and-ten, glistening once again….."

_____

Duck Trivia

1. On the TV show Duck Dynasty, how many Robertson men is the show centered around?

    A. Three   B. Four

    C. Five   D. Six

2. Which Robertson son said "Nothing makes a father happier than seeing his daughter with a smile on her face and her boyfriend with fear in his eyes."

    A. Willie   B. Jep

    C. Alan   D. Jase

3. Where does the Duck Dynasty family live?

    A. Georgia   B. Mississippi

    C. Louisiana   D. Texas

4. What did the Duck Dynasty family become wealthy manufacturing?

    A. Duck calls   B. Duck swimming fins

    C. Frozen duck meat   D. Plastic duck bills

5. Si Robertson carries around a Tupperware® cup his mom sent him while he was stationed in Vietnam. What does he always drink from that cup?

    A. Root beer   B. Iced tea

    C. Coke   D. Lemonade

6. Which Robertson is the CEO of the Duck Commander business?

    A. Jase   B. Jep

    C. Alan   D. Willie

7. Miss Kay is famous for her …
   - A. Cooking
   - B. Sewing
   - C. Dancing
   - E. Hog calling

8. The Robertson real life neighbor who appears on the show as himself is called:
   - A. Fish man
   - B. Dude Man
   - C. Mountain man
   - C. Gator man

9. Al the oldest Robertson son (and the only beardless one) did what as a profession for the last 25 years?
   - A. Fisherman
   - B. Minister
   - C. Fireman
   - D. Doctor

10. Which Robertson said "Uptown living, you've got to call 911. Where I am, I am 911."
    - A. Phil
    - B. Si
    - B. Willie
    - C. Jase

11. What pro football team wanted to get Phil Robertson on board when he was a junior at Louisiana Tech University?
    - A. Dallas Cowboys
    - B. Seattle Seahawks
    - C. New Orleans Saints
    - D. Washington Redskins

Name That Christmas Tune

See if you can think of the titles to these very familiar Christmas songs from the clues given below.

1. My Sole Desire for My Yuletide Season is Receipt of a Pair of Central Incisors
   _____

2. From Dark 'til Dawn, Soundless and Sanctimonious
   _____

3. Celestial Messengers from Splendid Empires
   _____

4. The Antlered Quadruped with the Crimson Proboscis
   _____

5. The Event Occurred at One Minute after 11:59 pm with Visibility Unlimited
   _____

6. Ornament the Enclosure with Large Sprigs of a Berry-Bearing Evergreen
   _____

7. Personal Hallucinations of an Alabaster December 25th
   _____

8. Anticipation of the Noel's Mementoes: Nil
   _____

9. Clappered Inverted Cups, Amalgamated
   _____

10. Testimony of Witness to Maternal Parent's Infidelity with Kris Kringle
    _____

11. In a Distant Bovine Diner

_____

12. Universal Elation

_____

13. O Miniature Nazarene Village

_____

14. The Approach of the Holiday Commemorating the Birth of Christ Is Become Evident

_____

15. Jehovah Grant unto You Happy Males Retirement

_____

16. Those of You Who Are True, Come Here!

_____

17. Are You Detecting the Same Aural Sensations as I Am?

_____

18. The Diminutive Male of Less than Adult Age Who Plays a Percussion Instrument

_____

19. Primary Yuletide

_____

20. Heavenly Cherubs Announcing in Song — Listen!

_____

21. Reigning Monarchs of the Far East

_____

22. Proclaim It to the Hills

_____ _____

23. Pastoral Woolies Nocturnally Observed in Vigilance by Herdsmen

_____

Christmas Trivia

1. After Jesus, Mary, and Joseph left Bethlehem, what country did they travel to? _____

2. What famous Christmas movie is the following line from? "Every time a bell rings an angel gets his wings!" _____

3. What are the names of Santa's reindeer? _____

4. What street does the miracle take place on in the 1947 film? _____

5. What country did the real St. Nicholas hail from? _____

6. True or False: The only female deer that grow antlers are reindeer. _____

7. In what country is Santa Claus know as Sinter Klaas? _____

8. Who directed It's a Wonderful Life? _____

9. Where did the Grinch steal Christmas? _____

10. True or False: The New England Puritans forbade Christmas celebrations. _____

Figure out THESE Holiday Songs!

The following words are alternate titles for several well-known Christmas Carols.

15–20 Correct – You don't need any Yuletide spirit!

10–14 Correct – You could use something in your stocking!

5–9 Correct – Are you sure you have the right holiday?

1–4 Correct – Surely you jest!

1. Antlered quadruped with crimson proboscis _____

2. 10pm or 11pm without noise _____

3. Miniscule hamlet in the Middle East _____

4. Happy ancient benevolent priest _____

5. Adorn the vestibule _____

6. Exuberance directed to the planet _____

7. Listen, aerial spirits harmonizing _____

8. Monarchical trio _____

9. Yonder in the haystack _____

10. Assembly, everyone who believes _____

11. Hallowed post meridian _____

12. Fantasies of a colorless December 25th _____

13. Tin tintinnabulums _____

14. A dozen 24-hour Yule periods _____

15. Befell during the transparent bewitching hour _____

16. Homo sapiens of crystallized vapor _____

17. I merely desire a pair of incisors _____

18. I spied my maternal parent osculating a fat man in red _____

19. Perambulating through a December solstice fantasy
    _____

20. Aloft on the apex of the abode _____

Christmas Charades Songs

1. "All I Want for Christmas Is My Two Front Teeth"
2. "Silent Night, Holy Night"
3. "Angels We Have Heard on High"
4. "Rudolph the Red-Nosed Reindeer"
5. "It Came upon a Midnight Clear"
6. "Deck the Halls with Boughs of Holly"
7. "I'm Dreaming of a White Christmas"
8. "Walking in a Winter Wonderland"
9. "Silver Bells"
10. "I Saw Mommy Kissing Santa Claus"
11. "Away in a Manger"
12. "Joy to the World"
13. "O Little Town of Bethlehem"
14. "It's Beginning to Look a Lot like Christmas"
15. "God Rest Ye Merry Gentlemen"
16. "O Come All Ye Faithful"
17. "Do You Hear What I Hear?"
18. "The Little Drummer Boy"
19. "The First Noel"
20. "Hark! The Herald Angels Sing"
21. "We Three Kings of Orient Are"
22. "What Child Is This?"
23. "Go Tell It on the Mountain"
24. "While Shepherds Watched Their Flocks By Night"
25. "I Saw Three Ships Come Sailing In"

Christmas Carol Match-up

Questions:

___ 1. No crib for a bed

___ 2. O holy child of Bethlehem

___ 3. All is calm; all is bright

___ 4. Oh what fun it is to ride

___ 5. City sidewalks, busy sidewalks

___ 6. Bearing gifts we traverse afar

___ 7. With a corn cob pipe and ….

___ 8. When they are both full grown

___ 9. Special night, beard that's white

___ 10. Hark! How the bells

___ 11. Jack Frost nipping at your nose

___ 12. She didn't see me creep

___ 13. Right down Santa Claus lane

___ 14. Had a very shiny nose

___ 15. Sweetly singing o'er the plains

___ 16. Come they told me

___ 17. In heaven the bells are ringing

___ 18. How are thy leaves so verdant

___ 19. You can count on me

Answers:

A. "Frosty the Snowman"

B. "Here Comes Santa Claus"

C. "Rudolph the Red-Nosed Reindeer"

D. "I Saw Mommy Kissing Santa Claus"

E. "Ding Dong! Merrily on High"

F. "Little Drummer Boy"

G. "O Christmas Tree"

H. "Angels We Have Heard on High"

I. "The Christmas Song" (Chestnuts..)

J. "Away in a Manger"

K. "We Three Kings of Orient Are"

L. "Carol of the Bells"

M. "O Little Town of Bethlehem"

N. "Silver Bells"

O. "The Holly and the Ivy"

P. "Silent Night"

Q. "I'll Be Home for Christmas"

R. "Jingle Bells"

S. "Must Be Santa"

Answers

Super Bowl Trivia: Answers (page 195)

1. 1967
2. B. NFL (National Football League)
3. True
4. Pittsburgh Steelers (six championships)
5. B. The Beatles
6. B. Rose Bowl, in Pasadena, California
7. C. Green Bay Packers
8. B. White jerseys
9. B. Montana

* * * * * * * *

Coin Collecting: How Much Do You Know? Answers (page 196-197)

1. b. Numismatics
2. True. At the time King George IV had his portrait on British coinage. Washington saw this as too much of a monarchial trait.
3. a. Kings
4. a. they cannot be run through coin sorters anymore. Coins can be circulated indefinitely.
5. True – they also mint commemorative coins as well. The mint in San Francisco mints proof coins and commemoratives.
6. c. Mesopotamia
7. c. 5 cents
8. False
9. False. The image is a composite of three Indians; a Cheyenne named Chief Two Moons, an Iroquois named Chief John Big Tree, and a Sioux named Chief Iron Tail.
10. c. Denver, CO.
11. True
12. b. they end up in pocket change bottles
13. b. George Washington
14. True.
15. Mint

* * * * * * * *

308 | DEUTSCH

Famous Animals: Answers (page 205-206)

1. Lassie
2. Bugs Bunny
3. Wilbur and Charlotte
4. Mickey and Minnie Mouse
5. Bagheera
6. Shamu
7. Pluto
8. Jiminy Cricket
9. Benji
10. Eeyore
11. Tigger
12. Winnie the Pooh
13. Moby Dick
14. Barney
15. Simba
16. Dumbo
17. Baloo
18. Bambi
19. Black Beauty
20. Daffy Duck
21. Babe
22. Garfield and Odie
23. Wile E. Coyote and the Road Runner
24. Brer Rabbit
25. Secretariat
26. Thumper

* * * * * * * *

Riddle Your Brain: Answers (page 209)

1. The third room. Lions that haven't eaten in three years are dead. That one was easy, right?
2. The woman was a photographer. She shot a picture of her husband, developed it, and hung it up to dry (shot; held under water; and hung).
3. Charcoal, as it is used in barbecuing.

4. Sure you can name three consecutive days: yesterday, today, and tomorrow!
5. The letter "e" which is the most common letter used in the English language, does not appear even once in the paragraph.

* * * * * * * *

Bible Pairs: Answers (page 212)

1. X. Andrew
2. N. Animals
3. I. Aquilla
4. P. Esau
5. W. Martha or Q. Joseph
6. T. Elisha
7. S. John
8. K. Sapphira
9. L. Phinehas
10. F. Ephraim
11. M. Naomi
12. R. Eve
13. U. Abel
14. Q. Joseph or W. Martha
15. A. Jonathan
16. G. Rebecca
17. H. Samuel
18. V. Miriam
19. E. Barnabas
20. O. Mordecai
21. C. Elizabeth
22. D. Nabal
23. Y. Caleb
24. B. Michael

* * * * * * * *

Answers

"Heart" Words: Answers (page 215)

1. Heartache
2. Kindhearted
3. Heartstrings
4. Halfhearted
5. Sweethearts
6. Coldhearted
7. Heartburn
8. Purple Heart
9. Heartworm
10. Hearty
11. Lionhearted
12. Heartthrobs
13. Bighearted
14. Fainthearted
15. Heartbroken or brokenhearted
16. Heartwarming
17. Lighthearted
18. Wholeheartedly

* * * * * * * *

Saint Patrick — How Much Do You Know? Answers (page 220)

1. c. Ireland
2. b. Maewyn Succat
3. c. a slave
4. c. Mochta
5. a. 120
6. a. nuns
7. b. Britain
8. b. financial impropriety
9. a. accept gifts from kings
10. d. a man calling him to come to his country

* * * * * * * *

Square Dancing Trivia: Answers (page 222)

1. a. Ronald Reagan in 1982.
2. a. True
3. c. Thomas Edison
4. f. Spare the Rod
5. b. Henry Ford
6. c. Peanuts
7. b. False. It had square dancing but not break dancing!
8. a. "The Brady Bunch" and b. "Lassie"
9. c. Li'l Abner Square Dance Book by Fred Leifer (1953)
10. Hoedown

* * * * * * * *

Take Your Foot out of Your Mouth!" Answers (page 223)

1. Foothold
2. Tenderfoot
3. Footstool
4. Football
5. Footwork
6. Fleet footed
7. Footlocker
8. Footings
9. Foothills
10. Bigfoot
11. a Foot
12. Footloose
13. Clubfoot
14. Footbridge
15. Footstep
16. Footpath
17. Footprints
18. Footage
19. Footsie
20. Footnote

* * * * * * * *

Science and the Bible -1: Answers
(page 230)

Java man: E. The first fossil specimen of Homo erectus
Radioisotope Dating: F. A process that determines the age of the earth
Paleontologist: H. Studies the forms of life existing in previous times
Stellar Evolution: G. The Big Bang
Archaeology: I. Digging to uncover past time period
Edward Blyth: D. A Creationist and Author
Interglacial: C. Short period of warming between glacier growth
Atheist: B. One who rejects the Bible
Humanism: M. A belief in mankind as the measure of all things
Charles Darwin: P. Evolutionist
Gap theory: N. A compromise belief that a vast period of time exists between Genesis 1:1 and 1:2
Clone: O. Organism that is genetically identical to its parent
Cosmology: J. Systematic study of the structure of the universe
Artifact: Q. An item or its remains produced in the past by humans
Josephus: K. Jewish historian around A.D. 90
Cro-Magnon man: L. An extinct group of Europe and Eastern Asia
Exegesis: A. Critical interpretation of Scripture

* * * * * * * *

Science and the Bible-2: Answers
(page 231)

Meshech: I. Is the old name for Moscow, Russia
Jesus: D. The "Last Adam"
Materialism: G. The assumption that all that exists is mass and energy (matter); says there are no supernatural forces
Septuagint: J. The translation of the Old Testament into Greek during the third century B.C.; the word itself means 70
Mutation: L. Any change in the sequence of DNA
Sir Isaac Newton: K. Invented calculus, and discovered the laws of gravity and motion

Answers

Pentateuch: M. Known as "The Law," the first five books of the Bible

Apocrypha: F. A group of about 14 books written between the close of the Old Testament and beginning of the New

Mizraim: H. The Hebrew name for Egypt

Tarsus: C. A mountain range in Turkey

Cush: B. Ancient name of Ethiopia

Canon: A. 66 books found in the Bible

Methuselah: E. Lived to be 969 years old

* * * * * * * *

Old West Trivia: Answers (page 235)

1. "Home on the Range" / "Yellow Rose of Texas" / "Red River Valley" / "Get along Little Doggies"
2. a. Around the campfire
3. Higher-heeled boots.
4. Rough Riders
5. b. 10
6. Longhorn
7. Yes
8. d. 1½
9. To calm the cattle; it settled them down at night because they were used to it.
10. "Gunfight at the OK Corral"
11. b. A cow that escaped
12. d. 5 miles

* * * * * * * *

Senior Student Exam: Answers (page 236)

1. How long did the Hundred Years War last? 116 years
2. Which country makes Panama hats? Ecuador

3. From which animal do we get cat gut? Sheep and Horses

4. In which month do Russians celebrate the October Revolution? November

5. What is a camel's hair brush made of? Squirrel fur

6. The Canary Islands in the Pacific are named after what animal? Dogs

7. What was King George VI's first name? Albert

8. What color is a purple finch? Crimson

9. Where are Chinese gooseberries from? New Zealand

10. What is the color of the black box in a commercial airplane? Orange (of course)

* * * * * * * *

Bible Testing Time: Answers (page 239)

1. 2
2. Neither, there is no book of Hezekiah
3. John 3:16
4. Gospels
5. 5 (The Gospel of John, 1st, 2nd, 3rd John, Revelation)
6. 27
7. 39
8. Joshua
9. Sinai
10. Pure, God
11. Door and knock
12. Ur.
13. Shortest verse in the Bible
14. No.
15. Elijah
16. False, it means "Good News"
17. False, from Mt. of Olives
18. False, in Jerusalem
19. False, in the Garden of Gethsemane
20. False, Antioch

* * * * * * * *

Answers

Advertising Slogans: Answers (page 240-241)

1. Kentucky Fried Chicken
2. Adidas
3. Allstate (Insurance)
4. Maxwell House Coffee
5. Pepsi
6. AT&T
7. M&Ms
8. Volkswagen
9. Raid
10. Rice Crispies Cereal
11. Taco Bell
12. Southwestern Bell Yellow Pages
13. Burger King
14. ESPN
15. Timex watch
16. Coke
17. Nike
18. Geico
19. John Deere
20. BMW
21. L'Oreal
22. Duracell
23. Kay Jewelers
24. General Electric
25. Kodak
26. United Airlines
27. Wal-Mart
28. Avis rent a car
29. Kellogg's Frosted Flakes Cereal
30. McDonald's
31. Federal Express
32. Bounty (paper towels)
33. Wheaties

* * * * * * * *

Famous Women Quiz: Answers (page 245)

1. Rachael Ray or Paula Deen (or formerly Julia Child)
2. Oprah Winfrey
3. Elizabeth Taylor
4. Marilyn Monroe
5. Golda Meir
6. Amelia Earhart
7. Hillary Clinton
8. Sarah Palin
9. Martha Stewart
10. Grace Kelly
11. Margaret Thatcher
12. Alice Walton
13. Indira Ghandi
14. Danielle Steel

* * * * * * * *

Famous Christian Women – Giving All to the Lord: Answers (page 246)

1. F. Mary Slessor
2. J. Elisabeth Elliott
3. K. Corrie Ten Boom
4. H. Gloria Gaither
5. L. Gladys Alyward
6. I. Fanny Crosby
7. M. Mrs. Smith Wigglesworth
8. D. Kathryn Kulhman
9. B. Joyce Meyer
10. A. Lillian Trasher
11. C. Huldah Buntain
12. G. Amee Simple McPherson
13. E. Anita Renfroe

* * * * * * * *

The Quiz for Those in the Know: Answers (page 249)

1. Boxing.
2. Niagara Falls ... The rim is worn down about two and a half feet each year because of the millions of gallons of water that rush over it every minute.
3. Asparagus and rhubarb.
4. Strawberry.
5. Dwarf, dwell and dwindle...
6. Period, comma, colon, semicolon, dash, hyphen, apostrophe, question mark, exclamation point, quotation mark, brackets, parenthesis, braces, and ellipses.
7. Lettuce & Watermelon
8. Shoes, socks, sandals, sneakers, slippers, skis, skates, snowshoes, stockings, stilts.

(www.mikeysFunnies.com. Used by Permission.)

* * * * * * * *

Geography Quiz: Answers (page 250-251)

1. Maine
2. Arizona
3. Pennsylvania (Hershey)
4. New Mexico
5. California
6. North Carolina. Sir Walter Raleigh founded the colony on Roanoke Island. The colony mysteriously vanished with no trace except for the word "Croatoan" scrawled on a nearby tree. The first permanent English settlement was in Jamestown, Virginia.
7. Nevada
8. California
9. Alaska (because grocery stores are scarce in parts)
10. Colorado
11. Wyoming (as of 2011 it was just 568,158 residents)
12. Nebraska
13. Key West, Florida
14. Hawaii
15. South Dakota
16. The sunshine state, Florida (with 1,350 miles of coast)
17. Maryland
18. Alaska
19. Rhode Island
20. New Hampshire (6 months before the Declaration of Independence was signed).

* * * * * * * *

Answers

Fantastic Flora Facts: Quiz Answers
(page 254 -255)

1. K. California Redwood trees
2. P. Soybeans
3. D. California Bristlecone pine (estimated to be 4,600 years old)
4. F. Onions
5. O. Corn
6. J. Peach
7. M. Broccoli
8. N. Vanilla Orchid (the pods from the flower)
9. B. Asparagus
10. L. Grapes
11. C. Bamboo
12. G. White Potatoes
13. H. Saffron
14. I. Strawberries
15. A. Bananas (The average person eats 33 pounds of them in a year)
16. E. Pineapples

* * * * * * * *

Theodore Roosevelt: Answers
(page 256-257)

1. a. Eleanor was the only child of Theodore's brother, Elliott. She was later married to her distant cousin Franklin D. Roosevelt.
2. True
3. a. The Rough Riders included several hundred cowboys, several dozen Indians, and any number of assorted athletes. Many of the rough riders knew T.R. from his time out West. He was said to treat all of the riders equally and they were very devoted to him.
4. d. His son Kermit broke his arm.
5. b. T.R. struggled with severe asthma as a child. His father is said to have told him, "Theodore, you have the mind, but you have not the body…you must make your

body." His father installed a gym in their home and T.R. spent great effort working out there.
6. True. He kept it secret for years, because he feared humiliation from it.
7. c. That is a Sir Winston Churchill quote.
8. c. T.R. attended Harvard.
9. c. T.R. was the first president to receive the Nobel Peace Prize (for diplomacy in the Russo-Japanese War, where Japan eventually forced Russia to abandon its expansion in the Far East).
10. c. Second rate …
11. b. Jonathan Edwards was a black bear cub, Bishop Doane was a guinea pig, and Eli Yale was a macaw, part of the large pet collection kept by T.R.'s children
12. d. T.R. drank large amounts of coffee. Once, after drinking a cup of coffee at the Hermitage (the home of Andrew Jackson in Nashville, Tenn.), he stated that it was "good to the last drop." The coffee had come from the Maxwell Hotel and was produced by a local family that later sold their business to General Mills. That particular phrase became the "sales theme" for Maxwell House coffee under General Mills!

✳ ✳ ✳ ✳ ✳ ✳ ✳

British Trivia: Answers (page 261)

1. England, Wales, Northern Ireland and Scotland
2. London
3. Sheppard's
4. Queen Elizabeth I
5. Scotland
6. Fox
7. Queen Mary 1st
8. Red, white and Blue
9. God save the Queen
10. Queen Victoria
11. Windsor

✳ ✳ ✳ ✳ ✳ ✳ ✳

Answers

Gents, Ladies and Language: Answers (page 262)

1. G. Princess Diana
2. M. William Shakespeare
3. I. Biscuit
4. H. Elizabeth Taylor
5. L. Rowan Atkinson
6. B. Lorry
7. N. Twiggy
8. O. Roger Moore
9. A. Chips
10. C. Julie Andrews
11. K. Sir Winston Churchill
12. E. Lift
13. F. Audrey Hepburn
14. J. Football
15. D. Sir. Lawrence Olivier

* * * * * * * *

"Hope" Trivia: Answers (page 264)

1. b. England. His dad was a stonemason and his mother an aspiring concert singer. Bob joked that he left England when he was four when he found out he couldn't be king.
2. d. all the above
3. Ethel Merman and Jimmy Durante
4. Dolores
5. Singapore
6. b. NBC
7. a. Harry Truman
8. a. World War I

9. Yes. Queen Elizabeth II bestowed on him an honorary knight-hood, the "Knight Commander of the most Excellent Order of the British Empire (KBE) in 1998. Upon hearing the news, Bob said, "I'm speechless. 70 years of ad lib material and I'm speechless."
* * * * * * * *

Webster's Words: Answers (page 268)

1. E. Stringent
2. K. Metadata
3. N. Riot act
4. B. Sacrilegious
5. H. Nepotism
6. A. Stalwart
7. C. Frugal
8. O. Bellwether
9. J. Gossamer
10. D. Thesaurus
11. G. Rambunctious
12. F. Libertine
13. M. Esoteric
14. L. Roustabout
15. I. Hoosegow

* * * * * * * *

Crime Doesn't Pay: Answers (page 269)

1. J. Bonnie Parker and Clyde Champion Barrow (they both died instantly when authorities ambushed their car.)
2. G. Columbine High School (The two teen killers killed themselves as well.)
3. B. Lizzy Borden (Found not guilty to all's surprise.)
4. H. Unabomber (went to Harvard at 16, earned his Ph.D. and wasa professor at Berkeley by age 25 – sentenced to life in prison.)
5. L. Butch Cassidy and the Sundance Kid (Escaped to South America and died in a shootout.)

Answers

6. K. Timothy McVeigh (Was executed in 2001.)
7. I. Lee Harvey Oswald (who was then shot by Jack Ruby two days later.)
8. D. Al (Scarface) Capone, ended up serving seven years at Alcatraz; however was so ill with syphilis that he went into seclusion in Florida and died of a stroke and pneumonia.
9. C. Charles Manson (Who is still in jail as of 2016, having been denied parole 12 times.
10. E. Jim Jones (909 of his followers died and he with a gunshot to the head.)
11. A. Frank and Jessie James (Spree ended when Jessie was killed by a gang member.)
12. F. O.J. Simpson (Found not guilty resulting in a stunned nation.)

****

Rodeo Lingo: Answers (page 270)

1. D. Box
2. F. Covered
3. E. Barrier
4. G. Rank
5. B. Judges
6. C. Mark Out
7. A. Wrangler

****

Elephants and Donkeys: Answers (page 271)

1. B. Andrew Jackson
2. True
3. A. Abraham Lincoln
4. C. Andrew Jackson
5. True
6. Democratic
7. False. It was formed by Thomas Jefferson and James Madison in opposition to the Federalists.
8. A. Democratic-Republican

****

Name that Game: Answers (page 282)

1. N. Clue
2. R. Life
3. K. Battleship
4. J. Parcheesi
5. O. Monopoly
6. P. Sorry
7. S. Candyland
8. M. Uno
9. Q. Rook
10. B. Twister
11. G. Chess
12. A. Trouble
13. D. Checkers
14. I. Scrabble
15. E. Connect 4
16. F. Marbles
17. C. Cribbage
18. H. Bridge
19. L. Jacks

✶ ✶ ✶ ✶ ✶ ✶ ✶

Word Puzzles: Answers (pages 283 - 284)
Game One:

1. bread (gingerbread, cornbread, breadcrumbs)
2. wood (woodwork, woodpile, woodworm)
3. fire (fireman, fireplace, fireproof)
4. head (headlight, headache, headmaster)
5. sand (sandbags, sandcastle, sandpaper)
6. door (doorbell, doorstep, doorway)

Game Two:

7. possessive
8. access
9. Mississippi
10. occurring
11. dumbbell
12. raccoon

Game Three:

13. A stitch in time saves nine.
14. Better late than never.
15. Make hay while the sun shines.
16. Do as I say, not as I do.
17. Waste not want not.
18. Don't cry over spilt milk.

Game Four:

19. fluff
20. thrift
21. rotator
22. dividend
23. trust
24. surpass

✶ ✶ ✶ ✶ ✶ ✶ ✶

Answers

Peanuts Trivia: Answers (page 290)

1. Snoopy
2. King Tut
3. Lucy
4. Pig Pen
5. Linus
6. Schroeder
7. Sally
8. Woodstock
9. Peppermint Patty
10. Charles M. Schultz
11. WW II Flying Ace

****

The Christmas Story: From A to Z: Answers (page 291-292)

A. Angels
B. Bethlehem
C. Cattle
D. David
E. East
F. Frankincense
G. God
H. Herod
I. Infant
J. Joseph
K. King
L. Love
M. Mary
N. Night
O. Omega
P. Prophet
Q. Quickly
R. Rejoice
S. Savior
T. Tidings
U. Us
V. Virgin
W. Wonderful
Y. Yes
Z. Zeal

****

Christmas Songwriter/Composer: Answers (page 295 - 296)

E. Gene Autry
G. Irving Berlin
F. George Frederick Handel
A. Martin Luther
D. Felix Mendelssohn
C. Peter Ilyich Tchaikovsky
B. Mel Torme

****

WHO SAID IT?

1. Elizabeth
2. Mary
3. Chief priests and scribes
4. Angel
5. Zachariah
6. Simeon
7. Wise men
8. A multitude of the heavenly hosts
9. Herod
10. Shepherds

****

Musical Lyrics: Answers (page 297-298)

1. My Two Front Teeth
2. Kissing Santa Claus
3. And since we've no place to go, let it snow, let it snow, let it snow.
4. Walking in a winter wonderland.
5. Frosty the Snowman.
6. White Christmas.
7. Yuletide carols
8. Jingle Bells
9. Sleigh Ride
10. I'm dreaming of a white Christmas.
11. I'll be home for Christmas.
12. Christmas Island
13. Santa Claus is coming to town.
14. with candy canes and silver lanes aglow.

* * * * * * * *

Duck Trivia: Answers (page 299-300)

1. B. Four
2. A. Willie
3. C. Louisiana
4. A. Duck calls
5. B. Iced tea
6. D. Willie
7. A. Cooking
8. C. Mountain man
9. B. Minister
10. A. Phil
11. D. Washington Redskins

* * * * * * * *

Name That Christmas Tune: Answers (page 301-302)

1. "All I Want for Christmas Is My Two Front Teeth
2. "Silent Night, Holy Night"
3. "Angels We Have Heard on High"
4. "Rudolph the Red-Nosed Reindeer"
5. "It Came Upon a Midnight Clear"
6. "Deck the Halls with Boughs of Holly"
7. "I'm Dreaming of a White Christmas"
8. "I'm Gettin' Nothin' for Christmas"
9. "Silver Bells"
8. Jingle bells
9. Sleigh ride
10. "I Saw Mommy Kissing Santa Claus"
11. "Away in a Manger"
12. "Joy to the World"
13. "O Little Town of Bethlehem"
14. "It's Beginning to Look a Lot like Christmas"
15. "God Rest Ye Merry Gentlemen"
16. "O Come All Ye Faithful"
17. "Do You Hear What I Hear?"
18. "The Little Drummer Boy"
19. "The First Noel"
20. "Hark! The Herald Angels Sing"
21. "We Three Kings of Orient Are"
22. Go Tell It on the Mountain"
23. "While Shepherds Watched Their Flocks by Night"

* * * * * * * *

Answers

Christmas Trivia: Answers (page 303)

1. Egypt
2. It's A Wonderful Life
3. Donner, Blitzen, Comet, Dancer, Prancer, Cupid, Vixen, Dasher, Rudolph
4. 34th Street
5. Turkey
6. True
7. Holland
8. Frank Capra
9. Whoville
10. True: The Puritans considered Christmas trees and decorations to be pagan, and outlawed them in Massachusetts until 1859

****

Figure out THESE Holiday Songs! Answers (page 304-305)

1. "Rudolph the Red-Nosed Reindeer"
2. "Silent Night"
3. "O Little Town of Bethlehem"
4. "Jolly Old St. Nicolas"
5. "Deck the Halls"
6. "Joy to the World"
7. "Hark! The Herald Angels Sing"
8. "We Three Kings"
9. "Away in a Manger"
10. "O Come All Ye Faithful"
11. "O Holy Night"
12. "I'm Dreaming of a White Christmas"
13. "Silver Bells"
14. "Twelve Days of Christmas"
15. "It Came upon a Midnight Clear"
16. "Frosty the Snowman"
17. "All I Want for Christmas"
18. "I Saw Momma Kissing Santa Claus"
19. "Walking in a Winter Wonderland"
20. "Up on the Housetop"

****

Christmas Carol Match-up: Answers (307)

1. J. "Away in a Manger"
2. M. "O Little Town of Bethlehem"
3. P. "Silent Night"
4. R. "Jingle Bells"
5. N. "Silver Bells"
6. K. "We Three Kings of Orient Are"
7. A. "Frosty the Snowman"
8. O. "The Holly and the Ivy"
9. S. "Must Be Santa"
10. L. "Carol of the Bells"
11. I. "The Christmas Song" (Chestnuts…)
12. D. "I Saw Mommy Kissing Santa Claus"
13. B. "Here Comes Santa Claus"
14. C. "Rudolph the Red-Nosed Reindeer"
15. H. "Angels We Have Heard on High"
16. F. "Little Drummer Boy"
17. E. "Ding Dong! Merrily on High"
18. G. "O Christmas Tree"
19. Q. "I'll Be Home for Christmas"

****

Copyright © by Lisa C. Deutsch 2016. All rights reserved. No part of this publication may be reproduced (with the exception of the handouts), stored in a retrieval system, or transmitted in any way by any means—electronic, mechanical, photocopy, recording, or otherwise—without the prior permission of the copyright holder, except as provided by USA copyright law.

Scripture quotations are taken from:
THE HOLY BIBLE, NEW INTERNATIONAL VERSION®, NIV® Copyright © 1973, 1978, 1984, 2011 by Biblica, Inc. ™ Used by permission. All rights reserved worldwide.

This is a compilation of ideas, stories, jokes, and activities collected from numerous sources over many years. Any use of original material that is unauthorized is unintentional. Unless otherwise attributed, the origin and authorship of jokes, stories, and poems is unknown and assumed to be in the public domain. Credit is given to as many original sources as are known.

CPSIA information can be obtained
at www.ICGtesting.com
Printed in the USA
LVOW01s0347081116
512024LV00006B/7/P